THE FERRIS CONSPIRACY

Disclaimer

This book tells true stories with actual people. In writing we set out to hide nothing and, by doing so, reveal something of the nature of justice in this country.

Some of these people, mainly current or former officers of Strathclyde Police, are well known for what they are by fellow officers, journalists, lawyers, the people of the housing schemes and of the prisons. Their activities and methods are corroborated by audio tapes, film, witnesses and court records. We decided to tell their story the way it is.

Where necessary the names of certain parties have been altered to protect the guilty. They know who they are – so do we.

Paul Ferris & Reg McKay
September 2000

THE FERRIS CONSPIRACY

Paul Ferris with Reg McKay

MAINSTREAM
PUBLISHING

EDINBURGH AND LONDON

Dedicated to the loving memory of the late
Bobby Glover and Joe Hanlon.

Copyright © Paul Ferris and Reg McKay, 2001
All rights reserved
The moral rights of the authors have been asserted

First published in Great Britain in 2001 by
MAINSTREAM PUBLISHING COMPANY (EDINBURGH) LTD
7 Albany Street
Edinburgh EH1 3UG

ISBN 1 84018 388 8

A catalogue record for this book is available
from the British Library

Typeset in Stone and Typewriter
Printed and bound in Great Britain by
Creative Print and Design Wales

CONTENTS

PROLOGUE

BILLY THE KID'S FRIENDS
(27 May 1997, London)

hen I saw the guns I thought I was a dead man. Somehow, I'd always known this would be the way. Whenever you were least expecting them and turned your back then they would appear. The car came screeching down the road swerving to form a blockade. Men in uniforms held the guns, police uniforms of skip hats and flak jackets. So what? It was the police I'd most feared for years. They'd tried before and had long memories.

I'd never been an angel – well, maybe years ago when I was a tot. But now I was trying to start afresh. So, I'd slipped back and thought a money scam would do no harm. Those suits all do it, so why shouldn't I? Rising above my station? Straying too far out of my territory? Or was it just that I'd thwarted the police before? A man put down stays down – isn't that the rule? Well, fuck that. I'd come too far, through too much, to lie down for anybody. Besides, they'd never succeeded in putting me down. So, that's it – I'm due and today is the day. Well, it's as good and bad a day as any.

With an innocent friend in the car and no gun I have no choice. I'll have to trust they really are police and not rogue police. Paul Ferris trusting the police! Who would have thought? Not me. Not Paul Ferris.

Here goes. Do as they say. Hands on the top of my head and slowly get out of the car. Fuck! Everything is in slow motion. The film reel is unwinding. I am being yanked through the car window – lifted out and through like a featherweight kid. Well, I was never that big or heavy and that used to annoy them too – those old-time wannabe gangsters and fat-arsed, corrupt cops. Easy, carefully, and try to ignore the barrels. Steady and slowly. Give them no excuse. I'd cross my fingers but I don't believe in luck.

How the fuck did I get here? Where the hell did this all start?

I awoke in that state hanging somewhere between dreams and tears. Sitting up, startled and bewildered, unsure of what was wrong but certain something was. The bedroom seemed to be the same, the familiar green and white décor reassuring through the night's darkness. This was my home and my parents were asleep next door, yet still I felt uneasy and fearful. A kid's nightmare, perhaps. I'd had them before, not often but you never forget that feeling – alone, hunted, scared of everything.

I could call out for my parents. 'It was just a nightmare, Paul,' my mother was certain to reassure me. 'There, there, son, everything's hunky-ma-dory. Your Mammy and Daddy are here. Just through the wall.' Just through the wall, of course they were. Nothing to worry about, Paul. Just relax and go back to sleep. As I lay down and snuggled into the warm blankets I heard the noise and was wide awake again.

It was coming from outside and terror forced me to look. Tiptoeing to the window I pulled back the curtain and scanned the wet street below. Parked in front of our house was a large white van. In the driver's seat I could make out a bulky, black shape, the white of a shirt collar and a lardy, potato-faced profile. He seemed to be bored, looking around and tapping his fingers on the steering wheel, an impatient motorist waiting for traffic lights to change. The back of the van moved from side to side and a howl filled the air. Low and high, sharp and blunt, grunting and squealing. They weren't human noises but stuck pig, snared animal bellows. A second or two of silence followed by another dull metal clump, a shimmy of the wagon and the wailing belted out again. The driver never stirred, rattling his one-handed tattoo on the wheel and pursing his lips in an accompanying whistle.

'Heeeelp. Stop. Pleeeease stop,' came the tinny echo before disintegrating back into inarticulate sobs.

'Shut the fuck up, you, or you'll get worse.'

'Heehaayyeeooooouuuuu . . .'

'You asking for a doing, ye wee cunt?'

The van gleamed white and glistened in the Glasgow rain falling gently and steadily. Even in the middle of the night the rain would feel warm. Not cold enough to bring on the miseries but wet enough to make you look forward to your own living-room, the fireside and your family. Weather like this made me feel sad and happy at the same time. That night I just felt sick.

I knew what was going on inside that van. I was five years old after all – not exactly a kid. Besides, you could hardly miss it. Most days they would drive about Blackhill; just cruising and looking during daylight. By dusk the trouble would start. They would park up at the top of the scheme, here in Hogganfield Street, hovering with the engine turning. When a stray appeared staggering up the road they gently eased the gears into action and moved off slowly, swooping down on the target like a seagull on a mess of fish entrails.

Drawing up alongside the lonesome drunk or a group of bored young guys hanging around a close mouth there were brief, stern words from the driver. The big double doors at the back would burst open and a group of them would spring out grabbing their prey, tossing him into the back of the Meat Wagon before driving off to a quieter nook. The police made no secret of their hit squads – quite the reverse. They paraded their logo on the vehicle, wore their uniforms and carried off screaming, complaining victims oblivious to witnesses.

Through the drizzle I watched the vehicle rock and thump once more before a silent lull invaded the street. Shivers trickled through my body with the cold of the late hour and I crept back to bed to keep warm. Lying awake, tormented shrieks still gnawed at my consciousness. In the back of the van, pleading for mercy, would be one of my friends' older brothers or fathers. This was Blackhill. Everybody knew everybody in Blackhill. It might be a teenager who sometimes let me join in with his street kick-about. It might be an adult who called my Da by his first name. Or one of the cousins from down the road in Germiston or Royston. Whoever it was, they would all feel the same now.

I imagined their faces, thought their names, praying it was none of them while knowing it would be. Futile, but I believed in prayer back then and tried harder. As the mug-shots ran through my mind sleep threatened to return hand-in-hand with the silence. In the distance of the shipyards the muffled boom of the hammer reassured, lulled. Struggling to stay awake, I was losing the fight and with every family, every litany, my head nodded and I drifted off to sleep.

'Aaayyyyyeee . . .'

'Keep the wee bastard still till I . . .'

'Hhhaaahheeessppooo . . .'

All that night I begged God to make the police stop. He didn't listen.

2.

THE LEPER COLONY
by Reg McKay

'You've got to be fucking joking, man.' The speaker was John and not accustomed to swearing or judging others. He surveyed the neighbourhood and blanched. John wasn't a prude or naïve. Like most people he had never been in the area before. You didn't stray into Blackhill by accident unless you were very careless or absolutely lost. This is the Blackhill of Paul Ferris's childhood.

Among the notorious schemes of Glasgow, Blackhill was the most of everything. According to the majority of Glaswegians it was the pits and its residents had made it that way. You could live in the most decrepit slum tenement anywhere else and console yourself that at least it wasn't Blackhill where everything was more – dead babies, violent deaths, unemployment, crime, prisoners, illness, malnutrition. Blackhill was the most deprived small urban area of Glasgow, Europe and probably much farther afield. The only produce the scheme was rich in was police attention and fighting spirit.

Built on a hill to the north of the city centre, Blackhill was sectioned off in a triangle by a motorway, a stinking canal and gasworks. It was distinct, separate and easy to avoid, making it an ideal dumping ground. Many centuries before it had been a leper colony, perched on high ground overlooking the Clyde and far enough away from the burgeoning towns that would eventually form the city of Glasgow. From the 1930s, the green slopes were built over to house the refugees from the slum clearances of Gorbals, Govan, the Garngad and other crumbling inner city communities. The people moved in, delighted with their inside toilets and the luxury of bedrooms, only to discover that was all they had. Almost immediately, the place disintegrated into the reputation it now carries like a long, deep facial scar.

The houses wavered from the terraced cottage flats at the top end to the grey-fronted tenement flats making up the majority. Strictly speaking, the upper scheme was Provanmill but you had to live locally to know the difference. Provanmill consisted of quiet streets, well-tended gardens and supportive neighbours. That is where Paul Ferris's family lived at 19 Hogganfield Street. But walk to the end of road, near where the police's Meat Wagon would park at night, and the scene changed to urban decay.

Dull-grey, scarred tenements with narrow, dark close mouths. Rusting corrugated iron for windows. Water flowing from houses stripped of the plumbing for the illicit profit of selling the copper and lead to scrap merchants. Burst sewers neglected for weeks spewing their filth all over the road where the kids played. Communal greens overgrown with weeds and rough grass harbouring broken glass, rusted metal, decaying corpses of dead dogs and every inconceivable form of hazard for the legion of youngsters to stumble into.

As the fabric of Blackhill crumbled so its infamy soared as the most vicious place in a city celebrated for its razor gangs, territorial warfare and unremitting violence. The Blackhill Toi was a street army of four hundred desperadoes feared everywhere. A small scheme of Glasgow with a population of only 6,500, Blackhill punched well above its weight. It was a no man's land where every stranger was clocked, tackled and robbed.

They stole from the goods trains as they trundled on their way, from nearby factories, from other schemes, but rarely from each other. It was a place where everybody shared and often the spoils were illegal. They made food and booze from the rhubarb snaffled from the acres of fields nearby. Dairy produce from the milk-marketing depot was another staple of their diet. When gallons of illicit alcohol disappeared from a Glasgow distillery one Hogmanay every family in Blackhill got their measure. It wasn't whisky, but poison, and the death toll rose to a hundred people from that tiny scheme.

Around the closes of Blackhill children and young adults gathered buzzing cheap glue. The health of women was so bad that Dr Mary Wilson introduced Deprovera, the long-term contraceptive injection, to Blackhill before the drug had been sanctioned in Britain. Diseases long vanished from most of the industrialised world hung on in the scheme taking lives, young and old.

In a city of religious division, Blackhill was primarily Roman Catholic, as were the adjoining territories. A corridor stretching from

Blackhill down to Royston towards the city centre, including Germiston, Roystonhill and Sighthill, was known as the Garngad. As you entered the area from the city end a gable wall declared FREE GARNGAD in the style and sentiment of the Irish struggles. In July, Glasgow reverberated with Orange Walks while Garngad had its Hibernian Walk – just as militaristic, just as threatening, only supporting the other side of the divide.

Over the years, Blackhill produced victims of poverty, disease, neglect, addiction and violence. It also produced one or two heroes. The police knew of them as villains but on the streets they were hailed as freedom fighters, men who refused to succumb and succeeded in making a career for themselves in the area's sole economic activity – crime.

Welcome to the Blackhill of Paul Ferris, born on 10 November 1963.

'**B**ut, Mammy, it is so Blackhill.' **WHACK!**
'No, it's not, Paul, it's High Riddrie.'
'But, Mammy, it is . . .' **WHACK!**

I was four years old and couldn't understand the problem. On the corporation bus rumbling towards the city centre a kindly old woman had asked me where I lived. My mother wasn't a snob, she loved Blackhill, but other people could have strange reactions to our part of the town. Riddrie existed but High Riddrie was a figment of imagination, a cover against prejudice and, finally, a local joke that meant Blackhill.

This isn't a story of a poor boy gone wrong. I had a splendidly happy, privileged and loving childhood and was pleased I lived in Blackhill. For a start our home was one of the posh houses at the top of the hill. My old man ran a small bus company and we were well off. Like other kids I took it all for granted and couldn't see the difference between my family and those of my friends, the crew from the tenements. I didn't notice that their buildings were falling apart, the closes stank of glue, their middens reeked of rot or that the arses hung out of their trousers permanently. They were and are good people, my people.

We used to laugh at folk because of eccentricities. Like the Murphy family who kept a horse in the tiny bathroom of their council flat. The poor mule pulled a small cart that the family used to collect scrap metal. That they were barely surviving on their meagre pickings wasn't the issue – a horse in the bog was funny.

Blackhill was an old-time place with a hangover from the traditional tenement life. Musicians and singers would come round the streets trailing their trombones, bagpipes or one-man-band paraphernalia. Traders would knock your door selling all sorts of goodies, though somehow I only remember the tablet so sweet you felt your teeth rotting even as you ate it. One time I smuggled a bundle of my good clothes to the rag and bone man, being dead chuffed with the gaudy bauble received in return till my Ma found out – then it was pelters.

My mother and father were as strict as hell. Hard love, you might call it. Jenny and Willie Ferris were tiny with the hearts of lions. They knew right from wrong and woe betide any child of theirs that crossed the line. They had a mixed marriage, which in Glasgow means my Da was Protestant and my Ma Roman Catholic, not easy in a city where you could get your throat cut for being of the wrong persuasion. It didn't bother them at all, with their first born being called Billy after William of Orange. While my older sisters Janet, Carol and Cath were given fairly noncommittal names, when I arrived on the scene it was time to right the balance. So I was named Paul John Ferris and raised a Catholic. Religion has never bothered me one way or another, though football is a much more serious matter. I left the Church when I was about nine years old but have never left the Celtic nor ever will.

My folk's values were the values of Blackhill: never tell on anyone, sort out your own problems, if somebody hits you hit them back twice as hard – even if you have to lift a brick. It wasn't just the police's policy of brutality that made them hated in Blackhill – they were the common enemy and quite unnecessary. The police made trouble for everyone while we made trouble for those who deserved it.

Like the Snowdroppers who broke the code against stealing from your own, in this case clothes off the washing lines. Clothes were precious in such a hard up place. Snowdropping was a vicious, low-level crime against your own people. A family called Welsh were regular clothes thieves but moved on to far more sinister activities in later years, as I found out to my cost. When a Snowdropper was caught they were never reported to the police. Their fate was far worse than the state could ever dish out – a good kicking from a bunch of women. No joke, I can tell you.

Life took a dizzy turn for me when my older brother, Billy, left home. As a teenager he went off to Corby, married and settled down. Billy was jailed for a robbery and when he was in prison his wife had been sleeping around. He's such a loving guy the news broke his heart, but he kept the grief locked inside him. A short while after his release he was in a pub when two blokes started goading him about his wife. A fight ensued and knives were drawn. All that pent-up hurt just spilled over and Billy stabbed one guy to death. When he appeared in court he refused to say why there had been a fight and he was sentenced to life for a motiveless murder. It was many years later before my big brother could share with his family what had really happened.

Shortly after that my father, Willie, was jailed for a short time for not paying his income taxes. While he was in Glasgow's infamous Barlinnie Prison, known as Bar-L, he and a few others planned a robbery. On his release he deliberately got a job driving the bus for nearby Smithycroft School. One day the bus had extra passengers – bank robbers. They used the bus full of schoolkids as a get-away motor while the police frantically combed the streets. A couple of the gang couldn't wait to spend the loot and soon after were seen splashing the cash too vigorously. The police pulled them in and they sang like canaries, shopping all the others. The enterprise cost my father five years in jail.

There was no secret about my Dad's predicament. It wasn't any type of embarrassment, quite the reverse given his inventive ploy. Most families in Blackhill had somebody in jail – in fact we were one of the better-behaved families. My old man had lost his business through the tax problems. Contemplating how to care for his family he chose a local option – robbery. In Blackhill crime was as respectable a life choice as accountancy, banking or law are for middle-class folk.

Overnight there was very little money coming into the house and I'd just lost my father. Aged eight, my life had changed dramatically. It didn't feel that way since Jenny worked at two menial jobs to keep us going and was parent enough for all of us, particularly me and my young sister Maureen. But your Da is your Da and I was a wee boy missing mine.

Around the same time I made the biggest mistake of my life – a schoolyard scrap. All flailing arms and slapping punches, I won over St Philomena school's bully, Martin Welsh. I knew the Welshes from Blackhill – the ugliest bunch of thugs I've ever met even to this day. It was a bigger than usual tribe with six boys and four lassies. I can recollect next to nothing about the girls, but the Welsh brothers are inscribed forever in my nut. Packie Welsh was younger than me, Martin and Henry a bit older, while George, Tam and John were a lot older. These guys acted as tough as they looked dim. They had a kind of institutional glower to their phizogs with eyes too close together and haircuts looking as if they belonged on somebody else. They always seemed manky. Okay, so did a lot of us, but it didn't matter what the Welshes did they always looked unwashed.

The day after my victory, I heard the call: 'Ho, Ferris, ya wee shite. C'mere.' Before I'd a chance to respond I was being pummelled on all sides by the flying fists and feet of all the Welsh bros.

'Think ye're a wide man, ye wee cunt? We'll show ye wide.' As I cowered and tried to protect my head with both hands, an uppercut flew into my face cracking my nose and splitting my lip. I went down.

'Ye don't fuckin' mess wi' us, ye wee wanker.' My back lay on the gritty tarmac and my vision spun as kicks rained into my ribs, legs, stomach, till finally the tacked sole of one heavy boot stamped once then twice down on my head.

'Serves ye right, ye wee bastard.' And it was over.

It was to happen every single day of my childhood. Some or all of the Welsh crew would come at me and beat me up, from a mild punching and dead-leg to stamping and jumping on my face and stomach. Once I ran away and received a worse doing when they caught up with me. That was the day I decided never to run away from anybody again – ever.

I made a point to keep my mates out of it since the Welshes terrorised the area. These were the people who would order grown up families out their homes so they could strip the rooms of the goodies, sometimes taking over the houses. There was nobody safe from them – young, old, male or female. My mother eventually sussed something was wrong – too many bruises, cuts and torn clothes too often. But she knew better than to interfere.

When the psoriasis arrived it was a different matter. I was covered in red, scaling, itchy blotches that the doctors couldn't understand. There was no history of skin complaints in my family. Years later the medics explained that my psoriasis was purely a psychological reaction to stress – the Welshes' bullying – something I'd never forget and neither would they. I made sure of that.

Psoriasis and hormones don't mix well. By the time I'd moved to St Roch's secondary school in Royston, in the heart of the Garngad, I had a strict policy of letting no one, but no one see any of my body aside from my face and my hands. Though I'd eventually learn how to keep the reptile skin in abeyance, it made my adolescent years more awkward than they needed to be. The Welshes provided me with two traits – psoriasis and an absolute hatred of bullies.

Secondary school was a hoot. I'd float around the huge building allowed to do my own thing but ignored academically. Thing is, I didn't truant more than most kids my age. I'd have an occasional spat with some older hardman, hitting him with an object fast and furious to his shock and my friends' relief or mirth. Being a wee guy, these wide boys couldn't quite believe it when I walloped them. But it was always for a reason and they always started it. Enough trouble followed me without me chasing it.

Unlike most of the other guys in school I didn't get inveigled into the gang warfare bit. It seemed childish and false to me. As for hunting the Proddies – well, that was for the birds. A huge mob of kids from St Roch's would regularly search out the neighbouring Protestant schools and battles ensued resulting in serious injuries, often in deaths. Every now and then the Hibs Walk would circle a block of flats in Roystonhill rumoured to be occupied entirely by Protestants. They would circle the place playing their flutes and drums for hours on end as the enraged flat dwellers threw down TVs, chairs, buckets of pish. Everybody took it all so seriously. I considered it a laugh and stayed away.

I did steal cars – everybody I knew did. We would drive them past speed cops so they'd give us a chase. We always won and just abandoned the motors. By the time I was 14 I could drive as well as I needed to. Shoplifting was a lark but I was never that good. My first offence was thieving two model cars, Jaguar XJS make. I never got carried away and avoided the heavy metal that dumped many friends in approved school, borstal or whatever they were being called at the time.

By the time I hit 14 or 15 the Welshes' attacks were becoming sporadic but fierce. One time three of them grabbed me in a narrow tenement close and attacked me with hammers. My mate, Eddie Deegan, begged me to run away but I didn't do that any more. So the ugly brothers belted into me and I tried a new tactic – laughing. Every time they smashed the metal down on my skull I laughed louder till eventually they freaked and wandered off. All right, I was a bit smashed about but I would've been anyway. Besides, I'd made the thick shits think.

We hung around neighbouring Riddrie for the talent, as young blades do, drinking, sniffing, swallowing, snorting any substance that came along. Compared with my mates I was downright cautious, but the combination of substances and women made for great impromptu parties. Finally I lost my aching virginity – though with trousers firmly on. It lasted minutes, if that, which was just as well since the man of the house returned home unexpectedly. We were all scrambling around hiding in wardrobes when Eddie decided to dive out the window. He hadn't looked first and ended up dangling by his throat from some telephone wires 30 feet off the ground.

Another time we'd stolen a case of brandy and taken it to a disused garage. Drunk as skunks, an orgy ensued. I was standing there snogging the face off this lassie while another of my mates was doing the dirty deed with a girl against a wall only two feet away. When the shout of 'Polis' went up I heard nothing and kept on chewing lip. The guy shagging did hear and took to his heels, deserting his partner where she stood. When the police burst in I was still winching my girl while the other leaned against the wall with a dreamy expression on her face, T-shirt tucked under her chin, legs wide apart, her knickers and jeans dangling around one ankle. The police charged me with trespassing then offered their congratulations. Two women at once . . . as if.

That was our style for a couple of years but it was all just *growing-up stuff in the style of Blackhill or any scheme in Glasgow. There are plenty of guys who lived the full teenage rampage then went on to university degrees, white-collar jobs and mortgages. There are others who used their adolescence as an apprenticeship for a life of crime. I was a quiet kid who turned away from plenty of opportunities to blow my stack.*

At school I was called in to the assistant head's room. On the way there I tried to work out what minor misdemeanour I was in trouble for but shouldn't have wasted my time worrying. Because my birthday fell in November I wasn't being allowed to leave that summer. No talk of education or qualifications, just of rules. Another eight months hanging around the playground and facing teachers who'd rather be drinking tea and dunking biscuits.

'It's the law, Paul, you must stay on till Christmas – no questions.' He might as well have said waste another six months of my life. I nodded, left the room, walked out of school and kept walking.

'Christmas, that'll be chookies.' I was ready to be a grown-up.

So, no sad story. No certificates and only casual learning, true. But no stint in child prison, no drug addiction, no mindless gang warfare. Just a wee guy with attitude determined to have a go at life.

5

STAND AND DELIVER

My first serious crime was committed in that twilight zone between leaving school and being old enough to work. In the dead of night along with two good friends from St Roch's – Bernard Gallacher and Jim Kelly – we stripped all the lead from the roof of Collins the publishers in Townhead. It netted us several hundred pounds each – a lot of dosh for kids in the 1970s. I wasn't a great reader or writer at the time so you could say that my first encounter with publishing was entirely profitable.

Another time, a new warehouse had just opened nearby – B&Q, selling everything from nails through to bathroom suites. The developers obviously didn't study their street maps very carefully and left the unit with piss-easy security and a short walking distance from Blackhill. As soon as it opened, the Blackhill mobs were regular after-hours visitors. Most nights young guys staggered down the back streets lugging a bath, a box of fitments, flat-packed furniture. It was so easy they were stealing to order, same-day delivery.

It became a nightly irritation to the local bizzies who needed to nail it on the head. When we turned up at the place these two uniforms jumped us even before we could do the door in. They took a crowbar off one of my friends, walked over to the store's gleaming glass front door and smashed it. They wanted to get someone for breaking and entering and without the damaged door it would have been a charge of loitering with intent only. When they humped a load of stuff into their squad car wherein we were held captive I protested. For my pains one of the bears skelped me on the side of the head with my own jemmy. The purloined goods were never produced as evidence, ending up in some cop's own home, no doubt.

The first legitimate job was quick in coming. With my father now released from prison things were looking up at home but the money was still tight. Van boy at Waverly Vintners and £180 gross per week would do nicely. My folks were proud of me for holding down a job and bringing in a man's wage. My father's spirit and self-respect had taken a hammering in prison and it was up to me to contribute as best I could. At first, I enjoyed the work, with most of the drivers being utter chancers with a first-class line in patter. Some of the old geezers had a well-practised daily routine doing the absolute minimum of work and hiding out in their favourite watering hole most of the time. Facing a future full of all that drudgery, who was to blame them?

By the age of 16 I'd secured a half-decent job but otherwise carried on as before and carried a knife. As yet the knife was for no greater purpose than to be one of the lads. To be without one would have been like John Wayne without a shooter – half-dressed. You got yourself a chib without plan or purpose of using it. But I knew the rules. Slashing was in and stabbing out. A knife wound could kill accidentally but a slash merely marked, albeit permanently. Go round sticking people they would assume you were out to end their lives and the rules also said you met fire with fire.

Young guys wore their scars like a symbol of respect, signifying they were up for anything and could be trusted in hard times. There was an urban myth of the young neds in hospital casualty wards of a busy weekend begging the doctors to make the stitches big and clumsy so they could impress their mates. Must have been a story made up by someone from the soft underbelly of town because there was absolutely no need to try to be marked – no need at all.

Late one night, my pal Stewarty and I had bought a Blackhill briefcase – a carrier bag full of booze – and were heading to a house where a party was promised. We'd already had a few drinks – in my case Irn Bru laced with vodka – and were feeling good with life. Aged 16 we were all grown up with cheeks full of pimples and clumsy razor nicks. Out of the shadows stepped Mick Kenna, a local hardman in his thirties and infamous for his viciousness. He claimed us or, more accurately, our bag of booze. When Stewarty resisted, Mick Kenna started to kick seven shades of shit out of him. All over the road rolled Stewarty with Kenna walking after him still stamping and booting though he'd won the fight a long time since.

As I watched I knew I had to do something to save my friend. If I'd gone in against Kenna he would've made mincemeat of us both without breaking sweat. Besides, he was just as likely to start cutting us up if he thought the odds were stacked against him. If I didn't do something he would stick Stewarty just for the hell of it. Reaching for the knife in my pocket, I flicked the blade open and stepped forward slashing at Kenna's face. A slash is not enough to stop someone unless they are worried for their looks and Kenna had lost his long ago. But he was hurting. As my arm thrust out again he shied away and my knife gored the side of his neck, sticking in his throat.

That first knifing had happened in a hurry as I'd worried for my pal. What spooked me later was how calm I'd been and how unmoved by the act of forcing a blade into someone's flesh. As Kenna gurgled, moaned and dropped to the ground it was like watching a film in slow motion. I couldn't have cared less whether he'd lived or died. Kenna had deliberately sought to inflict pain and damage on a couple of young guys minding their own business. That was his style and he deserved all he got. Then the thought occurred to me that wee Paul Ferris had just sorted out one of Blackhill's wide men. I would never compete with these guys physically but with a knife, a weapon, an equaliser, I could take care of anyone. I'd discovered a way of fighting back.

Kenna was rushed to hospital and survived, a situation that left Stewarty and myself in deep trouble. There would be no police inquiry, of course, since Mick Kenna would tell them nothing and make no complaint. But he and his would seek their own form of justice with all the Kennas after our hide – not a pleasant position to be in. As we fretted and watched, we got on with our lives.

At that time a brand of herbal cigarettes was being punted in the shops as a cancer-free alternative to the real thing. Smoking those fags was a disgusting, rancid experience, but someone had discovered they possessed magical attributes. Chewing the mixture brought on florid hallucinations, providing a cheap alternative to LSD and much more accessible than mushrooms. The local storekeeper must have thought the Blackhill guys had turned into health freaks. In truth, it was a better high than glue sniffing and you could still have a drink and a decent smoke while you were tripping.

I must have overdone it because the terrors rolled on over days. I was sick, babbling all over the shop with vivid flashbacks pulling my attention away from the here and now to a place where I was the only visitor. By the third day my worried parents thought I was ill and took me to a doctor who arranged for me to see a psychiatrist immediately. With my Dad leading me by the hand we went to Duke Street Hospital, an ancient loony bin on a main road not far from the Wills cigarette factory and almost next door to a slaughterhouse. We waltzed through the heavy swing doors, up some stairs and along lengths of corridor till we reached the waiting room. As we sat and waited I looked about me trying to work out who exactly was mad because I knew it wasn't me.

A door swung open and a man with an enormous shaggy beard entered rapidly, walking straight up to where I was sitting. Leaning over with his face close to mine, he jabbed his hand out to shake and said, 'Pleased to meet you, Paul. I'm Doctor Baird.' Instantly I melted into convulsions of laughter. Bent double, tears streaming down my face, I couldn't stop giggling and snorting. As the mirth subsided I looked up and saw my old man staring at me, embarrassed and totally pissed off, while the good doctor was scratching his chin thoughtfully, analytically.

'What are you laughing at, Paul?' someone asked and I was off again. I thought the guy had introduced himself as Dr Beard, an appropriate handle given the excessive bundle of hair he had dangling from his face. Not funny at all as I realised that I could be in deep trouble and they might, after all, think I'd lost the plot.

The session finished with my father and the psychiatrist, eyes heavy with serious meaning, mumbling at each other as I was permitted to leave the room. Rather than loiter I started walking towards the exit, with every step expecting beefy male nurses to jump out and wrap me up in a straitjacket. As I approached the front doors, my gut started to thump and my chest tighten till I found myself on the pavement in the open air. I didn't stop running till I arrived at my sister Cath's house in the Barrowfield area.

Cath was a kindly sister whom I trusted and I told her everything including the hallucinogenic herbs. That was okay by her and she allowed me to stay on as long as I behaved within certain limited rules. What with the Mick Kenna situation bubbling in Blackhill, the Welshes still on my trail, and a threat of a return visit to the mad doc, I accepted the refuge gratefully. It was meant to be a temporary escape but I'd never again live in Blackhill.

Barrowfield was no safe haven, with a reputation almost matching Blackhill's. A small area where the young guys were not satisfied with external territorial warfare but formed two factions – one at either end of the scheme. The gangs had romantic names like Lady Spur and Torch but there was nothing poetic about their action. A number of times, as I picked my way back to Cath's house in Stamford Street, I found myself caught in the middle of a pitched battle. All around me there were skirmishes where individuals separated from their troops were being slashed, hacked and kicked. There would be a charge and the two groups would sprint screaming and roaring towards each other up the main road as I dodged past on the way home. Never once was I stopped or challenged. Rules dictate that you stay out of other people's fights, so that's what I did along with showing no sign of fear. My years with the Welshes had taught me how to look calm and relaxed while doubting I was going to survive. It was an ability that would serve me well in years to come.

A group of friends had fallen into good times. One came to my house one night – pay night and I'd managed to hand my mother £80 from my weekly wage – and offered me £500 from a wee turn. I refused the cash on the basis that money was always scarce and he didn't owe me anything. He just laughed and took a wad from his pocket that would've choked a hungry donkey. I looked at the greenbacks and thought hard. Thought of the long hours at work humping crates of whisky and vodka down steep cellar steps, and the drivers no longer seeming like characters but lazy old bastards sitting on their fat, haemorrhoid-heavy arses watching the young guys sweat. For what – to pay the taxman and slip my mother 80 notes to keep the devil from the door, just from the door? That was the night I chose a life of crime. It didn't feel momentous and God didn't send down bolts of lightning. But that was the night right enough.

I took the £500, chucked the job and joined the syndicate. Our speciality was a crude form of smash and grab specialising in jewellers' shops throughout Glasgow. Night raids were safest so that's what we did – smash in the window or the door and lift as many goodies as we could while the alarm, if they had one, squealed for the cavalry. Hit and run, in and out, then nip round to the dealers to trade in the loot and pocket any cash we'd picked up. The older, more wizened people who were up for a little bit of reset – buying and selling on stolen goods – were probably ripping off us young pups. We didn't suspect and we didn't care. The money we earned was more than we'd ever hoped for and we felt as if we could do anything.

The confidence gleaned from my new profession spilled over into the rest of my life. Till now I'd been hanging around and experimenting in what was available. Overnight I adopted a full-time criminal and delinquent lifestyle. We still hung around nearby Riddrie a great deal of the time – frequently partying, buzzing the glue and hanging out with the local women. One time a few of us were loitering in Riddrie when we spotted a full-scale raiding party from Cranhill approaching. Well outnumbered, the others decided to retreat on the assumption that we were in for some serious damage. On point of principle I couldn't budge and stayed alone to face the marauders.

'Wee man, who was that shooting off?' asked one Cranhill brave.

'The Blackhill mob,' I replied helpfully.

''Where d'ye stay yersel', pal?' another enquired.

'Cross the road there,' I pointed to the first house I spotted.

'You're wi' us then if that lot come back. Right?' the pack leader was telling rather than asking.

'Sure thing,' I muttered with a smile. I hung around to see what was to happen, determined that my night's entertainment shouldn't be cut short, when I spotted Eddie Deegan coming tramping along the road with reinforcements. The Cranhill team prepared to charge.

'Right, wee man, you're wi' us against they Blackhill bastards,' the leader was calling me in.

'Sure thing,' I replied before pulling my blade and getting stuck into the Cranhill guys.

'What kept ye?' I asked Eddie as the others joined the fray, as if to suggest I'd been fighting on my own since they had fled.

Eventually I took up another legitimate job, van boy again but for Schafer of Glasgow, a high-class company specialising in expensive furs, leather coats and dress wear. The daily grind had become more boring than ever and my personal habits too well formed. So, for a time, I was both a holder of a respectable job by day and a tearaway by night. Then one Paul Ferris caught up with the other and a minor incident on the streets left me with a deep facial scar – not the company image at all. So, it was back to full-time participation in the free market. Not that it would be a sacrifice since my friends had continued to prosper and demonstrated such through small quirks like hiring taxis for the whole day, buying cars and being loose with their cash. I was invited.

George Redmond and I started to steal bank bags. It was a simple enough routine of working out when companies sent their staff to pay in the day's takings, turning up and snatching them. No fuss, no violence, no bother. It was almost too easy then. It has been made much harder now.

Violence and dealing with aggressors had become a more familiar part of my repertoire through a whole series of events. One night I was going to a party with a friend when an older guy tried to grab his record collection, so I stabbed the thief. Another time, sitting on a bus with Eddie Deegan and some others heading to a night out in a city centre disco, a bunch of hulking, winkle-picker-wearing Teddy Boys started to noise us up. Seeing it was going to lead to a massed brawl with us younger, smaller crew on the sharp end, I invited the Teddy Boys' leader to a square go – just him and me, head to head, settling the aggro. He was up for it and the bus driver, sensing the impending fracas, pulled the bus over by pure chance outside the Glasgow Royal Infirmary, which seemed appropriate. On the pavement, the big guy with the greasy quiff and broad, fuzzy sideburns sneered at the skinny young team and confidently stepped forward, whereupon I drew my Stanley blade down his face. His loudmouthed chorus went quiet as they huckled their leader through the doors of the Royal.

Bullies. Everywhere there were people trying to do the dirty on others just because they could. I wouldn't stand for it against me, mine or a stranger. Anger never entered my range of emotions – I was well past that. I just got even by whatever means necessary.

The Welshes were unfinished business and they were heavy on my mind. As a hairy-arsed 17-year-old I thought I was as grown up as I was ever going to be. Well, you do, don't you, till you later realise that you were nothing but a spindly kid learning the ropes. An accidental gain helped me on my way.

One day I popped into one of the few local stores to buy an apple and, as I waited to pay, watched a woman hand over £60 to the shopkeeper without return. The guy counted the money and placed it in a wallet in a drawer. I reckoned he was a moneylender and decided to take an interest-free loan. When he popped through to his other shop next door I leapt over the counter, grabbed the wallet and was out of the place in a flash. It was yet another unreported crime since he wasn't about to complain to the police about money he couldn't account for. There was about £700 in the wallet and I used it to buy my first car, an old-fashioned three-litre Wolsley and pure class. Too young to drive legally, no licence and no insurance, I had to take precautions. So, I parked my car in Germiston and walked up the road to Blackhill. That is when the first opportunity arose.

6.

A DISH BEST EATEN COLD

I'd recognise a Welsh anywhere, even at a distance on a dark night. Up ahead of me on Royston Road John Welsh was walking casually in my direction. He was one of the older members of the tribe, in his late thirties, and had never done me harm directly. Nevertheless he was a Welsh, contributing to their power and the scourge of anyone weaker. As I huddled into my jacket sheltering from the chill of the night's breeze we passed each other at a bus stop just across the road from the Provanmill Inn, Arthur Thompson's pub. Turning abruptly, I drew an open razor from my pocket and silently sliced his throat from ear-to-ear. As I walked smartly on I didn't look back but could hear him gurgle and rattle before falling to the deck. He almost died that night and never spoke normally again. He would carry the scar for the rest of his life and that was just fine by me.

'One down,' I mumbled to myself. 'More to follow.'

Nobody had a clue who slashed John Welsh till many months later. I didn't seek to boast about my exploits in taking care of one of the scheme's most despised figures. My closest mates were not even told. The business of Ferris and the Welshes was an entirely personal matter and would stay that way till I finished it, or, rather, them.

At this time I was still living with my sister Cath in Barrowfield but slipping in and out of Blackhill at will. The tactic rattled those hunting my hide since they'd no idea where to find me. While Barrowfield was useful for self-preservation it also stopped any possibility of those bastards going to my parents' house. They even left my friends' houses alone, knowing that I wasn't there. The brothers grim were beginning to realise that if they made trouble I would slip back into the scheme and create hell on wheels.

Other Welshes had to be had and I laid an ambush one night with my friend George Redmond backing me up. We crouched in the shadows opposite a tenement in Blackhill's Greenside Street where most of the Welsh brothers were attending a party. My game plan was simply to take them on in whatever order they emerged, waiting all night if needs be. As George and I hid in some bushes we heard a commotion.

A girl I'd known at school, Eileen Bonnar from Royston, had come from the party house. Eileen had been friendly towards me at a time when it would have been easier to freeze me out. I watched carefully as Tam Monaghan emerged, caught up with Eileen and tried to coax her into a bit of sex. She was having none of it. Monaghan began to pull at her clothing and push her about and Eileen was retaliating in what was bound to be a losing battle. A few other guys had turned up and were hovering nearby like gawky nooky-vultures waiting for the kill and their share of the pickings. For certain parties around those streets an enforced gang-bang was viewed as just a normal night's entertainment. Not while we were watching.

George and I nodded at each other and moved. As I walked quickly from my hiding place I was just in time to see Tam Monaghan punch Eileen over a hedge. Pulling out two knives I rammed one into Monaghan's chest then went after the others. Whitey, a well known glue-head, and this evil shite called Johnny Rotten, a cousin of the Welshes, squared up to me. These guys always went around tooled up and drew their blades. First Whitey rushed at me and after a flurry of thrusts and parries I managed to slice him down the arm, leaving him howling, retreating. Rotten charged me with his shoulder, sending me backwards on to a fence and jamming my neck between two spars. I looked up in time to see a Stanley blade slice down my cheek and chin. As Rotten, razor in hand, leaned over my prostrate body, I reached my arm out and round, thrusting my knife blade hard and deep up his arse. He buckled and screamed and I scrambled to my feet. Unknown to me, George Redmond had opted out and left the scene in a hurry, allowing a fourth rapist to escape. At the time I was angry with George but later understood that he didn't carry the same luggage as me, that unbearable intolerance of tormentors. There were angry shouts from the party close and it was time to vamoose.

The wound to my face was deeper and longer than the run-of-the-

mill battle scar so I took myself off to the casualty unit of the Royal. Later that night, lying on a bed in one of the hospital's curtain-partitioned cubicles, I heard familiar grunts from next door. It was the brothers grim, the Welshes, visiting one of their wounded comrades and asking about me.

'Where's the wee cunt staying?'

'D'ye think he'll be at his mother's hoose?'

'Whit aboot they fuckin' Redmonds or Deegans – he's close tae them, eh?'

Biting my lip to prevent the sniggers, I gripped my one remaining knife already open in my pocket. Earlier that night I would've had them right there in the disinfectant-smelling ward. But enough is enough and, besides, I liked to hoodwink the thick thugs.

The story of the battle spread and was to do us no harm in the Blackhill pecking order. Monaghan had almost died, my blade piercing his chest through a nipple and missing his heart by a fraction. Whitey had bled a lot but not as much as Johnny Rotten, who limped and stood up for months. All three of the scum were senior members of the Provan Young Team and were close to the Welshes who maintained their rummage for revenge

That was probably the first time that people in Blackhill viewed me as a contender. They were all terrified of the Welsh family, the Kennas and their assorted hangers-on but I was the one doing the fighting. It was a role that suited me better than that of the young Paul Ferris sent scampering for his life every day – at least now I had self-respect and dignity. I knew it was dangerous with every action inviting major grief, yet being quiet and passive was far from safe – those guys loved to attack a soft touch. I felt good about myself for the first time in many years. But I was far from finished with them.

Because of my growing reputation I was invited to join a select criminal syndicate run by two brothers, Harry and Frank. Good friends both, they specialised in cash bag snatches and described the routine. Maybe I was getting too cocky and didn't listen well enough. George Redmond and I were arrested and charged with assault and robbery for our totally fluffed efforts in grabbing a bank bag from travel agent staff in Airdrie. It was a lesson in the need for careful planning we were to pay heavily for. As a first offender I was sent to Longriggend Remand Centre to await trial while George, being older, was sent off to Bar-L. I was 17 years old and in prison for the first time.

When I went into the jail my feet seemed to become heavier, my senses stretched taut and I ached for something familiar. Of course the point is that there is nothing familiar or personal. Prisons were for punishment rather than detention, even on remand when you were yet to be tried and still innocent in the eyes of the law. The loss of liberty and the frustration of containment is a punishment whatever any old lag or right-wing politician tells you to the contrary. Loss of your freedom is punishment the first time and the last time. Eventually you learn how to cut off though never entirely to relax in your cage. Punishment enough without the extras of staff treating you like dog shite and the ever-present threat of violence from all quarters.

A few weeks later I was released on bail, trusted by the state to turn up voluntarily at my trial. George and I were for the high jump so I opted to give the court a body swerve. George was brought in on the Bar-L special bus, a prison on wheels, and sentenced to 22 months. The court issued a warrant for my arrest and now, for the first time, I was a wanted man.

Ducking and diving around the Glasgow area, certain parties asked me to carry out a little removal job that was to give me some spare money and my first, albeit brief, association with guns. Asked to move a shotgun and some knives, I packed them in my car and drove to the meeting place. A hundred yards behind me a police patrol car was parked and eyeballed my car. Knowing I was wanted on an outstanding warrant they started their car, dimmed their lights and sped up. I spied them and took off in the motor, bobbing and weaving through busy built-up areas till forced to concede that the Wolsley might be majestic but lacked manoeuvrability. Deserting the car, I'd just enough time to open the door and sprint for cover, leaving the police in possession of a boot-load of weapons, more than enough fingerprints and a half-eaten packet of potato crisps. Now after me for seriously heavy metal, they renewed their efforts and had me banged up back in Longriggend within weeks. This time there wasn't a snowball's hope in hell of bail.

Ferris, the rising hardman of Blackhill, didn't like prison one whit but was well used to adjusting to fear and uncertainty. Besides, there were plenty of faces I knew in there – one of the benefits of coming from an area like Blackhill. One face in particular shone out – Sid Johnstone, close associate of the Welsh brothers, cruel bastard and tyrant. He might as well have been one of the brothers for all I was concerned, and I noted with anger that he hadn't mended his ways inside the jail.

In my cell I pulled loose a metal slat from underneath my bed and worked on it till it would serve as a makeshift razor. In Longriggend the inmates were herded into an open-air enclosure and encouraged to walk round for their statutory exercise period. Waiting till the right moment I stepped up to Sid Johnstone and slashed him across his face. Prisoners milled all around us and some screws were meant to be watching from somewhere in the yard, yet no one witnessed the assault. I wandered away free to take my exercise, feeling good with myself.

Later, someone informed on me and I was confined to the cells. No charges were ever pressed, presumably because the grass was too cowardly to stand witness at a trial. Either way I was kept in the restrictive dogleg cells for the remainder of my stay in Longriggend. Some folk back in the scheme didn't think I'd received justice. Not that they cared too much for officialdom anyway. The rule was that we sorted out our own problems whatever the state might think or do. The ugly brothers were letting it be known that they were unhappy and exactly what they intended to do to me. I was 17 years old and the word on the streets of Blackhill was, 'Paul Ferris is a dead man.'

At my trial for the attempted theft of the bank bags my lawyer, Peter Forbes, tried to plea bargain using my age and lack of prior serious offences. He might as well have been whistling 'Dixie' since the sheriff, a senior judge in Scotland, handed down the standard sentence of three months in Glenochil Detention Centre. It was the era of an old-fashioned approach to bad boys – short, sharp shock. The terminology didn't comfort me but the knowledge that my older brother Billy was 11 years into a life sentence did. If he could survive that fit and well, so could I. And I did, but I blew the chance to be out in eight weeks by refusing to take orders or accept shit from other prisoners and generally acting the angry young man who didn't give a toss for any of them. Stupid really, since a day of freedom is worth a year in jail. But you're only young once and the young have to learn somehow, especially in prison.

A few months out of Glenochil the firearms charges came up and I appeared before a sheriff and jury in Glasgow. It was a scenario I was to become comfortable with but not on that day. The evidence was all on their side and I was sentenced to a year back in Glenochil but, this time, the more relaxed Young Offenders Institution. This was an entirely different matter from the torture wing, being closer to a standard adult prison in the length of sentences, activities and time spent doing hee-haw all. While there I formed a close bond with a group of young men. When I walked out of Glenochil I thought I'd seen the last of them forever but I was to meet the Glenochil Wolves sooner than I thought.

A few weeks out of prison and I was out to earn some money through a raid on a jeweller's store. My accomplice was to meet me at the scene when he realised he was being followed by the cops. He got off his mark, scadoodled, ran for the hills – leaving yours truly alone and blissfully ignorant. In the jeweller's shop I was hefting a weight of gold chains and sundry precious items across the counter, reckoning to myself that the haul was worth several thousand pounds, when the police burst in and bust me. It was a prompt return to Longriggend and an experience that came close to ruining my frail faith in human nature.

7.

HIPPOCRATIC OAF

The red spots had appeared a few weeks earlier. I'd noticed them and thought no more. By the time of my return to Longriggend I was furious, despondent and spitting blood. I didn't settle well at all and being inside was beginning to feel like a bad habit. My foul mood resulted in several fights with other prisoners and a gang of screws manhandling me into the restricted cells. In these cells there is no furniture or bedding and you are kept dressed in the regulation issue pyjamas that are as rough as sackcloth. The small red spots of the earlier weeks had served as a warning – my psoriasis had returned with a vengeance.

Periods in hospital and many years of self-treatment had taught me the simple care routine, but in prison everything requires medical sanction. Repeatedly I asked the prison doctor for treatment. Repeatedly the prison doctor refused. Within days the symptoms covered 90 per cent of my body, missing only my face, genitals and the soles of my feet. I couldn't lie down, sleep or rest. The pain prevented me from being interested in anything, even conversation. A seeping, ripe mass of red raw blisters, I paced the stone floor of the cell. At every joint my skin cracked and tore, creating a constant dull ache and a sequence of biting sharp pains. Leaning over to lift my food tray or to slop out the stinking chamber pot was agony. Crouching to crap broke and cracked the skin on my lower back, buttocks and on top of my knees. When I moved the coarse material of the institutional pyjamas rubbed like fire and broken glass yet I could not, would not, remove them for fear the wardens would see my body. I didn't want to look at myself. I was the reptile man. Repeatedly I asked the doctor for help. Repeatedly the doctor refused to help.

From hospital tests I'd learned that most people with psoriasis had inherited the condition through their families. There was no such pattern in my case, which was deemed to be purely psychological in cause. There was no need for a qualified doctor to help me trace back the origins of this infliction. It was like the Welshes had come back to haunt and bully the boy Paul anew. Growing up, growing away and exacting some revenge was not enough. Psoriasis had grown from my adolescence, a gift from the ugly brothers that would be with me all my days.

My hate for the Welshes reared up afresh with every painful step and every sleepless night. All I could do was revert to covering my embarrassment, refusing to remove the sharp teeth of the pyjamas and declining the obligatory showers for week after week. When, in desperation, I eventually opted for a shower in some crazed notion that it might reduce the heat and relieve the pain I recoiled in agony as the water jets hit my body, electric shocks shooting through my nerve ends, rattling the blisters and piercing my very testicles. I ran naked from the shower back to my cell, threw myself on the floor and rolled from side to side on the tempting cold of the stone. Far from helping, it made it worse – bursting the blisters and tearing at my skin. Still I was refused any medical treatment.

On the day of my trial and departure from Longriggend, I refused the obligatory naked walk through the prison reception area to put on my civilian clothes. I was desperate to leave but wanted no one – no one at all – to see the state of my body, especially the screws. The prison officers on reception are often an easier-going bunch for some reason and after some banter I was allowed the privacy of a cubicle in which to change. I was leaving Longriggend after one of the lowest points in my life, a time when I discovered that a doctor is not always a doctor but sometimes a soldier of the state, a lethal combatant, a torturer.

At Glasgow Sheriff Court I was ushered into a high-security cell – an unusual action when dealing with someone my young age not charged with armed murder or deemed to be a crazy psychopath. Someone had marked my card, but who and why? Because I'd been demanding a doctor and refused to walk naked in front of others? Upstairs in the dock, the sheriff reckoned I'd strayed from the fold too quickly and enthusiastically after release from Glenochil so promptly sent me back there for a further nine months.

With my three prison terms and long periods held on remand I'd *spent more of my short adult life inside prison than out. The thought of returning to Glenochil for an extended time did not warm the cockles of my heart. Little did I know that within hours I would feel almost grateful I'd been sent to prison and my waning faith in human nature would receive a timely boost.*

8

THE HOWL OF THE WOLVES

I n Glenochil's reception I was given the usual medical once over to ensure I wasn't carrying fleas, rampant pox or a heroin habit. I expected nothing more or less than a cursory glance and knew I'd have to undress in front of others. As soon as my shirt hit the deck one of the nursing officers, Davie McCallum, took one look at my livid flesh, glowered at his colleagues and snapped, 'Get this man into the hospital wing NOW.' Turning to me and dropping his tone to a reassuring burr, he said, 'Don't worry, son, you'll be fine here.' Then with a sly wink, 'We WILL take care of you.' And they did.

For three months I rested in the hospital wing with the treatment for my psoriasis carefully administered through the material of my clothes, ointments and diet. From the crawling reptilian state I'd been in they turned me back into a healthy young lad fit enough to face the day-to-day rigours of prison life. All medics had been in danger of being labelled by me as self-seeking cruel bastards on the side of the uniformed boot boys. Davie McCallum quietly went about changing my view. He must have known that his colleagues in Longriggend had neglected my condition. When I got to know Davie a wee bit, I reckon he was seething inside at what he considered unprofessional conduct. Typical of his principles, he never mentioned the Longriggend creeps in front of me, ever. Davie McCallum taught the young Paul Ferris not to judge a person by his title, position or qualifications but to judge everyone on their actions.

Back in the mainstream prison I was delighted to be reunited with many old comrades from my earlier sentence in Glenochil. Most of them had been released, misbehaved and returned, though some hadn't even achieved a walk beyond the gates. Not that they let on that they were bothered one way or another. Mainly from Glasgow, though others were from Edinburgh and smaller places, the group had been a natural coming together of those most likely to have a go. At first glance a patchwork quilt of physical attributes and variations on Scottish dialects, we'd a great deal in common. All hardened criminals, street-taught to fight, wise to a fly move, very young, we were locked up and angry as fuck. Fencing us all in like that was asking for trouble and we were the very ones to dish it out. We became known as The Glenochil Wolves.

We'd all been through the non-cooperation route and realised that while it was fun the system reeled you in eventually, adding time to your sentence and removing the little remaining flexibility you had within those walls. While not about to kowtow to anyone we found another target to vent our spleen on. At that time sex offenders and police informers were detained alongside us in the open prison. They would do nicely.

Big Eck from Dundee was desperate to join The Wolves and today was the day of his initiation test in the textile shop. Eck wasn't called Big for a joke. He was a hulking monster of a man and still in his teens. His biceps were thicker than my thighs and his shoulders strained any shirt the institution could provide. Still, he had to prove he was tough enough and had a strong enough stomach for The Wolves.

As the machinery purred and rattled and the steam presses spluttered and hissed, Big Eck drifted quietly away from his position and hovered behind a prisoner seated at his workstation intent on his needlework. This was a guy who'd sat close to Eck and chatted with him every day for months. You might say they were acquaintances and had never before exchanged a hostile word. Without a cheep, Big Eck picked up the entire top section of an industrial sewing machine, held it at full stretch and slammed it down on the bloke's head which split wide open, spilling blood and scattering bone splinters across the bench. The riot alarms wailed while the screws team-handled Eck out of the way with a broad grin on his face. We punched a few faces and kicked balls – till the screws regained some order.

Eck was offered membership of The Wolves. His victim was hospitalised, surviving long enough to be brought back to prison to face an assault on his cracked skull that very same day. A few mornings later we were all kept in our cells beyond slop-out time.

The word floated down the wing that Big Eck's pal had been found in his cell swinging by his neck, his swollen tongue slobbering down his chin. A cheer rang out and spread from wing to wing till the whole prison celebrated. But it was only another sex offender down with many more to go.

Eck's victim was not the first or the last. His story is only of interest because the big man had the strength to lug a piece of industrial machinery at the pederast. Killing the sex offenders wasn't what we were after at all – they could do that themselves. We hounded them into suicide and we were good at it. Every day we took every chance to assault the vermin. Sometimes we would target one in particular, taking turns to thump or cosh him at regular, five-minute intervals. We didn't administer anything strong enough to ruin the guys physically. Within time we wrecked most of them psychologically.

Nonces and ponces, we despised them all and wreaked our frustration and anger on them. What's that I hear them say – psychological problems, deprived childhoods, treatment, change, control, sympathy? Fair do's, but does any of that stop them torturing kids, blackmailing infants, ravishing women, doing it all again and again and again? Well, does it? Chemically castrate the fuckers and some of them just keep on at it. No hard-on. No orgasm. No feeling. But they keep on at it.

Why did we bother? Because it was and remains the ultimate breach of our code, our ethics and our moral guide to day-to-day living. Lowlife like us have standards. We don't grass, we don't hurt non-combatants, we do time rather than put our comrades down, we tell the police sweet fuck all and we don't hurt women and kids. To sexually assault them is the ultimate breach and we don't care who the perpetrator is.

I feel the same way about sex abusers almost 20 years later. Okay, so I know a bit more about containment, treatment and so on. But tell me, why is it the quacks, the shrinks and the social workers still haven't found a cure or anything that vaguely works? While we play catch-up the abuse just goes on and on and on. Shame on us all for allowing that to happen, but those 18-year-old cons knew how to stop the sex abuse of women and children.

Over a short time in Glenochil there were around ten suicides. The Scottish Prison Service tried to hush it up but eventually the public found out, not that the suicides were all sex offenders or were encouraged on their way by The Wolves. The screws gave us very little hassle over our little campaign while it was going on. In fact, I believe the average prison officer held child abusers in even greater contempt than we did and turned a very blatant blind eye. Isn't it curious that not one of the dear departed sex abusers left a farewell note pointing the finger at The Wolves? Or did they? Collusion – you find it in the most unexpected quarters sometimes.

The only sex offender that held out and resisted our charm was a bloke called Raymond Gilmour who had been jailed for the murder of young Pamela Hastie in Linwood near Paisley. Gilmour received as much violence as anyone else. I remember participating in systematic repeat beatings of him over several days. He was scalded and badly burned on numerous occasions. His drinks were spat in. Rat droppings were mixed in with his food at every meal. If he hesitated in a corridor somebody kicked him up the arse or punched him in the kidneys. As he passed the other prisoners he would hear a cacophony of threats:

'Dead man walking, Gilmour.'

'We're gonnae cut yer cock off in yer sleep.'

'This blade's for you, Gilmour.'

Never once did he cease his protestations of innocence. Young Pamela's death had produced a public outcry and a great deal of media pressure on the police to identify a culprit. Raymond Gilmour was quite specific in blaming Charlie Craig, a senior detective with Strathclyde Police, for using psychological and physical torture to force a confession out of him. Eventually I got to the stage of accepting that people can be wrongfully convicted of anything, even child abuse and murder. Later, I found out that Craig was in the habit of fitting people up and was protected by some very interesting villains. I regret the suffering Gilmour faced. The Wolves should have been targeting Craig and his like.

My nine months served, I was led on to the prison bus at the gates of Glenochil. A silent ride down the winding rural roads soon took us to Stirling Station where the doors of the bus swung open spewing me out into the British Rail car park. No sooner had my feet touched the ground than the hatchet-faced driver drove off. For a second or two I watched the prison-blue bus with dark painted windows manoeuvre through the small-town traffic and thought, 'Is that it?'

It must have been how it felt to be driven out of town in the old days of America's Wild West. No horse, no saddle, no gun. Just a one-way ticket.

When I arrived on the platform I was delighted to be greeted by an old friend from Blackhill, Alco MacDonald. As we rode the train together towards Glasgow, word emerged that there had been yet another suicide in Glenochil that day. The newspapers were calling for an immediate investigation. When the self-serving bureaucracy eventually kicked in, the formal inquiry made no mention of The Wolves or our leader, Neily the Bomb, but pointed blame at the prison staff. True to form, they were right but for all the wrong reasons.

9

FORT APACHE, BLACKHILL

T he bottle smashed, sending a blue-yellow flame flaring upwards with a whoosh and the door of the police station started to burn.

'Roast, ye bastards.'

'Cook . . . cook . . . cook.'

Life in Blackhill had changed, the kids were fighting back. Young adults like me and even totty teenagers had had enough of The Untouchables and their ever-circling Meat Wagon, the beatings, false charges and the occasional missing body. A whole generation had grown up with it and had nothing to lose. If a Blackhill guy was picked up the call went out and the troops mustered. It was going to get even hotter. But first I'd to take care of more personal needs.

Shortly after Glenochil I was admitted to Stobhill Hospital's ward 20 for treatment for my psoriasis as arranged by the bold Davie McCallum. The ward at Stobhill had become almost comforting as I'd grown familiar with the staff. Given that I was usually ill when admitted it was never entirely a pleasure – till this time.

'Cracker,' I thought. 'She's a real doll and no mistake.' It wasn't a great compliment given the general state of the company and the all-pervading reek of disinfectant and tar ointments. But a young man ill is a young man nevertheless and hormones will be hormones.

I was a few years older than Anne Marie McCafferty but she could hold her own. During that short stay in hospital we shared time walking the walk, talking the game and sneaking a smoke in the patients' room. Like me she had psoriasis and, for the first time ever, I felt relaxed about my skin condition. With Anne Marie I saw a good-looking, lively young woman – who happened to have psoriasis. At last I didn't need to hide away or double check my topmost button was securely fastened. When I looked at her I saw a beautiful young woman. Maybe she could see beyond the state of my skin.

When we parted company and left the hospital we agreed to stay in touch as friends. She lived close to Blackhill in the housing scheme of Balornock to the northernmost city boundary. In territorial terms we were almost neighbours. Within weeks we were more than friends and became lovers. This was a good time for the young Paul Ferris.

Only a few days after my release from hospital, an opportunity for some old business presented itself. One mild evening I'd just ambled past the smoky invitation of the Provanmill Inn and was strolling down Royston Road feeling content with the world, glad to be free, when I spotted an old school chum. Martin Welsh was taking the air on the opposite pavement and heading my way. Over time he'd not grown any prettier. Of all the Welshes he was the one I wanted most – my adversary in that first schoolyard punch up and the harbinger of ill on my person for years. If only Martin Welsh had fought his own battles the years of daily bullying wouldn't have happened. Then again, he was a Welsh.

With a quick look around for patrolling police cars, I stepped smartly across the road. As I stood in front of him his face twisted into the belligerent sneer I knew so well, his hand reaching inside his jacket going for his weapon. Without breaking stride, I slid my brand new Bowie knife from the back of my belt, grabbed him by his thick, greasy forelock and sliced. Screaming like a banshee he dropped to his knees, his hands clawing up in a vain attempt to protect his head. Standing over him I wrenched his hair back and kept cutting till his scalp hung in a loose flap and the bloody rose of his skull shone in the late evening sun. Wiping my blade on his jacket, I crossed the road and continued on my way.

A few hundred yards down the street I stopped to light a cigarette, protecting the match's sulphur flurry with cupped hands and standing side-on as if sheltering the flame from a breeze. The Welsh was squatting on the pavement, slumped against a wall, both hands clutching at his temples in a long, silent howl. It had been due for years and was over in seconds. Paul Ferris was a happier man that night.

With my return to freedom I quickly arranged to visit my brother, Billy, then in Maidstone Prison. Billy had been moved around the most secure and notorious prisons in England that were then powder-keg tense, primed to explode into riots. He'd met some of the people described by the media as the most vicious and feared in Britain – murderers, IRA and UDA bombers and snipers, big-time gangsters from the London scene. The length of Billy's sentence had made him an old hand but still a very young lag. Wise to the ways of penal regimes, he'd kept his dignity and his honour. In doing so he'd inevitably tripped into scrapes with the screws and with some other prisoners. But he'd kept the code and, as such, had made many friends, some in the most surprising quarters. I was proud of my big brother and fully intended to get to know him as well as I could in the circumstances.

One of Billy's good friends was a bloke called Ben Al Agha, also known as Ben Nodjumi. Ben was a grandson of the Shah of Iran, one of the most powerful men in the world. When the Shah was deposed by the ranting Ayatollah and those fanatical fundamentalists, Ben had been Minister of the Interior in the government. The entire royal family fled the country and entered exile in different parts of the world. Ben had come to the UK and set about earning himself a living. Being an Iranian businessman was a fraught enough existence in those times but also being a member of the exiled Iranian royal family was truly swimming in the alligator swamp. People were out to get Ben and get him they did. He ended up entrapped in a web of deceit, including rape charges brought against him by a high-class call girl who'd been paid for by someone else. Eventually Ben was sent down for 16 years on charges of kidnapping two diplomats. Even in prison he wasn't safe and another prisoner tried to set him up as planning an escape. Brother Billy knew better and stood on the line giving evidence on Ben's behalf. The charges were dropped. For Billy this was a simple point of honour but for Ben it was a mark that he could trust this man and all who stood with him.

On one of my visits to Billy he made a point of introducing me to Ben, a handsome man with gentle, sophisticated ways, even dressed in the drab prison garb and surrounded by those thick brick walls. After the bogus escape incident, Ben had been sent to Albany Prison on the Isle of Wight and I was delighted when Billy asked me to visit his friend. Ben needed someone he could trust on the outside and very soon asked me to become involved in a business venture – my first legitimate earner beyond the van boy jobs.

Ben was owed about £4 million by two men of Iraqi origin called the Gogal brothers. On learning of his conviction the Gogals had refused to pay Ben, taking advantage of his lack of friends and associates in the UK at that time. Ben sued them and won his civil case from his prison cell. Still the Gogals were refusing to stump up the cash. Like any good strategist Ben had no intention of leaving it at that. The Gogals' business empire included cargo ships and Ben intended to find a way of recouping the debt through that route. While he was devising specific plans he wanted to know if I would be willing to accept his power of attorney and act on his behalf.

'Yes,' I replied without a blink of hesitation, looking calmly across the table. We came from different worlds – one raised in palaces and the other in the shittiest area of Glasgow. One educated by private tutors and who had played a part on the stage of world politics. And me – I was nothing but a skinny little kid who'd just found his way on the streets of Glasgow. I was still too busy thinking what to do about the no-hoper Welsh brothers yet here I was being asked to take on major responsibility for substantial reward. I knew nothing about big business but had the confidence and arrogance of youth. Of course I would do it. Of course I could do it. We all wanted a way up and out. A legal venture was always preferred but seldom available. The plans would unfold soon – I couldn't wait.

Back in Blackhill the Meat Wagon's appearance had become nothing more than sporadic. A local police station had been opened a few years before in the middle of tenement land and was the centre of attention. Local coppers used their station as a cosy little sanctuary while coppers coming in to carry out most of the arrests dished out merciless thrashings to the kids on the block. Police tactics hadn't changed, just the location. Enough was enough. We were going to rescue people.

Rush squads armed with staves, coshes or half bricks dashed into the police station creating mayhem. The station was a converted shop that had lain derelict for years as no right-minded small businessman wanted to run the commercial risk. This meant there was limited space and we knew that our captive comrade could be accessed through one simple plywood door. The bizzies got wise to this, installing more secure internal devices and being sure to draft in extra bodies from neighbouring stations whenever a Blackhill name was being arrested.

Frustrated by the security measures, the team turned their

attention to the police cars and wrecked them. The best at this was a bloke called Duncy McIntyre, one of Ma McIntyre the glue seller's older offspring. Duncy just didn't seem to care about pain. While others thumped the reinforced windscreen with hammers or poles, Duncy used his fists or his head. If he got inside the motor he kept going, biting and tearing at the radio, steering wheel, the seats. All the while blood would be flowing from his shredded mitts and the open wounds in his forehead and face.

Duncy McIntyre was a hoot and deemed to be totally mental – one of the greatest compliments on the streets. Around that time a few of us were trying to break into a jeweller's shop by the less than subtle method of smashing the plate-glass window. A couple of hard taps with a hammer and the bloody thing still hadn't cracked or budged. We were all for abandoning it when Duncy took a few steps back on to the road and charged at the shop head down. The window shattered, sending a cascade of lethal shards down on Duncy. Bleeding and cut, he stood with a smile of satisfaction splitting his face, oblivious to his wounds.

Years later I crossed paths with Duncy in prison, his arms, face and torso a mess of scars from repeated and deliberate self-mutilation. The behaviour we'd seen as a laugh and the police viewed as a menace was a cry for help that nobody listened to. He was a McIntyre from Blackhill, after all. A miracle he'd survived into adulthood and bound to be a nuisance – end of story. Shame on us all for not seeing the real Duncy McIntyre – a good guy who deserved better.

When the police hid their cars the bombs started. A Molotov cocktail is simple enough to make. A hose into the fuel tank of a car, an empty bottle, a strip of rag, a box of matches and you are equipped. At first they were simply flung at the doorway but the cops just sweated it out till the fire brigade and reinforcements arrived. Then volunteers dashed in through the front doors and lobbed the bombs over the counter. Much better, the coppers shifting their arses, grabbing their suspect, clambering through the fire exit at the back door on to a stretch of wasteland. Foiled, the boys were quick to learn a lesson. On the next arrest, a stolen car was driven across the rough ground and smashed against the wall blocking the rear exit. Kamikaze bombers rushed the front door slinging petrol bombs. The cops almost died that day and their prisoners escaped –

a major victory for the boys of Blackhill but one that had serious and lasting repercussions.

Blackhill was endowed with the first bombproof local police station in Britain. It was designed to a model copied on the war-torn streets of Belfast. While the brick maze entry and three layers of wall frontage protected the police, it didn't deter the Blackhill guys in their efforts. At the same time, a sinister unmarked van reappeared on the streets every night. The Meat Wagon had returned with a vengeance.

Approaching the age of 19 I had somehow outgrown these youthful skirmishes, looking more towards earning a living through my energies. By accident the offer was about to be made that no ambitious young man could refuse. It wasn't Ben's cargo ships but much closer to home.

10

HEAD HUNTED

he car swerved erratically through the narrow streets. Women and children scurried off the pavement, jumping into closes and gardens to shelter from the danger. As the drunken driver turned the car into Greenside Street there was a scream of tyres skidding and spinning before revving and accelerating. Too slow and too close, the pedestrian was hit square on and sent flying through the air before landing with a crunch of bones. The car didn't hesitate and sped on.

My young sister Maureen, then aged about 14 years, was spending a great deal of time with our granny in Greenside Street, often staying over to keep the old lady company since the death of our grandfather. Maureen witnessed the sorry affair, and, as ever, the police were hassling the young girl for a full statement and a dose of finger-pointing in court. Was it the right thing to do in helping the police track down the hit-and-run killer? Not in Blackhill. The driver's behaviour was outrageous and he deserved to be punished but not by the police. Giving information to the authorities on any pretext was breaching the code and you were stepping over a line into the enemy camp. Such a move drew suspicion, hostility and a removal of community support overnight. In the scheme, life was hard enough without losing the trust of your neighbours. In Blackhill we took care of all our own problems.

As soon as I heard that Maureen had been interviewed I went round to see her. We'd never got on too well but I dismissed it all as just part of the baggage of a brother and sister too close in age. Maureen was young and was family. I was relieved to hear she wasn't going to make a statement, more for her welfare than for anyone else. It was then I learned that the driver was a cousin of Arthur Thompson senior.

To uphold the family's honour I needed to ensure the alleged culprit's side knew we wouldn't help the police. So off I traipsed to see the old man Thompson, knocking on his door for the first time. Then I knew of Arthur Thompson by reputation only as the major player on the scene. His status didn't faze me in any way since his world was of the oldies and established, organised crime while mine was about young guys with street credibility. The two were distinct, separate worlds. As far as I was concerned the Thompsons were just another local family.

Thompson greeted me formally and politely. When I told him of the nature of my business he said he knew my father well and spoke fondly of him as a good man. Then he asked me to call to see him around 7 p.m. that night at the Provanmill Inn, a local pub known to have been run by Arthur, though not officially.

That night, standing at the bar, we had a drink and chatted. I reassured him that as far as my family were concerned they would not now and never would stand as prosecution witnesses against his family or anyone else. I guessed the car involved had been stolen and was already destroyed so its identification posed no threat. I reassured Thompson that under no circumstances could Maureen recognise the driver and that was exactly what she would tell the police. It is an absolute taboo among the criminal fraternity to stand as a Crown witness. All the fresh-faced young Ferris was telling the wily old Thompson was that we knew the rules and would abide by them. We would have done the same for a nonentity of a low-life.

Arthur Thompson said he was grateful then handed over one hundred fags and a half-bottle of whisky for my father. It was a small token, and an unnecessary show of appreciation. With the gifts under my arm I headed home to my parents' house to give over the goodies and, more importantly, reassure them that the family's honour was intact. Like me, Jenny and Willie couldn't give a toss for Arthur Thompson but they cared for their family above and beyond anything else.

Nothing ever came of the police inquiry. As for any punishment handed out to the erring Thompson cousin, well, he was seen marauding the streets showing no signs of remorse for years to come. The victim was dead and that was tragic. They couldn't be brought back to life regardless of who was punished. My expectation was that Arthur Thompson would provide the bereaved family with some generous compensation. The most important issue was that the Ferris family was seen as being trustworthy. In schemes like Blackhill sometimes that is all you have and, just as often, all you need.

From the day of my release from Glenochil and the shared train journey from Stirling I'd renewed my acquaintance with Alco McDonald and his brothers, Blink and Gash. They were a local family from Greenrig Street, a short stroll away from my parents' house. I was particularly fond of old Alco – named for an early predilection and capacity for the falling-down liquid. The McDonalds were nobody's mugs and were planning a bit of business. One night I popped in to the Provanmill Inn to discuss the enterprise with Blink over a few drinks.

The Provanmill Inn was the kind of place you felt safe in. A den of thieves, you might say. If a stranger walked in they'd be spotted pronto and the buzz of chat would dribble into strained silence, hard eyes would turn on him, the bar staff would ignore his drinks order till he got the message and vamoosed. The clientele of that bar summed up an essential part of the local code and trust. All it would take would be for one loose-lipped bevvy merchant to spill the beans on an overheard conversation and the shit would start flying. Trust broken is a great betrayal and those suspected would pay the heaviest of penalties. You still had to be cautious not to broadcast your plans but at least you felt relaxed and comfortable in the Provanmill Inn.

Blink hadn't kept our rendezvous and had still not turned up one slow drink later. Standing at the bar was Arthur Thompson junior, old Arthur's son. I asked him if he had seen hide or hair of Blink and he said, 'Naw, but listen, A wis looking for ye any roads.' I looked at the small fat man with an open but distanced stare – the kind that portrays you're listening but are yet to be impressed. Arthur Thompson junior was older than me, ran with a different crowd and, while I recognised him, I wouldn't have described him as an acquaintance let alone a friend. We called him Arty as in Arty Farty. So, my look conveyed, 'I'm listening. No more, no less.'

He didn't give a bugger what expression I was wearing. This was the centre of his father's kingdom and he was well at ease. He continued, 'C'mere a bit closer. We were wondering if ye'd be interested in earning a bit money working fur us? It would be nothin' ye're no' used to. Whit dae ye think?' He went on to explain that my talents had been noticed, 'We heard whit ye done tae that Martin Welsh bastard. Heh, heh – could hear the fucker squeal frae in here that night. When the story reached the pub door the Godfather bought a round a drinks fur every wanker in the place. The old man! Fuckin' unheard o', A'm tellin' ye. What dae ye think, eh?'

I winced at a grown man calling his father by a media-hyped nickname but listened on. The Thompsons were impressed by certain of my violent escapades and took great satisfaction in my campaign against the Welsh brothers – a mob they were having a little local difficulty with themselves and less success than they'd ever admit. My reputation was sky high and that was as important to them as my capacity for action. All the while Arthur Thompson junior was droning on like a gangster. It was embarrassing. The criminal fraternity in Glasgow don't speak as if they have a bit part in a low budget B-film about Al Capone. Arthur Thompson junior did speak like his life imitated cheap, shitty art. Still, he was making me an offer on behalf of his old man. So, I listened.

A short time later I left the Provanmill Inn and sauntered up the road, my eyes blinking as they adjusted to daylight. In half an hour I'd been both stood up and employed. As of now I was working for Arthur Thompson – not the junior variation but Big Arthur. The opportunity for regular good money was too tempting to pass over and I'd simply and quickly agreed. I'd recently turned 19 years old, and was capable of anything. What had Arty asked?

'What dae ye think?' Of course, I hadn't thought at all, not wasted a second. In years to come I'd make up for the lack of thinking time but now, as far as I was concerned, I'd just been promoted to the premier division.

11

GODFATHER OF CRIME - MAN OR MYTH?
by Reg McKay

In the windowless pubs of Glasgow's broken-backed communities men with scarlet-pocked faces, weary eyes and shaky tumbler hands sat and growled in voices ravaged by smoke, dampness and too many years spent in too many jails. It was the early 1980s and the old school of survivors from the razor gangs, the rackets and the gambling dens had taken to enforced early retirement in the only refuges that would have them.

They spoke of heroes and men who stood apart in their own world. Men they claimed to have fought alongside or against too many years ago. Men who had got one over on them. Men who had perished on the way. But mainly they spoke of the men who had won the day and climbed to the top, one boot firmly in the world of the gangster and one moccasin placed politely on the rug of respectability. There were few of these men and they straddled the public consciousness. Contrary to the media view, Arthur Thompson was not the sole topic of conversation.

Everyone who wasn't anyone in Glasgow claimed allegiance or blood link to Arthur Thompson. Claims of being Thompson's cousin or nephew were a sure sign of a lack of influence or power. Still, a number of scams were pulled off for a profitable period using this one lie. Protection rackets were set up and paid out with no more recommendation than Thompson's involvement. Chibbings were postponed till the blade man checked out whether his target really was a relative of Thompson's wife, Rita. Postponed, mind you, rarely cancelled. Police would interrupt a raid to make a discreet telephone call to ascertain if Big Arthur actually owned the business. By the early 1980s Arthur Thompson had influence all right, and not just in Glasgow.

Thompson had been born and brought up in the north of Glasgow before moving to Provanmill with his mother and brothers. Born in 1931, his childhood was spent in austere times for anyone with a need to work for a living. By the 1940s his brothers had become barmen and bouncers in the Provanmill Inn and Arthur had entered a life of crime. In that city of diminutive fly men during an era of malnutrition, TB, rickets, means-tested benefits, cod liver oil and orange juice, the young Arthur was physically impressive, being around five foot ten inches in height and muscular. Hardmen in Glasgow were two-a-penny but Thompson used his brain as well as his knuckles.

Even in the harsh days of the 1940s and 1950s Thompson was renowned to have ambition and a ruthless streak in disposing of anyone who got in his way. An early effort at making his fortune ended in farce. Along with Paddy Meehan, a well-known safecracker, he tackled the Commercial Bank in Beauly, a prosperous but very small burgh in rural Inverness-shire. In that little hick town they found not one safe but six and were awarded with a haul of £400, way below the expected tally. On the long road back to Glasgow, a petrol attendant noted the number of their upmarket Humber Snipe car, too good for such rough-and-ready working-class types he reckoned. Within a few days Thompson's house keys were found lying on the road outside the robbed bank. For his pains Thompson received three years in prison while the unfortunate Meehan suffered double the sentence.

It was to be one of the few prison terms served by Arthur Thompson, a fact usually put down to his cunning – but was it? Arthur Thompson had proven from an early age that he was prepared to play many roles. TC Campbell remembers his late father, Bobby Campbell, and his associates, a successful and ingenious team of bank robbers and hijackers, recruiting Thompson as a junior partner in the 1950s. 'They'd be sitting on tens of thousands of pounds of hot money, a helluva pile for those days,' TC Campbell recalls. 'You can only leave it stuffed under the mattress for so long and they needed legitimate businesses to circulate it through.'

Thompson had been taking over a variety of businesses for many years – by fair means or foul. Sawmills, pubs, casinos, garages, car showrooms, scrap yards and others were acquired by a combination of a series of accidents followed up by an offer of a rock-bottom price. Anyone intent on survival sold to Arthur Thompson. The businesses were never in his name but fronted by other family members or sleeping partners – often the dispossessed owners now working for a minimum wage. For all of his life, Arthur Thompson had no visible means of financial support apart from the particular welfare benefit he was claiming from the government at any time.

Violence was always part of Thompson's repertoire and he used to associate with legendary hardmen like Teddy Martin, then king of the Gorbals. In 1954 Martin was the first man ever to escape from the notoriously strict regime of Peterhead Prison. Once over the prison walls, Martin was collected by Paddy Meehan and a man called John Harvey while Thompson was setting up an effective decoy. Some time before he had arranged for articles of prison clothing to be smuggled out of Barlinnie Prison and had them marked with Martin's prison number. With Martin safely ensconced in a local Peterhead hotel hundreds of miles from Glasgow, the police received an anonymous tip-off that he was hiding in the loft of a house in Blackhill. When the police raided the house they found the prison clothes with Martin's number and as they meticulously searched every house in the Glasgow scheme, Martin went about his business safe from scrutiny or fear of being caught.

In contrast to this picture of honour among thieves there were early signs that Arthur Thompson could not be trusted by anyone. When planning to rob a branch of the Westminster Bank in London, Thompson offered to pay his part of the expenses with a £100 note – at that time very rare, most likely stolen and easily traced. Teddy Martin, the very man rescued from Peterhead, would have been the fall guy of a fit-up and said so. This dispute resulted in Thompson shooting Martin who fell into a coma.

Thompson was renowned for being tight with his money – someone reluctant to buy a round of drinks or pay his way and a formidable negotiator. The kind of man who would reward the teenaged Paul Ferris for saving a close relative from a certain jail sentence by lifting one hundred fags and a half bottle of whisky off the shelves of his own pub. A meagre trade-off calculated at impressing the young man at the cheapest price possible. Penny-pinching and tight-fisted – far from admirable, but harmless really. All that was true but Thompson was mean in a more ominous sense too.

Archie Rollo was a well-known player from the Bridgeton area of Glasgow. Archie and his brothers were highly respected by the city's fraternity, especially in that Protestant stronghold of the east end, the origins of the Billy Boys razor gang and not a place for the faint of heart. Archie was no pushover and was an expert in demolition, earning a reasonable living from it. He had the type of practised eye that could take a sweeping glance at a building and within minutes know the scrap value and the time and cost involved in accessing it. As Glasgow's housing policy had more to do with slum clearance than providing decent homes, Archie Rollo's business thrived till Thompson paid him a visit.

The value of wood had soared as had the profit from recycling high-quality timber salvaged from old buildings. Thompson proposed to take all the wood off Archie's hands. He should deliver it to one of Thompson's wood merchant yards. After the first consignments, Archie sought payment and thought Big Arthur had made a mistake missing out a few loads in his calculations. No mistake. That was the price Thompson proposed to pay and that was the price Archie Rollo would accept – wouldn't he? The cash in his hand didn't cover delivery let alone dismantling, loading and the wood itself. Archie Rollo was nobody's mug and knew the score. As he walked away, a proud man silently accepting a blow to his dignity, Thompson called after him. In future all the planks should be delivered with the nails removed – see to it. Salt in the wound and more money to Thompson.

That was Thompson's business style, turning on many close to him who considered themselves allies, for a while. The remarkable aspect of Archie Rollo's account is that it involved Thompson himself. Usually he paid someone else to pass on the message, hand out the threat and deliver the punishment.

From the early days of his career, Thompson made links with the London mobs and maintained them throughout his life. Such is the Thompson mythology in Glasgow that a common tale does the rounds of those who know little of the scene. It goes like this:

Sometime in the 1960s, when the Krays were recognised as the leading gang in Britain, a lone Scotsman disembarks from the Glasgow train. He rides a black Hackney cab to the Krays' club and walks in as the brothers and their entourage are holding court. He stands in the middle of the floor among swinging sixties trendies, out of place in his checked coat buttoned high at the neck and with a stern, unsmiling face pitted with old battle scars. When the waiter approaches him the Scotsman declines to order a drink and, instead, asks to speak to Ron or Reg. One of the twins appears with a smile whereupon the Scotsman reaches into his coat, drawing out a sawn-off shotgun, cocking the trigger and aiming at his host's head.

At that the Scotsman spots the other twin and signals for him to come close. 'Right you, kiss his arse,' he growls and jabs the shotgun into the face of the first twin. Nobody in the bar knows who the stranger is but all realise he has to be a desperado to walk into their place looking for grief. The second twin obliges, kneels down and kisses his brother's arse.

'Thompson. Arthur Thompson. Ye'll no forget me and ye'll no fuckin mess wi me.' At that the intruder backs off towards the door, the snub-nose shotgun still aimed at the twins, slips in to his waiting taxi and disappears.

This tale is undoubtedly untrue but is a mark of the Thompson legend among ordinary citizens of Glasgow. While he was capable of acts of horrifying violence, bravado and cunning, the signs are that Thompson agreed a business deal with the Krays and other London firms from an early stage. Frankie Fraser, professional torturer and peer of the Krays and the Richardsons, remembers the friendly cooperation between the London and Glasgow teams going back to the 1950s. By Glasgow, Fraser means Arthur Thompson.

Thompson was a close friend of Billy Hill and a regular visitor to Frankie Fraser whenever he was in prison. A mutual convenience arrangement was allegedly set up with an exchange of hit-men. When Andy Anderson escaped from jail along with Ronnie Biggs, the great train robber, and turned up at the premises of his erstwhile boss, Eddie Richardson, he had to be hidden. Richardson asked his number-one minder, Frankie Fraser, to get him safely out of the way. A few days later, Anderson was comfortably ensconced in Edinburgh where he remained for a few months till moved on by Richardson. His host was Thompson who didn't hesitate to help in spite of the public hue and cry and countrywide police efforts to track the escapees down.

When they were erecting the Kingston Bridge across the Clyde – a huge structure built on enormous stanchions – word went out that people were disappearing. The concrete legs of the bridge were considered very convenient cemeteries from which the corpses would never emerge. The name attached to this little municipal service was Arthur Thompson. Whether the bridge story was true or not remains conjecture but no surprise. Thompson and his henchmen had been helping competitors disappear for years – how else was he to become kingpin?

Yet it wasn't everyone who was terrified of Arthur Thompson. Blackhill's Welsh brothers were too dull to be scared of anyone. Having ruled the streets and playgrounds of the scheme they tried to take over organised crime. In that there was only one man, Thompson, and a feud commenced that dragged on for a generation.

The fatalities were high. First James Welsh and his friend Patrick Goldie were killed when their car was run off the road. Thompson was prosecuted but found not guilty by the jury in less than an hour. During the trial, one senior police officer evacuated his home, while after the verdict another hastily emigrated. What were they scared of – reprisals? Police going about their work in a legal and professional manner rarely have had anything to fear from gangsters in Scotland. Was Thompson really beyond those standards or might it be that he was double-crossed by people in his employ – the police?

A few months later, Thompson and his mother-in-law clambered into his MG sports car outside his home in Provanmill Road. When he turned the ignition the car exploded, badly injuring the man but killing the woman. For months the city reverberated with Arthur Thompson's mother-in-law jokes – whispered of course. Three of the Welsh clan were tried and found not guilty.

The Thompsons demonstrated a capacity for family unity when Big Arthur's wife, Rita, was found guilty and imprisoned for leading an armed raid on the Welshes' home. Was Mrs Thompson as much involved in the family business as Arthur himself? Was she plotting a revenge for the death of her mother? It is common knowledge on the streets of Blackhill that the Welshes blew up the Thompsons' car along with shootings, stabbings, slashing and trashings that never reached the police records or the public domain. Rita Thompson had been acting in the true tradition of the Blackhill community in sorting out her own problems.

By the early 1980s Arthur Thompson had been around for so long that the media had grown almost fond of him. He had provided many a hack with good copy as he was charged with offence after offence, achieving acquittal after acquittal. Part of his charm wasn't luck but the skill of his lawyer, Joe Beltrami. Such was Beltrami's success that 'Get Me Beltrami' became a catchphrase for seeking help in desperate circumstances.

While Beltrami prospered and Thompson stayed free, Arthur junior was going around bad mouthing the lawyer – clearly scurrilous treatment of an honourable man – but that was Arthur junior's style. Still, Arthur junior, nicknamed Fatboy by the press for obvious reasons, would tell stories over and over to anyone who would listen, biting the hand of the man who helped his father out of many a hole. As Big Arthur was a man of few words, feared by all, Arthur junior was a loose-mouthed joker feared by no one. Trouble was brewing from within the Thompson empire.

Thompson had helped Beltrami in his campaign to have Paddy Meehan pardoned of his wrongful conviction for the murder of Rachel Ross. Tank McGuiness, long time associate of Thompson and a client of Beltrami, was one of the unconvicted murderers. McGuiness was coming close to a full, public explanation when he was found battered to death in the city's Janefield Street in 1976. Years later, an ex-policeman would publicly confess that in spite of an outstanding arrest warrant he and a colleague had been ordered to deposit McGuiness in Janefield Street that same night. Much later, Arthur Thompson junior gleefully revealed that his father had paid John 'Gypsy' Winning to kill McGuiness. Tank McGuiness's death hastened Meehan's pardon by freeing Beltrami from confidentiality restrictions. More important to Thompson it protected Charlie Craig, a senior detective with Strathclyde Police. Craig had been a close associate of Thompson for most of his career and was renowned on the streets for fitting people up to secure convictions. The policeman was more precious to Arthur Thompson than McGuiness, his long-time friend.

Still, the press had labelled Thompson as The Godfather, a benign gangster of the old school who had scruples and moral standards. This was the type of man you didn't cross but who would have nothing to do with drug dealing or hurting innocent parties. His home – a gaudily decorated, heavily extended, fortified council house – they titled the Ponderosa or South Fork, depending on which television programme they favoured.

Local people and other gangsters didn't recognise any of this or use any of those names. They didn't recognise Big Arthur from his coverage in the media. Sooner or later the truth would emerge. In the meantime, the 19-year-old Paul Ferris had just walked into the lions' den.

12

THE FIRST RUNG

By the time Paul Ferris entered the Thompsons' scene the family were involved in the drugs trade. Whether this business had been instigated by Arty or the old man remains unclear. By the early 1980s there was no family dispute about their involvement in the trade. Young Arty had previously served as a courier for a drug trafficker by the name of Martin Ross, then believed to be the top man in the Glasgow supply chain. Martin had come from a fine tradition with his grandmother, old Granny Ross, still continuing a thriving drug operation from her house in the traditional tenement land of Maryhill in Glasgow. Arty noted the high profit margin in return for little effort and started his own drug dealing. Predictably, Martin Ross told Arty to behave himself and to back off from his territory. Greed maketh the man in this instance and Arty ignored his ex-colleague's protestations.

By Reg McKay

Arthur Thompson junior was never called Fatboy in the scheme – many things much worse but never that. It was only later when high-profile trials caught the media's attention that I became aware of the nickname invented by some frustrated pulp fiction writer. On the streets we called him Arty but he was no good at drawing as far as I'm aware. The full handle was Arty Farty due to his constant wind problem and the rancid fug that would follow him like a bad-tempered mongrel. The fat man could clear a room with one long, squeaking ripper and honestly declare, 'Look, no hands.'

Arty was fat, no fighter, loudmouthed, brash and a boast. His one redeeming feature was his sense of humour and he was constantly on the wind-up, taking the mickey. Glasgow is full of guys who survive on the streets in just that way. They are usually skinny, little weak guys who cover their timidity by becoming the jester of the pack. Quick with their lip, a few became some of the most accomplished wisecracking comics I've had the pleasure to encounter. Arty was more of a practical joker, setting up some weaker git to fall flat on his arse and laughing at his expense. Put simply, Arty was too lazy and too stupid to make a good comedian. Besides, he didn't have to try – he was Arthur Thompson's son and everyone knew it.

A few days after our verbal handshake in the Provanmill Inn I was called to the Thompsons' house. They'd now taken over two homes at opposite ends of the same terrace separated by two run-of-the-mill council houses. The second house was for Arty and his wife. The rumour was that the Thompsons had persuaded the previous tenants to move out sharpish. At one time a close neighbour was a policeman who did a lot of complaining about the other neighbour who ran a hairdressing business from a spare room. Nobody seemed to complain about old Arthur, not even when gunfire and bombs ricocheted off the brickwork.

The fancy stone cladding and big expensive cars made the houses stick out in Blackhill like angels in hell. I'd become so accustomed to seeing those places I didn't notice them any more but had never before crossed the threshold. Inside, I walked on a carpet so thick it sucked on my shoes, the upholstery on the massive suite bruised as you sat on it and the whole place was decorated in garish though expensive taste. Tacky, yes, but the whole place shouted, 'Money, money, money.' I was 19 years old and had only ever been in low-budget council houses and institutions. I was impressed.

The first few jobs were easy and trouble-free. The people paid up in a sullen though uncomplaining manner. They obviously owed Thompson and no argument. I never asked what the payments were for – that would display a lack of trust in my employer. Obviously, I knew the debts would be for some illegal enterprise since why else would yours truly be collecting the cash? I took my orders, collected and was paid generously for trouble-free expeditions. Then Arty introduced me to Tam Bagan and work changed.

A few years earlier in the sprawling township of Easterhouse on the north-eastern border of the city Bagan had shot a couple of brothers, doing an eight-year stretch for his troubles. So I knew of him and already held him in some degree of esteem. Someone had told me Bagan was Arty's cousin, a relationship qualifying him for respect. Later, I ascertained that there were no blood ties but that the Bagan brood had been taken in by the Thompsons when in dire need and catered for over many years. One of the Thompsons had actually adopted one of Tam's family. Not so much a cousin through birth, more a chosen member of the family.

From the off I wasn't keen on Tam Bagan. His style was too clinical and cold. Tam was all black leather gloves clasping a polished revolver and I sensed he was capable of anything. I suppose he fitted young Arty's view of a Mafia hit-man. Maybe they'd read the same gangster comics and watched the same movies? Tam Bagan was seriously dangerous and worth the watching. Arty and old Thompson occasionally paired us up as bagmen to collect hefty, illicit debts from resentful and menacing parties. Just like the good-cop bad-cop routine Bagan was the financial courier and Ferris the enforcer. The approach was simple and effective – pay up or be hurt. Pay up or you die. Choose now and choose quickly. Usually the spiel was unnecessary. Usually they paid up.

We didn't need to be business analysts to work out the gist and the scale of the operations involved, walking away from our house visits with bulky bags loaded with £20,000 to £80,000, often more. Occasionally we walked away empty-handed but left in our wake a calling card of broken bones, slashed faces and wreckage. Such inflictions were only ever meted out to aggressive buggers telling us to take a hike or stupid enough to have a go. A promise of payment at a later date would result in a sound reminder that the money had better be available then and no later. With a few words and a hard, cold look from me I watched the customer paint a graphic, mental picture of the consequences before my eyes. I was very young and small for this work and that alone spooked the older, hardened men we dealt with. But there would never be any violence if the man's wife or kids were around or if non-combatants were bound to get hurt. Rules were rules regardless of the bloke's arrogance. They always knew their reprieve would be short-lived. They had to emerge on the street sometime and we ruled the streets.

We'd often return to the Thompson house to pay in the proceeds of our labours in the early evening. The family would be gathered in their lounge watching their favourite soap series on TV. Rita Thompson was a Coronation Street addict. The Thompsons had a villa in Spain that the family hardly ever visited because Thompson hated leaving his business and Rita refused to miss her weekly quota of Coronation Street. They'd sit glued to the badly acted renditions of low-key human drama. Who was pregnant, who was leaving whom, who'd lost their job – all make believe and in the fictitious setting of a drab Manchester backwater. That fluff intrigued the Thompsons more than the real-life dramas Ferris was dishing out in their name on Glasgow's sordid streets. But I was being paid well.

My father didn't see it that way. One day he took me aside and asked, 'Paul, what you doing working for that fucking grass?' He was referring to old Arthur. 'He'll do nothing but bring you grief, for Christ sake.'

My father wasn't the only one ringing my alarm bell. An old mentor, Bertie Connor, also wanted a word, 'Anybody I know in the past that's got involved with the Thompsons has either finished up doing a heavy prison sentence or becoming a victim of a serious assault.' I respected my father and Bertie but was a young man who'd worked out my reasons. I replied, 'Well, the way I see it I'll have money. I won't need to beg, borrow or steal.'

As usual Bertie gave my opinions some thought before replying, 'Fair enough, but what good's a salary if you're in jail or on a slab in the morgue?'

Bertie and my father had given me strong warnings and I should have listened. I believed I was working for the city's top team run by people of standing and integrity. The Thompsons were successful and I wanted a slice of their success. I was nothing more than a kid and like all kids was certain I knew better than anyone else.

A few years before old Arthur had muscled in on a decent thriving business called Maryhill Cash and Carry Carpets owned by a genial giant of a character called Peter Ferguson. Big Peter was larger than life, decent and generous. Thompson's demands put too much pressure on Peter who committed suicide one night – a waste and an outrage. That left the carpet place and the garage next door, Maryhill Autos, fully under the Thompsons' control. In a flat above the garage lived a guy called Joe Hanlon, whom I would later come to know very well. Joe's father, Shoulders Hanlon, had been an associate of old Arthur till one night he'd been found up a close.

Some evil bastards had stuffed his fish and chip supper, newspaper wrappings and all, down his throat, choking him to a brutal and slow death.

In the meantime, young Arty had control over the garage and had designs on his old gaffer, Martin Ross. In the criminal world you give known players your business and they guarantee good terms in return. Ross had taken advantage of this convention to have his car fixed at Maryhill Autos. A few days later, Ross was sailing on Loch Lomond, a scenic freshwater loch not far from Glasgow. His sport over, he returned to the Duck Bay Marina where a police squad jumped him and searched his car. Popping off the steering column they found it packed solid with heroin. Word on the street was that the police had been informed of the drugs by someone called Wattie Douglas, a name that meant nothing to me or anyone I knew, so we dismissed it as another rumour.

One day Arty asked me for a meeting to discuss a little business. Arty claimed he'd been cheated in a deal involving John Friel, known as The Irishman, and Martin Ross. Some goods were to be purchased by the Thompsons for £50,000. As is the routine on these occasions, the two sides had apparently met at a prearranged spot. The Thompsons handed over their bag with the cash and a sealed holdall was passed back. Don't believe the Hollywood myth on these scenarios. No one checks the goods or the money – that would be to break trust and increase the risks of detection while you're at it. You grab your bundle and hightail it away from the locus as quickly as possible. In a city where you're dealing with familiar people, you know where to find them and they're only too aware of that. When Arty got home, he cut open the sports bag to discover two bricks and a bottle of Irn Bru. Now the bricks I could understand but the bottle of soft drink was someone taking the piss.

The Thompsons had deployed their own resources to retrieve the money and failed. While they hated to lose as much as a brown coin their reputation was also at stake. Whatever the price, they had to be seen coming out on top. So, young Arty wanted me to go on their trail. Call me arrogant or call me naïve but I didn't stop to wonder why they handed the job over to a young guy like me. My back-up was to be Tam Bagan and our task was to inflict as much damage on the other side as possible – the type of remit I was comfortable with. It was almost a return to my ned days. This group and their associates had cheated our team and, in doing so, declared war. They were combatants who had started the hostilities and I was back in the old position of finishing them.

All hell broke loose. The first incident involved us driving alongside a carload of them and forcing it off the road, wrecking the motor and causing serious damage to the crew. A few days later I was driving with Arty in the passenger seat when we spotted one of the team we were hunting. Giving chase, I caught up with his car, bombing along on the wrong side of the road as my fat passenger eyeballed the guy. I thought we were just giving him a threatener when Arty pulled this .357 Magnum revolver from his jacket and started firing. He shot as the other car went spinning round a corner in a desperate effort to escape. The bullet went into the back of the car, through all the seats and hit the guy in the back before exiting through his stomach.

Life was becoming hectic and I felt wound up, always alert for attack or ambush. One night Bagan and I went into a pub searching for a contender but could see no sign. As we were edging our way through the crowd of drinkers a man beside me smacked me hard on the face. Like a flash I drew my blade, stabbing him repeatedly and his mate for good measure. I expected to be attacked at any second and thought the time had arrived.

This guy I was knifing didn't look familiar to me but that meant little with the other side likely to pull in all sorts for handers. What had happened was that the unfortunate bloke had been having a quiet drink with his pal when suddenly they were attacked by a gang with baseball bats, an act I hadn't noticed in the mêlée and rumble of shoulder-to-shoulder boozers. Naturally, the guy threw up his hands to protect his skull but accidentally struck me hard in the face. I was so wired I just got stuck right in there pronto. Night by night the tally was growing.

In the middle of all this, a man well known in the world of boxing approached old Arthur to ask for his help sorting out a little professional difficulty and I was asked to go along to see if I could be of assistance. Knowing next to nothing about boxing, I'd heard of this man in other spheres.

Wondering why he could possibly need my help I headed for his office full of curiosity. 'Good o' ye tae come, son,' he greeted me warmly.

'No worries. What can I do for you?' I replied brusquely, not yet having learned the place for pleasantries in discussing business.

'Need a young boxer slashed, son. Shouldnae be too hard for a boy wi' your talents.' I looked at him straight on, cold-eyed and he got the message, continuing, 'He's saying he's no gonnae box for me any longer. Gonnae sign wi' another guy. A've put a lot o' time and money into training him up, son. Cannae jist let him get off scot-free but.'

His plan disgusted me. This boxer, whom I'd never heard of, was just changing teams, not declaring war. He'd every right to box for anyone he wanted. But the Thompsons had asked me to help. At that time I was prepared to do anything for the Thompsons – burn, knife, shoot, wreck, bomb. I was loyal and dedicated to my work. During this period I didn't drink, smoke hash, socialise or anything that might distract me. My full concentration and energy were focused on my work. Every time they sent me on a job I would complete it and return to report. I'd watch their expressions flicker with surprise as if to say, 'Fuck me, he's done it again,' before handing me my next task. I was a success and they knew it. Should I carry out this slashing then – mild in comparison to my repertoire so far?

'No' a lot o' damage, son. Case he changes his mind like. I dinnae want him back a bleeder in the ring, son. Heh, heh, heh . . . ' I stared at the man with as much contempt as I felt, turned on my heels and marched out. This job was outwith my agreement with the Thompsons and the boxer didn't deserve any trouble. He was a sportsman, not a gangster. Besides, the arrogant bastard of a man kept calling me son and I hated that.

Years later I learned that the boxer did in fact get slashed. It isn't hard in Glasgow to find a queue of guys who'll do such deeds for the price of a couple of drinks. The young sportsman went on to sign with another team and did very well in his professional career. It was one decision of the time that I never regretted and left me with a healthy dose of cynicism about all the hype surrounding the boxing game.

I was beginning to develop a fuller picture of young Arty Thompson. Most of the time Arty could be found in his room that stank with the gasses from his constant thundering belches and mushy farts. He was an overgrown man poring over his collection of gun magazines, dreaming of the latest killing technology. Repeat viewings of his Mafia videos or almost anything to do with organised crime in America was his other pastime. The 'Godfather' series was his favourite and he watched them again and again. While the screen action unfolded his wet lips silently mouthed the script and when the gunfire started he would be up on his feet making realistic rat-a-ta-tat noises improvising a machine gun, revolver or rifle. Mostly he sat slouched in an armchair noisily eating an endless stream of chocolate bars washed down with sugary soft drinks.

All of this may seem no more than pathetic but this was a man with an illegal cache of arms downstairs and the power to deal out death – or pay someone else to play executioner. At the time I was too obsessed with my own progress and ideals of loyalty but a man with a cartoon cavalcade mentality and a loaded pistol was bound to prove dangerous sooner or later. Events from Arty's past were about to catch up with him and bring that red alert to my door.

Working for Arty at Maryhill Autos a few years earlier had been a guy by the name of Willie Gibson. While Gibson did basic mechanics he was part of a syndicate ringing stolen cars – changing their serial numbers, colour and registration plates before selling them in the open market at a knock-down rate. Isn't it funny how few questions people ask when they know they've saved some dough? The racket is run in every city in Britain, all over the world probably, is lucrative and works well till you're rumbled.

One day Arty asked Willie Gibson to go to the local car auction pitch to pick up a cheque for the sale of a car. Gibson obliged, no doubt preferring a drive to being stuck under the oil-dripping innards of some motor. As he picked up the cheque he was arrested by the police for selling a stolen car. Down at the station, Gibson became convinced he'd been fitted up by Arty and he started singing. In particular, he told a detective sergeant we'll call Wylie McIlvain of the contents of Arty's lockers at Maryhill Autos containing more guns and ammunition than overalls, girlie pictures or sandwich boxes.

One warrant later and Arty was in custody heading towards court and a ten-year jail term, assisted along the way by evidence from Willie Gibson. Gibson had just breached two golden rules – he'd informed and stood as a prosecution witness. On appeal, the family's trusted lawyer, Joe Beltrami, secured Arty a reduction to four years in jail – an excellent result under the circumstances.

Arty hadn't forgotten the debt he owed to Gibson who paid homage to the Thompson dignity by moving away from Glasgow and taking up permanent residence in England. This appeased the Thompsons till Gibson decided to visit his family in Glasgow. Now fleeing a city is one thing, but it's not meant to be a holiday. It shouldn't be treated as if you've got a job on the oilrigs or moved towns through free choice. Banished is banished and to breach that sentence is punishable.

When Arty heard that Gibson was back in town visiting relatives in Blackhill, he scratched his fat arse and contemplated what to do. That's when things started to get really hot between the police and me.

13.

ONE-WAY BRIDGE TO NOWHERE
by Reg McKay

It had been a pleasant night out for William Gibson. English pubs were fine but the warm beer couldn't replace his fondness for cold lager and the rowdy, slagging patter of Glasgow drinking dens. Down south also suffered a dire lack of his family like those with him tonight – his brother, John, his sister-in-law as well as his own father-in-law, John Hogg. They couldn't drink in any of the Blackhill pubs run by the Thompsons and the Shields family and full of men who would lift the telephone to old Arthur or, worse, damage him themselves right on the spot. He knew that every drinker in any of the Blackhill pubs would be struck temporarily but completely blind, deaf and mute for the duration of any such assault.

The Open Arms in Riddrie was a good enough pub but a bit of a distance from Blackhill. With no car and no spare cash for a taxi, even if any had been willing to risk working the area, the Gibsons would have to walk home. Never mind, they had supped well and walked that walk many a time.

There was a long way and a short way back to the house in Maxwelton Road, Blackhill. The long way was safer but a pain in the bunions. Besides, this was their home territory where they were well known and had long outgrown the rituals of the teenage gangs. The shortcut involved crossing a bridge over the M8 motorway and was infamous for trouble. Rival young teams frequently clashed bloodily and fatally in the centre of the bridge, fighting for nothing more precious than control of the footway. Groups of armed muggers would collar lonely souls halfway across giving them a choice of passing the cash, a chibbing or free fall into the stream of speeding traffic thirty feet below. Bands of teeny tots, barely into school, would hurl chunks of breezeblock at the car windscreens and giggle at the ensuing chaos till fleeing down their foolproof escape routes. No, the bridge wasn't a safe place to be but they had little to fear, a group of grown adults like them.

Crossing the narrow construction two by two, the whishing of the motorway speedsters hit a crescendo as they reached halfway, in sight of home territory and the comfort of their house. Ahead a lone man appeared on the bridge walking rapidly towards them. At first sight he appeared innocuous, being of small enough build to be a teenager and dressed in a trendy blue tracksuit like all the kids were wearing. Just some youngster returning late from winching a Blackhill lass. Young love always seemed to find a way round the inter-area violence and rivalry. Then they spotted the ski mask pulled down over his face. The men braced themselves to deal with the trouble, then they saw the pistol in his hand.

In an instant the masked man strode across the bridge and stood legs apart, the .45 automatic clenched in two hands at arm's length, pointed straight at Willie Gibson's head. The group froze. Instinctively, Gibson grabbed his protesting sister-in-law and held her in front of him, ducking behind her and cringing. The gunman hesitated though he knew he could shoot through the whimpering woman's body and still hit his target. For a second it looked as if he would do just that then he raised the pistol and fired into the air. John Gibson was already panicking but the blast of the gun sent him over the edge, literally. Grasping the metal spar of the bridge he swung his legs up and round tumbling down thirty feet into what could have been certain death in the path of the rushing traffic. As luck would have it he landed on the hard shoulder of the motorway, missing death by mere feet. Still he howled on impact, having shattered his legs. Nobody was paying any heed to John's agonised screams, least of all his brother, Willie.

Willie Gibson threw his hapless, shrieking sister-in-law at the gunman, turned and ran for it. Ahead of him was his father-in-law, John Hogg. The older man couldn't run fast and it almost cost him his life. Willie Gibson was going to live and he didn't care who else died. He grabbed John Hogg by the shoulders, turned and held him as a human shield just as the masked man fired. Shots rang out and a bullet struck the older man in the upper thigh, smashing his femur before exiting from the other side. John Hogg buckled and collapsed as Willie Gibson kept moving on to the Blackhill side and galloped to safety.

The gunman stood and through the narrow slit of his mask watched Willie Gibson scampering away as the old man groaned close by his feet. Down below, John Gibson was pleading for help as he crawled and edged inch by inch away from the bridge. Nearby the woman was sobbing. The smell of gunpowder wafted in the air replacing the chemical bite of exhaust fumes from the unheeding lorries and speeding cars. Just for a second it looked as if the hit-man might continue the chase, then he spun on his heels and headed back across the bridge towards Riddrie.

In all their panic and pain, the victims knew that the gunman was intent on one target only, Willie Gibson. At any time he could have picked off the other three and declined the opportunity. So, it was only Willie they were after and, to his mind, there could only be one paymaster, the Thompsons. From the build of the assailant he was clearly not old Arthur or young Arty. Besides, they employed other people to do this kind of work. Who would they pay to shoot someone? The whole city knew who the Thompsons' enforcer was these days – Paul Ferris.

Armed police were scouring the streets searching for me. A few telephone calls later I'd sussed that Arty and his 16-year-old brother, Billy, had been arrested in connection with the shooting of the Gibson family the night before. Armed police are no joke and even at 20 years old I knew efforts to escape were likely to lead to one fatality – mine. A call to Peter Forbes, my solicitor at the time, and soon we were headed together to Baird Street police station where the Thompson brothers were being held.

The police noted my alibi then locked me in a cell. Later that day the three prisoners were put on identity parades. Willie Gibson came in first and fingered us all – me as the one who tried to shoot him while Arty and Billy were accused of driving past the scene in a car at the time of the action. The rest of the Gibson clan failed to point any of us out. Of course, Willie Gibson was very familiar with all our ugly mugs.

The lack of corroboration from Gibson's relatives might have influenced the police's decision about pressing charges. But they had two well-known targets and one's gangly little brother in their sights so there was little doubt as to what they would do. Arty and Billy were charged with conspiracy to murder while I hit the jackpot and stood accused of four attempted murders.

Arty was driven off to Barlinnie to stink on remand while Billy and I were rewarded with the human refuge dump of Longriggend because of our youthful years. Returning to the old routine was probably the spell of incarceration when I finally and fully became immune to the deprivations and boredom of prison existence. Aged 20 I'd graduated with first-class honours as an experienced con.

A week later, without as a much as by your leave, Joe Beltrami secured a procurator fiscal release for the Thompsons. This is a curious Scottish set-up which amounts to the prosecution changing their mind mid-flow and dropping all charges. While I was left to rot out in the wilds of Lanarkshire in dingy Longriggend, I never found out exactly what new information, if any, had emerged to result in serious charges being dropped against the Thompsons.

Apart from resenting every second spent behind bars there was an additional reason I was hacked off. Ben had come up with a plan on how to recoup the £4 million owed to him. From a friend in the insurance business he'd ascertained that two of the Gogals' cargo ships would dock at a British port on a particular date. Legal bods would seize the ships and their loads worth over £100 million in total. The ships' captains would be served with a seizing order, a marine mechanic would disable the engines and there they would stay till the debt was paid up in full. Acting with Ben's power of attorney I'd be on hand to sign, seal and receive – except I was banged up. My commission was substantial and if the deal had come off I would've kissed the streets goodbye. Three extra days of freedom and my life would have followed a different path.

After some months in Longriggend, the trial was held at Lanarkshire House, a decrepit old court building acting as an overspill to the High Court. Glasgow's courts are among the busiest in the world and every inch of space is used. In Scotland, the most serious criminal charges are dealt with by a judge and jury, 15 good men and women true who decided whom to believe.

I was to be represented by an advocate known as a Queen's Counsel – the highest form of legal representation possible. The skill of my lawyer was crucial and I was determined to have the best. That was when I met Donald Findlay QC. Taking one look at Findlay my jaw dropped as I wondered if I'd made the biggest mistake of my life.

A tall, slim man, Findlay wore what I took to be the traditional garb of a QC – frockcoat, pinstripe trousers, wing-collared shirt with what appeared to be ruffles at the front. Gloriously full handlebar whiskers flowed across his face. Elaborate watch chains drooped from his waistcoat pockets. Clenched in his teeth was a curved pipe, ornate and heavy. In court the outfit would be set off by a short, grey-white, chalked wig and flowing black cloak somehow putting me in mind of the priesthood. Findlay entered the room trailing a slither of aromatic tobacco smoke smelling expensive, classy and

somehow reliable. If he'd marched through Blackhill looking like
that they would've stoned him before they robbed him.

Findlay appeared like a character out of a period play – maybe a
First World War pilot or big game hunter in the heyday of the British
Empire. But a lawyer who was going to save my bacon? I didn't think
so. I'd no alternative but to go along with him, judging the man on
what he did rather than his eccentric appearance. It wasn't long
before I learned that no other QC looks like Donald Findlay or
matches his prowess in a courtroom.

As the events unfolded, Willie Gibson gave evidence first and
fingered me. No shocks there then. John Gibson and the woman also
picked me out in the dock in spite of having failed to identify me
only hours after the incident. Remarkably their memories had
improved with time rather than the normal human frailty of failing
with each tick of the clock. John Hogg consistently stated he couldn't
identify the masked gunman yet he was the only one to have been
shot and had more reasons than most to seek revenge.

The prosecutor sensed the case would need more proving and dug
deeper. The Gibsons revealed that bullets had been pushed through
their letterbox days before the trial. This is a standard threatening
message that conveys, 'Say the right things or you are dead.' The
judiciary take a dim view of intimidating witnesses and it's easy for
the jury to assume that the little present had been sent by the
accused, the alleged gunman, me. There was another purpose in
posting bullets through the letterbox of a family hellbent on
cooperating with the police – to make me look bad. That type of
threat wasn't my style – I preferred the strictly personal approach.
Hollywood Mafia gangsters post bullets. In my real world we have a
friend or two make a house call. The evidence was having the desired
effect on the jury, good people feeling the pressure of dealing with
low-life like us.

The prosecutor dug too deep. Soon Willie Gibson was bleating
that the gunman had passed them on the bridge barefaced before
pulling the mask down and coming at them from behind. I was
sitting in the hot seat muttering under my breath, 'Must've been a
right stupid fucker. Deserves to be caught.' As the thought passed
through my mind Donald Findlay was on his feet encouraging the
witness to point out exactly that.

The Gibsons weren't finished. When the masked man was

pointing the gun at them they noticed he had tattoos across his hand. Apparently one read FERGIE in big, bold letters. On cue, the prosecutor enquired, 'What is the significance of that name?' In parrot fashion the witness replied, 'It's a name some of the local men call Paul Ferris.' Call me stupid or call me tense but my first reaction was to think, 'Fuckers. You really want me to go down.' It was true. On the streets some people reckoned that my recent activities had earned me more respect than the Wee Paul label suggested. So, Fergie it was – for a while. I sat there fizzing then realised they'd hoisted themselves with the noose they were preparing for my neck.

I didn't have any tattoos then or now. If I should ever consider getting one I'll be sure not to have some nickname emblazoned across my skin for the simple reason that I'm not called Fergie any more. Close shave in more ways than one. I mean, imagine me an old man lying on my deathbed with some football manager's nickname adorning my paw.

In the dock, I felt as if Donald Findlay was playing me like a musical instrument he'd practised on since childhood. Every question called for a specific answer that seemed telegraphed to me and to the jury. His voice resonated with a range of emotions – disbelief, incredulity, outrage and anger.

By the time I'd stepped down from the witness box the jury were wondering about non-existent tattoos, a gunman who shows his face to all four people but tries to shoot one of them only, the Gibsons failing to notice the prominent scar on my chin and the fact that I had an alibi of being at my sister Cath's house in Barrowfield. Nor were they too impressed by two of the party failing to identify me in a formal ID parade but somehow managing to finger me when I was standing in the dock flanked by two overweight and fully uniformed cops.

Throughout, I'd been impressed by the old man, John Hogg. Here was a guy with his thighbone smashed by a gunman just because he went out for a pint with the wrong relative on the wrong night, yet his evidence was unshakeable. He couldn't recognise the gunman at the time and he still couldn't at the trial. The only thing he would concede was that the unidentified shooter was of a similar build to me and that covered half the male population of Glasgow.

After deliberating for a short time the jury returned and announced their verdict on four charges of attempted murder: Not

PAUL FERRIS & REG McKAY

Proven. It's been described as 'that bastard verdict' and has stirred fierce debates in the Scottish legal system. I could never decide whether it was deemed to be a bastard because it was neither one thing nor another or as a curse when an injured party has been looking for a hanging. Either way I think it was the right decision in this instance with the Gibsons and the prosecutor failing to prove I'd committed any crime.

Afterwards, a member of the press approached me suggesting that Not Proven meant that the jury thought I was the man but never quite believed it.

'Neither did I,' was my tight-lipped answer and off I sauntered. So, Not Proven of attempted murder it was and I went back to freedom and work.

Some time after the trial, John Hogg received a generous compensation from the masked gunman as an apology for being unintentionally shot and for the honourable manner in which he conducted himself throughout the trial. The gunman respected John Hogg.

By Reg McKay

DANCING IN THE STREETS

They staggered out of Panama Jax so late at night it was nearly morning. Flocks of birds chirped on the roofs and window ledges wakening to their daily chore of shitting on the smoke-stained stone of the tenements. A dawn veil of grey-blue light spread over Govan warehouses, shimmering and skipping on the thick, trundling waters of the Clyde.

In a dark doorway a young couple canoodled, his damp shirt clinging to the curve of his spine, her short skirt riding higher with each booze-fuelled burst of passion. Straggling groups of too-young teenagers, drunk and loud, staggered in the direction of the all-night buses in George Square, pausing only to shout encouragement to the jaw-locked couple. One boy broke away and stood by the doorway miming what he would do to her if given half a chance. Now and then, platoons of schoolgirls dolled up for the night hobbled down the pavement in too-high shoes, linked arms and chasséd up the road singing their favourite pop songs. In the distance somebody hollered, 'CHIPS,' and received a prompt reply, 'Naaaw. KEBABS,' as the drink hunger and the chill of the night bit home. I wished them luck in their search for food at that hour and waited and watched.

Maybe they thought I'd go down for the attempted murders. Maybe they'd become used to me not being around. Maybe they thought the dispute was finished. Maybe they thought I wouldn't have been back on the streets so soon after my trial. When I popped up in front of their faces they must've shit themselves. The crew I was chasing hung out in city centre clubs – the new, trendy wine bar type and not the tepid lager and knee trembler discos my mates and I would occasionally venture into. Venues for poseurs with too much dosh were what my targets preferred. In those days in Glasgow there seemed to be a new club opening every week and I got to know them all – from the outside.

I continued the unfinished business exactly where I'd left off, refusing to stop for the usual fortnight's bender in celebration of my court victory. Buckling down, I went straight back at it that day. In prison I'd kept myself fit and healthy. Not pumping iron every day like those cons with their bulging biceps and glistening triceps. They might be able to bench-press their own weight but could they handle themselves in a knife fight? I just kept disciplined and fit, passing on the wacky-baccy, keeping the cigarettes to a reasonable level, eating well and sleeping well. As soon as I was out of those gates I was going after those guys.

Eventually they would emerge in company or alone – either way would do. More often than not they were stoned on coke, uppers, alcohol or some combination of all that and more. I was cold sober and deadly serious. This was work. As soon as I spotted them I'd spring from the car and head across the street feeling for the knife or gun in my pocket. Usually it was quick. I'd call out their name in a friendly greeting and they'd answer cheerfully, unthinking and unguarded. Grab them by the throat, utter a terse warning, slash and off – that was the quick visit. Sometimes it was slow.

I'd lead them into my car or up an alleyway and ask for information. Sometimes Tam Bagan was there, sometimes not, and I didn't care much either way when dealing with people who didn't expect me. If they told me what I wanted to know they didn't get hurt. If they dallied they were hurt just enough to jog their memories. If they spilled the beans and I shot off chasing shadows – I came back. Maybe not that night or the next but I always came back. Word was you were either in or you were out of the club scene in the early 1980s. I was out and still had a good time.

Mission accomplished I'd head back to report to the Thompsons. They'd greet me cordially demanding the gory details. Arty made sick jokes and old Arthur, if he was there, said little and what he did utter was growled out in gruff, short fragments. It always ended in the same way, 'Get that fucking toerag . . .' And I did.

Not that I forgot about old enemies and they hadn't forgotten about me. Giving young Arty a lift back from his girlfriend's house up in Barmulloch, I spied a group of five or six men up ahead all wearing thick, ankle-length coats – not exactly the height of fashion at the time. It was the Welsh brothers, scuttling back to their den from their weekly ritual of signing on the dole together.

As we drew alongside them the Welshes turned, flipped open their long coats and drew out full-barrelled shotguns in one sweeping movement. A volley of shots rang out, shattering the windows and blasting several ragged holes in the metal bodywork. I booted the accelerator and the back tyres spun and whistled as more shots blasted past.

'My good fucking car,' I roared. 'Bastards.' It was a high calibre Volvo but I think our survival had less to do with its reputation for safety than the Welshes being lousy marksmen. I was furious, 'Got to get the fuckers, Arty, once and for all. Let's get tooled up and go back for them.' The Welshes had just tried to kill me and the heir apparent to Thompson's kingdom. We couldn't let it lie.

'Naw. Need tae tell ma Da. See whit he says,' Arty stuttered in reply and I looked across at him hunched down in the passenger seat. His podgy cheeks had drained of colour, his fat lips were dry for once and gnawed red, while his chins visibly trembled.

'Suit yourself, but we can't let them off with this. It's a right fucking liberty.' He needed to discuss the matter with his gaffer. I needed to get armed. Dropping Arty off at his house I sped round to a safe location where I'd planted a shotgun, loaded both barrels, shoved a handful of cartridges in my pocket and headed towards the Welshes' house.

Parked by the kerb, I hooted the horn again and again. Eventually a couple of the ugly brothers came to the window looking annoyed at first and then startled as I pointed the gun towards them. In my wing mirror I spotted a police van coming fast up the road heading in my direction. Change of plan. I scooted off at speed and managed to deposit the gun with a friend before driving on again quickly. I reckoned the police must have seen me aiming the gun so I couldn't risk being found anywhere near such a weapon. The police huckled me, searched me and impounded the car, clearly the worse for wear, being full of holes. Nobody had tried to shoot me, I saw no one with a shotgun and I certainly hadn't noticed the Welshes. All they found was a pickaxe handle in the boot, a couple of Stanley knives and a stave. Deeply disappointed, they charged me with possession of offensive weapons, letting me off lightly in the circumstances, or so I thought. I didn't know that same pickaxe *would be used by the courts to wreak their revenge on me in the not too distant future.*

When I caught up with Arty later that night he was in a relaxed frame of mind, pursuing his favourite hobbies of chocolate and gangster videos. 'It's aw settled, Paul,' he yawned. 'The Welshes didnae know it wis me in the motor. Mistake like.'

I shook my head in disbelief. Was he talking about the same Welshes who shot his father, killed his granny and terrorised the area for a generation? My guess was that he had told old Arthur absolutely zilch.

Another local diversion came in the form of Jazza Welsh, cousin and associate of the ugly brothers. I'd heard he was taxing people at local service stations, helping himself to free petrol and the cash contents of the tills. Call it a protection racket. I called it bad for business. Spotting Jazza at a garage one afternoon I drove in. While his back-up man, Paddy Bain, was filling their big Audi with petrol I strolled over to Jazza at the kiosk, hustling the young woman behind the counter.

'Can I have word in private?'

'Sure, no worries,' he smiled while turning to the frightened young woman and adding, 'Mind whit I said. I'll be back in a minute.'

As soon as he sat in the passenger seat of my car I locked the doors and drove off at speed to a soundtrack of Jazza Welsh's entire vocabulary of curses. I was trying to tell him to desist from threatening the locals and he was having none of it. Noticing first that he'd omitted to fasten his seat belt, stupid given the speed we were doing, I then saw that he'd pulled out a large knife. Holding him with one hand while steering with the other, the Mexican stand-off went on for miles. 'Put the blade away or you go through the windscreen,' was my final ultimatum and one he realised I could deliver in an instant. We made arrangements for the Glaswegian equivalent of a duel.

'Get tooled up with whatever you need and meet me at the Three Hills at the rhubarb fields,' I offered.

'Right,' was all he said.

I sped off to the safe house where I stored my weapons. Armed with a gun and a knife I was heading back to my car when the Audi came screeching up with Paddy Bain at the wheel and Jazza in the back. The window was down and the barrel of a shotgun pointed at me from a few feet. If he'd pulled the trigger they would've needed tweezers to pick my remains off the tenement wall.

'Ready?' he asked.

'Aye, ready,' I replied, wondering what the hell that show was all about. But if I thought he was going to play entirely by the rules I was soon to be disappointed.

Once we hit a country road, the Audi kept trying to pass me – a manoeuvre that would allow Jazza a free shot at me. Swerving across both lanes I led us away from Blackhill towards Stepps. The big Audi was pushing me very hard so I slammed the brakes, swung the car round to block the road and shot. In his panic, Jazza fired his shotgun forgetting to open his window. The spray skimmed my car but the broken glass scattered, slashing a vein in the driver's throat. Paddy Bain clutched his neck trying to stem the blood flow, turned down a side road and booted it. Furious, I drew level with them on the wrong side of the road and was trying to get steady enough to take decent one-handed aims. I hit the car but was well off the passengers. A taxi appeared from the opposite direction and I edged over to let it through. Paddy Bain hit the brakes so all three of us came to a halt, side by side on that narrow road.

The poor taxi driver looked to his left then his right. The blood was spouting out of Bain's neck. Guns were jutting out of both cars. Windows were smashed and body panels pock-marked. Bain and Jazza Welsh were refusing to move, the taxi driver couldn't move and I wasn't about to endanger an innocent party. I shrugged at Welsh, gave him the viccies, turned my car and drove off.

A while later Jazza was badly stabbed in prison by someone who'd heard about our dispute and assumed he was one of the ugly brothers. But he was just another scheme guy going about his business like any other. Jazza was an okay guy who didn't deserve the knifing.

It was time to invest in some new wheels. Through Arty I was put in touch with someone who had a three-litre Renault for sale. Now, I wouldn't have recognised one of those if it had run me over in broad daylight with its beams full on but it sounded good and the price sounded better. Its dull appearance and shape bored me for I reckoned I was due something a bit flash. Against my better judgement I was persuaded to take the car for a test drive and fell in love. The power of the machine was outrageous, with the automatic transmission booting it into overdrive like jet propulsion. The wheels looked ordinary but could move – just the type of deception that might be useful to me in my business. A bit like me, I suppose – wee, slight and unthreatening. I'd bought the car and been driving it for a while when someone pointed out the registration number – 666.

Anne Marie McCafferty was my solace and relaxation. We'd been going steady since a few weeks after we met. Anne Marie gave me the freedom to get on with my business and I made sure she knew nothing about the details. Increasingly, I was spending time with her at her mother's house up in Balornock. Still people were unsure where I lived and that was the way I liked it. In those pre-mobile phone days, they saw me by arrangement or when I deigned to turn up. I preferred it that way and it was safer all round – except for Jenny and Willie Ferris.

Now that I was earning good money, I wanted to give something back to the parents I loved. As proud as ever, my folks refused any cash or new gear – a three-piece suite, sound system or whatever. They always refused, suspecting that the goods might have been provided through one of my sources. Out of one back door and into their front room. Jenny wouldn't have any of that. Then the police raids were landing on them. As I'd become more active, the police searched harder and they'd only one address in their files – Jenny and Willie's. It was a problem that would become more severe with every passing month.

My car was proving as useful an addition to my armoury as any blade or gun. One night on the hunt, I spotted four targets passing by in a Ford Fiesta, a car I'd become very familiar with. Tarted-up to look like a high-powered XR2, it was in fact a humble, basic car with next to no horsepower under the bonnet. We chased them through the city and out on to the motorway. Before long I'd edged up bumper-to-bumper and started accelerating. We drove at one hundred miles per hour, nose to rear, with the Fiesta's brake lights gleaming red and the bitter stink of burning rubber wafting into the car. As the Fiesta slithered and swerved from side to side, I booted the accelerator, sending the car and its four occupants into a full spin and crashing into the barriers. In my rear view mirror I watched the car bounce out, round and overturn as we headed away.

What amazed me about the people I was after was that they didn't seem prepared to alter their lifestyles which made them sitting ducks. They saw me as a vengeful poltergeist and thought they could protect themselves by relying on good-luck charms and prayer. Word got back to me that this bloke called Raymond Bonnar, who hung around with the crew I was after, had been badmouthing me. 'If that wee bastard comes near me looking for his fifty grand I'm gonnae shoot him,' was the gist. Mr Bonnar had declared war and was added to my list.

A few days later I was driving with Tam Bagan by my side when we pulled up at some traffic lights near the city centre. Who should be alone in his car ahead of us but Raymond Bonnar. I nipped out of my car and rattled on Bonnar's window asking in a friendly tone, 'Are you Raymond Bonnar?' 'Who the fuck are you?' he replied, frowning and rolling down his window. I reached inside the car and stabbed him. 'I'm the wee bastard you were going to shoot,' and, as he sat trapped in his car, continued stabbing him.

The Alsatian in the back seat didn't take kindly to my actions, gripped my arm in his jaw, tugging, twisting and biting as his master howled for help. I'd no choice but to stab the brave dog who loosened his hold enough for me to free my mauled arm. As the traffic lights changed through amber to green, Bonnar slammed his foot on the accelerator and spun off at speed. I wasn't finished with him yet and gave chase up Bell Street and around Glasgow Cross.

Madness took over Bonnar who stopped at a set of red lights with us sitting on his tail. Ahead of him, the cars and buses were streaming past at some speed so I improvised by revving up the big Renault and ramming the rear of his car, trying to shunt him forward. The wounded Alsatian barked in the back seat and the cars were making enough noise for a warm-up at a Grand Prix. Pedestrians were stopping to watch the action and I decided it was time to scarper before someone called the bizzies. Swinging my car out I passed Bonnar and away.

A few hundred yards up the road I spotted Bonnar in my rear-view mirror tight in the Renault's slipstream, blasting his horn, hunched over the steering wheel, blood seeping from his wounds and the silhouette of one angry, big dog just over his shoulder. He kept up his antics through congested city traffic till finally I shook him off. Bonnar was either too brave for his own survival or had totally

PAUL FERRIS & REG MCKAY

flipped. When he lost us he proceeded to London Road police station and staggered in to the front desk. 'Paul Ferris,' he gasped before collapsing in a pool of his own gore.

A few years later I was to learn that Raymond Bonnar had nothing to do with the £50,000 which Arty claimed he had been cheated out of by Friel and Ross, and had never uttered the threat against my life. A female friend had known him well during those years, describing him as, 'A womaniser, maybe, but no gangster – it just wasn't his style.' She explained this to me one night when we were in a pub and Bonnar was at the other end of the bar. When I appeared in front of him he flinched and recoiled, the years between our meetings having done little to obliterate the memory of that first encounter.

'About that time, I'm sorry. It should never have happened,' I said as I stuck my hand out in the offer of a handshake.

Bonnar hesitated and his eye twitched before he took my hand and replied, 'No harm done now.' We stood in each other's company for a while, just another two guys sharing a social drink.

I despise those who habitually injured non-combatants. The Thompsons had told me of Bonnar's declaration of war and I can only surmise that they were trying to create additional difficulties for me or that young Arty had a grudge against the harmless guy. I hated mistakes and made very few even when others had been trying to set me against other people. In those days I trusted the Thompsons implicitly, was blinded by my sense of loyalty.

The same day of the Bonnar incident I tracked down a guy called Spot Henry who knew the whereabouts of some blokes I was chasing.

'Fuck off and find them yourself, ye wee bastard,' Spot Henry muttered two minutes before I knifed him. He was just one of many faceless characters I damaged on the way to my main targets. By now the opposition had got the sense that I wasn't going to stop till I got them all. My old mates in Blackhill were adjusting to my lifestyle. They introduced a new nickname for me, Robot, like a machine that just kept going. Thankfully, this nickname lasted just about as long as Fergie and I still hadn't changed my mind about tattoos.

My car had turned into a liability, the 666 proving more of a help to the police than a hoot for me. The evening of the Bonnar chase I parked my car at the back of the Thompsons' and was in their house *discussing just that difficulty. The information about Bonnar's bloody collapse in the police station had already percolated through the street tom-toms. We agreed my next action was to take a different car, the only one available and parked at the front of the house. I bid farewell, walked out the front door and into a Volkswagen Beetle, more often identified with latter-day hippies than Glasgow gangsters. As I drove off, I passed two police cars and heard a commotion behind me. Comfortable in the seat of the car with the most innocent reputation in the world, I drove on anonymous and free from detection.*

Two minutes after I'd walked out of the Thompsons' front door the police had burst in through the rear looking for me, while a squad of bluecoats were all over my Renault. About 30 police were deployed in the operation rather than the usual two or three and my car was towed away for forensic tests. Clearly they were out to get me.

Arty agreed and next day along with old Arthur suggested I lie low for a while. The old man threw me the keys and the address to his holiday home in Rothesay on the Isle of Bute, a short drive and ferry ride away at the mouth of the Clyde. It was a sleepy little backwater used to tourists and would be ideal. When old Arthur tossed me the keys to his Daimler I got a real sense of being taken care of and protected by the firm. The Thompsons were looking after me and I was safe from the police. Or was I?

Fourteen attempted murders against my name. The police flashed the paperwork at old Arthur who was taking such care of me because everyone listed was part of young Arty's vendetta. Fourteen attempted murders sounded a lot but after a quick tally in my head I reckoned there was some chaos that hadn't found its way on to their books. I'd always known I was playing for big stakes, so my situation was serious but not unexpected.

'A wee break,' I suggested to Anne Marie as I chatted to her in her mother's house. 'We could use it. Besides, things are a bit hot for me in Glasgow right now.' True to form, she asked nothing and packed a bag to join me later in the day, travelling down on her own. It would be good to get away to Rothesay for a while and the only significance to Anne Marie of the number 14 was the days we might spend there. Anne Marie was heavily pregnant and I hadn't been able to spend much time with her lately. As I headed the car down the Clyde coast I was genuinely looking forward to some relaxation.

Rothesay is on the Isle of Bute in the wide Clyde estuary. Till cheap flights to Spain became available, it had been a traditional holiday spot for Glaswegians who could afford any sort of holiday. During the second fortnight in July, the Glasgow Fair, the shipyards and factories shut down and Glaswegians trundled down in their droves even for one day if their purse couldn't stretch any further. We called it going 'doon the watter' since all you did was follow the River Clyde down towards the sea. As you progressed, the scenery changed from the smoke and grind of urban wasteland to the jagged crags, heather-strewn hills and rolling waters of picture postcard Scotland. It was a good place to have a holiday. It was a better place than most to hide out.

Later that night, well ensconced in the Thompsons' holiday home, Anne Marie was in the kitchen making a pot of tea as I sat in the lounge watching a football match on television. Minute by minute I could feel the pressure reduce and almost stopped thinking about what was going on up the road in Glasgow. The telephone rang and a deep male voice asked for someone I'd never heard of. A wrong number and just the low-level hassle of an ordinary life I could get used to.

With a thud and a crack the house door flew open and from the hall I heard, 'ARMED POLICE! ARMED POLICE! FERRIS COME OUT . . . NOW!' Message received. I was on my feet and out into the hall in one movement, palms open and arms outstretched. They yelled and screamed and were all around me, three of them in plain clothes with pistols aiming at me. From the right, a guy kicked me behind the knees, downing me in one. Face flattened against the floor, I felt a great weight on my back, my arms twisted behind me and the metal handcuffs clamping my wrists. In the mêlée I recognised one copper by reputation alone. Greg Diddle, as we'll call him, stood at well over six feet in height, broad and hefty with a shock of white hair. Once seen never forgotten.

As Anne Marie stepped out of the kitchen, one of the cops shouted, 'There's a fuckin' woman in the house. Get a WPC. We should've brought a woman wi' us. Fuck sake get oan the blower now.'

Diddle replied with one word. 'BASTARD,' he spat.

As his colleagues fretted at Anne Marie's presence, Diddle went about his preferred activity. Kneeling between my shoulder blades with my head twisted to one side and flattened against the floor, he rammed his pistol hard into the back of my head growling, 'Know what this is, don't ya, ye wee cunt?'

Anne Marie had recovered from the shock of the rumble and sussed the situation immediately. Trying to shield me from the guns, she threw herself across my body. Diddle soon got Anne Marie out of his way and pulled me from the ground using my handcuffed arms as a lever. Dragging me through to the bedroom, he dumped me on the bed sitting up facing the window. Behind me I could hear the police searching the house while Anne Marie protested. Diddle yanked me to my feet and started to rummage through my clothes and the crevices of my body. As he leaned over to shake down my legs, a gun slipped to the ground with a heavy clatter. Quickly, I kicked the gun, sending it skidding across the floor. Diddle looked down at me as if he wanted to rip my skull off my neck and bluntly I told him, 'Better no' be any accidents in here. There's a woman in the house. My woman and she's pregnant with my baby. There better no' be any fucking accidents. Right? I said RIGHT, you?'

Diddle looked irritated but continued with his body search, rifling my upper garments. Still he remained tight-lipped and pulled a plastic bankcard holder out of my trouser pocket. I knew it contained nothing more heinous than a few credit cards and about £50 in spare notes but I resented the intrusion of this man, any man, going through my possessions – always did, always will. Turning his back on me for a couple of minutes, he threw the bankcards and cash to the floor before swinging around to face me again. 'Whose is the brown powder, son?' he asked, with his eyebrows raised, dangling a small plastic bag from two meaty fingers.

'Fuck knows,' I replied honestly.

'Must be yours in that case, eh?' and he winced in what passed for a smile on his ugly mug. I lost it again, shouting and swearing and ranting with the only available weapon – my gob.

In the middle of my outburst, another cop we'll call DS Trickey, came into the room waving a bundle of cash he'd found lying on top of the mantelpiece. Trying to calm me down, he asked if I could sit back down on the bed and count the money. It took me no more than a minute or so to confirm there was about £500. By the time I'd finished, Trickey came back into the room with a collection of assorted goods in a transparent evidence bag – telephone directories, several sheets of notepaper, a brown envelope. Those bits of paper had to be significant, yet I'd made a point of going to that house in Rothesay absolutely clean. Whatever it was, they must've turned up while I was being a good little boy sitting quietly on the bed and counting the money for DS Trickey. That's when I lost the place again.

'Shut it, son. Just fucking shut your trap.' Diddle wasn't for listening.

'Come bursting in here with all your fucking guns clueless about Anne Marie being here – you're not just dangerous you're out of fucking order,' I rumbled, warming to my theme.

'Jist be quiet, ye wee shite,' Diddle shouted, the colour rushing to his face.

'If I go down I'll blow your fucking head off. I'll fucking blow you away, you evil bastard, and that's a promise.'

I'd gone too far in my rant. Diddle wasn't used to being threatened, 'Who the fuck do ye think ye are exactly, ye little shit? Ye cannae go about threatening the polis, son. If ye think ye can ye're aff your little fucking nut.' He was spitting blood, clenching and unclenching his fists, desperate to give me a good doing.

Riling him helped me cool down but not drop the subject, 'We both know what's going on here. So get the picture – I meant what I said. If I go down I'm coming after you. Got it?' Lowering my tone but not my stare had the desired effect of unnerving the big thug. His pallor turned a shade of jaundice-stained milk and sweat trickled down his greasy forehead.

'Look, son, nobody's getting fitted up here,' he muttered, attempting to make peace.

Far too late. I sat on the bed and looked up at the giant of a man and repeated, 'I meant what I said.'

Both Anne Marie and I were huckled out of the house and driven to the tiny police station in Rothesay. The local uniforms seemed ill at ease, being more accustomed to dealing with a little vandalism by holidaying riff-raff and the regular punch-up after the Friday night dance. I almost felt sorry for them. Almost. I did feel sorry for Anne Marie. In spite of how well she'd handled herself she wasn't used to such goings on and looked shell-shocked. My personal life was kept very far from my business but that didn't stop Diddle and company from grilling Anne Marie over many hours. By the end they discovered she knew nothing about anything. Did they release her, a captive on a small island where the ferries had stopped for the night? Did they consider the advanced state of her pregnancy and the well-being of our unborn child? Did they what. Guilt-free and under no suspicion, she was locked in a damp cell in that cold, depressing jailhouse. Me – they proposed to charge with attempting to murder the demented Raymond Bonnar amongst a list of other things.

The next day, Anne Marie was sent packing while I was driven back up the water to Glasgow for an ID parade.

'That's the little bastard,' Bonnar screamed and pointed. No doubts there then. Formally charged and a short drive to Barlinnie Prison's C Hall. I was 21 years old, had graduated to the adult regime and Scotland's most infamous jail, Bar-L. Whereas just a short year before I dreaded the prospect of a sojourn in Bar-L, it was now water off a duck's back.

A week later I was taken back to court and advised that the charge of attempted murder was being dropped on Bonnar's insistence. Instead, I stood accused of possessing offensive weapons in the form of two Stanley knives and a pickaxe handle, of a few other minor offences and of being in possession of diamorphine with intent to supply. So there it was, the little plastic bag of powder. Diddle's words rung in my head, 'Look, son, no one's getting fitted up here.' I was fuming by the time they headed me out to the Bar-L special.

Back in the jail I was put in the Sweat Box, a small, airless cell where they hold you until they decide where to dump you. Along with me were three other remand prisoners and we got chatting about what we'd been put in for. The others' charges ranged from assault to shoplifting. One of the other guys said he'd been done for possessing drugs but added, 'A wis fitted up by the bizzies, man.' One of the alleged thieves winked, 'I'm saying that too, pal,' and the other guys laughed. I decided to hold my tongue and say nothing.

In Longriggend and Glenochil I'd looked down on the prisoners always moaning about being set up. Prisons are loaded with men *claiming to be innocent and you soon get to the stage of disconnecting your brain from their griping. I thought of all those others I'd refused to listen to, how many of them were actually innocent. If it could happen to me, then why not to them? In the sweat box I resolved to keep my trap shut and concentrate on winning my trial.*

WALKING THE WALK

C Hall in Bar-L is the font of knowledge of all things criminal. Spend a few weeks there and you can learn more than a year at any university – on specialist subjects, of course. Individuals awaiting trial and considered too great a risk of absconding or a danger to the community are locked up there rather than trusted to turn up at court. It's like a busy air terminal with a constant toing and froing of any criminal's friends and enemies. It's a prison with extras as the cons bring in their feuds from the outside and continue them unabated. Almost everyone is driven to a nervy edge at the prospect of being sent down big style and the increasing tension of waiting to find out. C Hall is a prison with dangerous, anxious, angry men capable of anything.

C Hall is usually packed to the gunnels, housing many more men than it was designed to cater for. I was lucky, if that is the right word, since my psoriasis had flared up again qualifying me for a cell on my own. Sheer luxury in a place where the imposed presence of others, always somebody else around, is one of the constant nagging pressures.

Arty and Tam Bagan paid me a visit as part of the routine obligation paid to team members when in the clink. Make contact and make sure they and theirs are all right. I can't remember Arty offering assistance to Anne Marie but he did ask a favour of me. One of the guys we were after, Mark Watt, was in Bar-L. Arty thought that some pressure on their isolated gang member might encourage the return of the £50,000 he felt he had been cheated out of by Friel and Ross. Fat chance.

'Just lean on him a bit, Paul,' the plump joker directed. In other words, assault him.

I searched Watt out at the first opportunity, being told he was in *the exercise yard where someone pointed him out, 'There! That big, baldy bastard wearing the blue overalls.' The helpful stranger wasn't exaggerating. Watt was a colossus of a bloke, an enormous bruiser whose frame cast a menacing shadow over my flyweight status. I needed a plan and needed to act quickly.*

A weapon would be essential and I made discreet enquiries about getting my mitts on a knife. Being new to Bar-L, I hadn't worked out the connections, so by lock-up that night, alone in my cell, I was no further forward. My spy-hole was lifted and this deep voice boomed, 'You looking for me?'

Asking the enquirer to step back from the door so I could see who it was, sure enough there was the full-moon noggin of Watt himself. We conversed.

'I'm Paul Ferris.'

'Whit dae ye want me tae dae? Panic?'

'We've business that needs settled.'

'I've nae business wi' you, ye wee shite.'

'You're tied in with that 50 grand.'

'So, whit are ye proposing?'

'We want it paid up.'

'Or whit?'

'Or we sort it out in other ways.'

'Fuck the hanging around, Ferris. I'll sort you right out o' the game the morrow morning. I'll fuckin' see to you then . . . ' His voice trailed off abruptly as a screw started patrolling the gantry. I lay down on my bunk and contemplated the heap of smelly stuff I'd just landed in. Watt would make mincemeat patties of me and not break sweat. Think, Paul, think.

I'd no blade so I tested out the might of the pen. I scribbled a fake letter from Arthur Thompson junior to Mark Watt. It read:

> Mark Watt,
> Who the fuck do you think you are fucking me for 50 grand? You will end up in a coffin if you're lucky enough and by the way I know where you live and when you get out.
> See you soon,
> Arthur Thompson.

Writing a letter in Arty's name gave me a chuckle, since the self-

proclaimed Godfather's son was nearly illiterate, sticking his tongue out with the effort of scribbling basic, almost illegible words. The ploy was simple. In the morning I'd say to Watt that I only wanted to deliver the letter and hand it over. As he read it I'd jump him.

Still, I'd need a weapon if I were to stand any chance. Prisons are great places for improvisation. Most of my cell was taken up with spare beds and chairs with metal legs. Prising a leg from a chair provided me with a too-light but better-than-nothing assister. Then I covered the adaptation to the chair with a spar from under one of the beds. It looked okay but I'd have to remind myself not to sit down on it. I was as prepared as I could be in the circumstances. Watt was a first offender and I prayed that his lack of experience resulted in a lack of preparation. It was the only way I could envisage me surviving the joust.

Next morning Watt arrived at my cell door minutes after it had been unlocked. I passed him the letter as planned and as he read I smacked him as hard as I could on the head with the metal rod. Nothing. Not a flicker. Except he had noticed that I'd thumped him. Slowly, so slowly, he turned towards me and frowned. It was a long second before he grabbed me by the neck and rammed me against the brick wall of the cell. Winded, I was powerless to stop him clenching my throat in his left hand while pounding his right fist into the back of my skull. As my chest heaved for air my head rattled with every strike. I was losing consciousness fast but still managed to whack him on the head, blow for blow. As he moved me effortlessly about the cell my hand struck against the door, knocking the steel chair leg out of my grip, soaring through the air and tangling in the suicide net. Sinking down and down, getting dizzy and weak-legged, I was losing more than the fight. In dire need you have to deploy every wile in your book. 'Edge up. Here's the screws,' I lied in one last desperate ploy. Watt's lack of prison experience showed, thank God, and he dropped me in a heap before heading out and off.

I'd taken some doing and struggled to gain my feet. Warm blood, my blood, dampened my face and my head. I should've cleaned up fast and taken the day off from all hostilities. Then, 'What the fuck.' I was out of the cell, retrieved my metal rod from the net and off down the gantry. The wing was crowded with cons there for the show since Watt had broadcast he was going to give Ferris a doing. If I failed, everybody would know about it. It must have looked comical, a totty guy like me haring after a lumbering giant like Watt.

In front of me I could see Watt, his baldy head smeared in blood, walking slowly away. As I caught up with him, I leapt into the air bringing the metal rod down on his skull with both hands. If he survived that wallop I was a dead man and no question. He went down and so did I – right on top him, raining in as many blows as my spinning head would allow. Within a minute a pile of screws had jumped on us and pulled me off. They delivered Watt to the hospital and me to seven days in solitary confinement. It would've been much longer but Watt was persuaded by someone loyal to me to drop all charges. His very welcome change of heart didn't prevent me from spending my first Christmas in solitary – my first Christmas but not my last.

As is the prison authorities' style they moved me upstairs to a shared cell, probably as a punishment after my escapade with Watt. It was a lucky move, allowing me to renew an old acquaintanceship with James O'Neil, the infamous Neily the Bomb of the Glenochil Wolves. As with so many of the teenaged Wolves, he had graduated into a life of serious adult crime and was on remand with another two guys for charges of armed robbery. When their trial came up they were dished out 50 years between them. As Neily went off to do a long stretch, I was left with a close bond to another cellmate, Ricky Taylor, who'd connected with me since my fluke victory over Mark Watt.

Word reached me that another old acquaintance was in Bar-L, George Welsh of the ugly brothers from Blackhill. He was doing time for breaking into an old woman's house and ripping off her electricity meter – a typical Welsh crime, nothing being too low for that pile of slugs. To think at one time they'd ambitions to take over Glasgow from the Thompsons while they were clearly incapable of crawling out of the gutter. On my personal list from the years of childhood bullying, Welsh's treatment of the old woman had done nothing to endear him towards me either.

Taylor and I devised a simple and, I thought, foolproof plan. Welsh was on the landing directly below us. After the communal exercise period the following day, Taylor would track him back from the yard, nip into his cell behind him and pull a pillowcase over his head. Then enters Ferris to do the nasty. The pillowcase was a simple device to prevent Welsh from singing to the screws, a bad habit of all the brothers. I constructed a homemade razor and had a device with a long, sharpened nail embedded in a wooden handle smuggled out of the workshop. The evening before the proposed strike, Taylor and I practised the hooding routine over and over in our locked cell before settling to some sleep.

In the middle of the night, I was standing in the pitch-dark cell urinating into the chamber pot when the bold Taylor sprang from his bunk, throwing the pillowcase over my head – a perfect execution even in his sleep. Trouble was, in the commotion, I had managed to piss down his leg and all over his bedding. I was beginning to get an uneasy feeling about this plan and Ricky Taylor had a long, damp uncomfortable night to ponder over his doubts.

Trooping out of the exercise yard with five bodies separating Welsh from Taylor and Taylor from me, all seemed to be going to plan. Pushing my way down the crowded gallery, Welsh and Taylor fell out of sight momentarily. Turning sharply into the prescribed cell, there was George Welsh, sitting on his bed with a look of horror on his phizog but no pillowcase. Too late for turning back, I smartly slashed Welsh across the face with the nail device and tried to do him with the razor. Alerted of approaching screws, I retreated from the cell, the job half done. Taylor was full of apologies for entering the wrong cell. A prison is an anonymous place and in the heat of the chase, poor Ricky Taylor had just turned left too early.

I didn't have to wait long for another go at George Welsh. Sid Johnstone from Blackhill, the friend of the Welshes I'd slashed in the exercise yard at Longriggend, approached me. For reasons known only to him, Johnstone had turned against the brothers grim and wanted to make his peace with me. Trust is something you earn so I put a proposition to him. Johnstone could prove his hatred of the brothers by organising a little surprise. Put simply, attack George Welsh or be attacked by me. Johnstone agreed.

In prison there are no conventions except necessity. The long curved shard of mirror with a taped handgrip at one end looked as dangerous and lethal as any blade. When I handed it to Sid Johnstone, he appreciated the effort that had gone into tooling his equaliser. As he left my cell he hesitated, turned round and with a serious expression said, 'Even if I kill the bastard I'll just plead guilty to comical homicide.' As he stropped off to do the business I hoped *his knife skills were better than his vocabulary. If he killed Welsh I would find it comical, but I reckoned the authorities would consider Johnstone culpable.*

George Welsh was sitting eating his lunch when Sid Johnstone marched swiftly up and plunged the glass dagger straight through his throat. Welsh wouldn't laugh for a while, though he survived long enough to test out an old superstition – the one about broken mirrors bringing seven years' bad luck. The Welshes power was beginning to fade as my actions and those of others picked them off. As the brothers' numbers dwindled so they were increasingly revealed for what they were – heartless bullies.

Seven years after the attack in Bar-L he tried to jump the queue at the local ice-cream van in Blackhill. A local bloke called Brian Redmond didn't like it. Years of merciless pressure welled up inside Redmond and he went for broke. In the midst of a vicious fight he gained the upper hand, cutting Welsh's throat, hacking deeper and deeper till the man was dead and his head hung by a thread of gristle, skin and tendon. They may have ended public beheadings many centuries ago but in places like Blackhill anything goes.

Redmond was sentenced to life and I'm sure the wider public groaned in disgust at that type of crime. But in Blackhill a cheer went up not just from the players like me but from the ordinary citizens, old women, vulnerable families, the young men and women too fearful to walk the streets on their own. Brian Redmond had weakened a tyranny the police had failed to dent. Well done, Brian Redmond. Long live street justice.

Tam Bagan came to visit me on his own one day and reported that life on the outside had taken a curious turn. He had been instructed by Arty to drop off a stolen car outside the house of John Friel, The Irishman, in the city's salubrious St Andrews Drive. Delivery made, Arty telephoned the police notifying them of the offending vehicle, adding that it had a MI6 machine-gun in the boot – and it had. This was hardly a surprise since the routine fitted Arty's cowardly style, but there was more.

Arty had been arranging for guns to be planted in certain pubs owned by rivals who were getting too big for their boots. One place in particular was called Michelle's, across from Pier Thirty-Nine on the city's Clydeside. A gun was planted and a young woman paid to drop some live bullets into a cistern in the ladies' toilets. The donations were always promptly followed up by a call to a detective with Strathclyde Police.

A detective I'll call Sergeant Wylie McIlvain, a name I was to become increasingly familiar with, had apparently interviewed John Friel after the incident with the car and gun planted outside his home. As Bagan was talking, I wondered where I'd heard McIlvain's name before. Apparently the copper didn't just hassle Friel, he weaved a tale about the Grey Wolves, a middle-eastern gang scouring Glasgow a little upset at being cheated over a drugs deal. McIlvain leaned on Friel, suggesting that it might be safer for him to cough up on any recent transactions he'd been involved with rather than hang around a free man with these dangerous people in town.

Then it clicked that McIlvain had been involved following the arrest of Arty after Gibson had grassed him over the arms being stored in Maryhill Autos. Now you may ask how the detective knew about any botched drugs deal. You may ask why Arty planted a gun in a car outside of Friel's house. You may ask about the connection with Arty. You may enquire how Tam Bagan and Arty knew the details of the detective's interview with Friel. You may ask but, in my blissful ignorance, I ploughed on asking nothing, taking everything on trust and doing my job. I had a trial to prepare for and was more concerned to secure my freedom than analysing somebody else's behaviour. Unless, that is, we were talking about people intent on putting me in jail for something I didn't do.

he police were issued with two guns that day,' said Peter
Forbes, my highly efficient solicitor, in his usual straight-
laced, dour manner.

'No. Three guns,' I replied, certain of my facts as I'd run and re-
run the police action over in my head every day in Bar-L.

Peter had sifted through all the formal documents painstakingly.
Now he was trying to square up the police's account with mine,
looking for cracks. He rustled through the huge pile of documents till
he found the right ones. 'There were only two warrants of
authorisation issued for guns that day,' he confirmed, looking me
straight in the eye.

'Peter, there were three guns pointing at me as soon as they bust
in. Ask Anne Marie,' I suggested.

'I already have,' was the unsurprising response from a man
thorough in his work.

'And what did she say?'

'There were three guns.'

I sighed that sigh which says you are not losing your marbles, you
haven't imagined something that never actually happened.

One of the side-effects of going on trial facing serious charges is
that you mull over and over every possible detail till your brain
aches and your palms sweat and still you're not done till the bloke
in the long wig sings. So, there was a phantom gun. Interesting,
but it would have to wait to take second place to my defence,
especially against the allegation of possessing heroin with intent
to supply.

Accepting the heroin was mine but for personal consumption was
never considered. At that time, I had the occasional snort of cocaine
but heroin users were getting off very lightly while dealers were

jailed for ten years. If found guilty of intent to supply heroin I would never be able to get the police off my back for years.

Donald Findlay QC represented me again. He and Peter Forbes made a great team, one as sharp as the other was thorough, both on the same wavelength, contributing their particular skills unencumbered by ego. It transpired that the envelope was the main case against me for dealing. On one of the envelopes was scribbled:

> Sulph 10
> Black 50
> Coke 4
> £50,000
> £75,000.

This little message was interpreted by the police as absolute proof I'd been trafficking in drugs on a scale beyond what was necessary or possible to sniff up my nose or mainline into my body and my body alone. Trouble was, their forensic tests had thrown up a couple of complications – the fingerprints on the note belonged to Arthur Thompson senior and the handwriting belonged to the almost illiterate Arty. It was only then I recalled the police handing me that piece of paper during my arrest and thanked my good judgement in refusing to touch it. No trace of Paul Ferris's mitts anywhere on the paper. Round one to my team.

Possessing the heroin would prove more difficult to dismiss with the courts preferring to believe the police over everyone else, especially people with criminal records. The bizzies alleged they discovered the heroin in the pocket of my tracksuit bottoms, the same trousers they'd sent for forensic tests in connection with the attempted murder of Raymond Bonnar. In discussion with Donald Findlay, we decided on the unusual step of sending the same tracksuit for independent forensic tests. Gangsters view forensics as their most feared enemy. Wise enough in the ways of the police, the average criminal finds it impossible to avoid scientific detection. I knew I was innocent of the heroin so was happy and confident to arrange our own tests. I prayed that forensics would be my ally in this instance.

A foremost forensic toxicologist at Glasgow University carried out the tests by detaching the pocket from the tracksuit and subjecting the material to microscopic examination at something like 1,000 times thinner than the average human hair. He discovered the brown powder was very pure heroin and searched the plastic bag, bankcard holder and trousers for traces.

The plastic bag was green, meaning it would be impossible to judge the colour of the contents from the outside. What was it Diddle had said down in Rothesay? 'Whose is the brown powder, son?' How did he know it was brown? The bag would have made white powder appear light green and brown powder dark green. It made everything look green.

The bag was designed to keep small denominations of coins, had traces of the heroin on the outside and was bound to leak on to anything it made contact with. The credit card holder was smeared with fine particles of heroin. The tracksuit pocket was found to have no traces at all. The forensic bod went on to say that that the credit card holder's narrow fitments weren't designed to hold even a little bulk and would've squeezed the drugs out and into the pocket.

In the witness box, I was in full flow of a description of the actions of Diddle. Laughter broke out through the galleries and I thought I could see the flicker of a smile on the face of Lord Murray, the august judge. But all he said was, 'Thank you, Mr Ferris. Proceed.'

Making a courtroom laugh can be a dodgy business with the judge and jury likely to take the view of the accused being flippant or too bloody smart for his own good. Towards the end, when the judge was ready to give his charge to the jury, I held my breath anxiously, unnecessarily. Over many hours spanning two days, Lord Murray gave the jury a detailed analysis of the case for and against. He pointed out that one policeman claimed to have found the drugs in my tracksuit pocket yet the forensic test found no trace of heroin on the material. The jury were directed to consider carefully the role of DS Greg Diddle of whom Lord Murray said, 'I make no bones about it, that's the man who is criticised. That's the man at whom the finger is pointed.' The judge went on that the police search warrant was on the basis of drugs and not the attempted murder of Raymond Bonnar, for which I was being actively pursued. He referred to Diddle being 'painted as the villain of the piece' by Donald Findlay QC and charged the jury to make a decision about that view.

By the final strains of his very lengthy speech, it was clear to everyone that Lord Murray had given the jury a stark choice – if you believe Diddle then convict Ferris of the charges. If you don't, set Ferris free.

If the jury couldn't decide who to believe they would opt for a Not Proven verdict. As I waited for their decision this was one occasion where Not Proven wouldn't do me at all. The heroin wasn't mine and I wanted a clear-cut outcome.

Forty-one minutes is all the jury took. Not Guilty was called out and I scanned the room for the police. I wanted to look them in the eye and smile. Of course, the police were well out of the way, like lily-livered football supporters leaving the match early rather than watch their side being beaten. It was probably just as well. While at the end of the trial I was still fuming at the whole sorry charade, I should've thanked them for teaching me the methods of the police.

But how had they known of my flight to Rothesay? Arty insisted they must have tracked Anne Marie down that day since she travelled after me. Trouble was the police warrants had been issued at 1 p.m. while Anne Marie knew nothing about the trip till 2 p.m. Besides, the bizzies couldn't hide their shock and anger at finding Anne Marie in the house – not the reaction of people who'd used her to locate me. At 1 p.m. that day the only people who knew of my little trip to Rothesay were the Thompsons – old Arthur and Arty – and the police.

Then there was the mystery of the phantom gun – you don't carry a revolver around by accident, believe me. They had denied its existence, of course, but take it from me you don't miss a gun that's being pointed at you. Kept apart since my arrest, Anne Marie and I had both reported three guns and we said as much at my trial but then I was on trial and not the police. Why exactly was there an extra shooter? Why were they so furious when they discovered Anne Marie's presence? Not annoyance that she was a woman and they would need a WPC but that she was human and had eyes – the perfect attributes of a witness?

The court had seen fit to find me guilty on a couple of other charges including possession of a small amount of cocaine and that bloody pickaxe handle from the incident with the Welshes. Normally it would have been dealt with by a lower court and carry six months in jail at most. Visibly annoyed that I'd slipped away from the drugs *allegations the judge decided to whack me on the knuckles and handed out 18 months in prison.*

As I was stung by the blow, Donald Findlay reached for his pipe and said, 'Cruel result but at least you got a first.' My puzzled look made him continue, 'Never before in Scottish criminal law has anyone used such a defence and been found not guilty. It's little consolation but it's something.'

So, it was back to Bar-L with plenty of time to mull over all the unanswered questions about the police, the Thompsons, the drugs and the phantom gun – particularly the phantom gun. I should've thanked those policemen for opening my eyes to the world of official corruption and unholy alliances. For saving my life.

POST-MORTEM

Under Scots law, accused have a right to make a statement on the charges faced, called a Judicial Declaration. Paul Ferris made the longest, frankest Judicial Declaration in the history of Scottish criminal law. During the trial, after giving evidence, the policeman we are calling Diddle was kept in the courtroom at Donald Findlay's request, to prevent him speaking to other witnesses. Based on police evidence, Paul Ferris was charged with possessing heroin with intent to supply. The jury could have chosen a Not Proven verdict if uncertain who to believe. In less than an hour, by majority decision, they found Paul Ferris Not Guilty – a clear-cut verdict. At the back of the courtroom, two members of the Police Complaints Authority sat for the full duration of the trial, unusually. We are unaware of what subsequent action they took, if any.

by Reg McKay

NEW BABIES AND PAID BULLIES

My son Paul was born while I was in the prison. There's something universally painful about separation from your partner and your newborn baby. They can have their debates about criminal responsibility, whose fault it was and didn't it just serve me right. I don't seek their sympathy. The reasons for my absence made no difference to how I felt.

I cursed myself for not being around for him, for my boy. Then I swore to be there for him regardless of how far we might be separated, in spite of stone walls. One day I would be there for him to explain how all of this came about and, if he knew that I loved him, I knew he'd understand. Anne Marie had probably saved my life that night in Rothesay. Our son, Paul junior, gave me a future worth fighting for.

And fight you had to in Bar-L. While I now lived among men whose sentences were settled, some couldn't conceive of their future freedom. A date years away was beyond their grasp and they couldn't give a toss if the trouble and grief they caused added a few more months or years. Then there were others who just didn't give a toss anyway.

Some prisoners tried to blend into the background hoping the marauders wouldn't notice them. For some it worked but for most it simply placed them at the bottom of the food chain, easy pickings for any scabby vulture. The easiest way to avoid trouble was to create it. Dish out some of the verbals and follow them through fast and furious. An empty threat is worse than useless. Make alliances with others but only with those you would trust anywhere. Live up to your outside reputation. Proclaim that you may have lost your liberty but not your free will. Every now and then remind them of what you are capable of.

Well settled to prison life, I managed to cross swords with the screws too often. It seemed to me they'd do their damnedest to keep me in jail till the last second anyway so I declared, 'Fuck it, Paul. Take no shit.' I was always ending up isolated in the segregation unit, known as the Wendy House, for some misdemeanour or another.

Bar-L was a harsh Victorian regime matching the crumbling, rat-infested building that it was. The food was pig slop quality and repetitive. Educational and leisure facilities were so scarce they caused more strife between the prisoners than anything else. The place resonated with the constant noise of rattling metal doors and men bawling, arguing or shouting for the sake of being heard.

Many prisoners were mentally ill or had severe learning difficulties and should've been cared for rather than locked up. The prison reformers bleat on about the daily indignity of slopping out your own piss and shit and the need to end it. Now I can't disagree but it's slightly less significant than brutal staff and Bar-L had its share. At one time, the tabloid newspapers ran articles about Bar-L staff having their own battalion of the UDA. I've no idea if that was accurate or not but I do know the journalists missed the point. Politics and religion didn't matter a toss.

After lock-up at night the noise of the men shouting from their barren, boring cells would rumble on for ages till exhaustion took its toll and peace engulfed the Big House. Out in the corridor you could hear the shuffling of many heavy feet marching rapidly across the stone floor. We lay still listening, trying to suss out the direction of the hit squad by sound alone. Voices barked out and quietly grumbling prisoners were led out of their cell and out of the way. We knew there would be one man left alone, for the moment.

The creak of the door closing, then the angry shouts, howls of pain and the THUD-THUMP-STAMP of evil bastards belting into one man. The dull bump of his skull being knocked against the brick walls, the muffled squelch of blows to his stomach, the slow deliberate echo as they jumped on his body. Wailing and pleading. A grown man whimpering for his Mammy. Wordless screams. A man reduced to pulp. An animal bleating in terror.

'Leave him alone, you bastards.'

'A know who it is.'

'We'll fucking get you, ya pricks.'

The men raised a rumpus – cursing, swearing, rattling metal against metal, splashing their pish-filled pails over the walls, kicking cell doors, threatening, calling out the names of the screws known to love the violence. All useless, but we had to do something. I joined in with the rest but through it all the bestial howls of agony took me back to a wet night in Blackhill many years before and the booming horror of the Meat Wagon.

In the morning the screws demanded respect and expected fear. Fuck that, we gave them what they deserved at every chance we got.

I spotted a known face in a uniform, not an unusual occurrence given the proximity of Bar-L to Blackhill. When I'd been in his company before he'd taken off the peaked hat and thrown an anorak over his service shirt. Not that he went too far from his work. On a regular basis, on behalf of Arthur Thompson, I used to meet up with a prison officer we'll call Grant Kidd in Bar-L's car park. He would shuffle his frame into the passenger seat of my car and chat for a while

I didn't ask about the connection between Arthur Thompson senior and the screw. Kidd obviously thought it was worth whatever risks he was taking. Old Arthur obviously got a return for his friendship – he always did. Kidd didn't bother me or help me that time in prison. Not that time, but I'd meet him again in more threatening circumstances.

20

ONE BAD TURN DESERVES ANOTHER
by Reg McKay

The principles of commerce are the same the world over and stop for no man. So, with Paul Ferris cooked up in Bar-L Arty and company just continued as before – well, not quite.

During the mid-1980s in Glasgow there were still uncharted territories with regard to the drug trade. The city's vast peripheral housing estates were producing thousands of young people with no education, no jobs, no hope and some of them had yet to discover heroin. Outside dealers spotted the potential and were trying to move in by bankrolling known faces. TC Campbell recalls being approached numerous times by traffickers from London and the USA in the early 1980s. The most generous offer he received was the first £1,000,000 of smack put up for no deposit and vigorous profits all round. TC hated heroin and knocked back this sweetener with the same verve he had repelled all the others. Not everyone in the city had the same scruples as Tommy Campbell.

Arty was pushing the boat out on the drugs front. With Paul in jail he used Tam Bagan in his deals as a courier and a new recruit, Jonah McKenzie, for handling the smack. Carrying the wounds of many an affray, Jonah had moved around between teams in the north and east of the city chasing the bigger rewards. He was a different kettle of fish from Paul Ferris.

Arty was removing the competition like Ted Hughes. Hughes bought a black Mercedes off Arty and headed south to pick up a consignment of drugs. Arty telephoned the police, giving the car details and itinerary. Hughes and his co-accused were jailed for 22 years but there was only one man knew about the car. Hughes made loud, angry death threats against Arty. The Thompsons delivered bullets and a message to Ted Hughes' wife and children – then he shut up. Maybe it was time to ask questions. The drugs squad were displaying curiosity from their pitch directly across from Jonah McKenzie's house.

A man we'll call Detective Sergeant Duff Idle tracked Arty and Bagan on the short journey to the latter's house. Bagan disembarked and was allowed to proceed unheeded. Following on the trail, the police would report that Arty spotted them and was bailing out his car, throwing small packages on to the street as he sped along at 80 miles per hour. The police were not happy with Arthur Thompson junior. His turn had arrived.

The girlie magazine in the laundry basket did for Arty. It's not some local anti-obscenity law, though some of the civic leaders would have it that way given half the chance. The police had trailed him through the city streets claiming he chucked little bags of heroin out his car window in panic. Free £10 bags for the denizens of Blackhill. The bizzies claim they found heroin in his car and a CB radio tuned into the same frequency as one found in Jonah's pad. Jonah McKenzie had already been raided, was sitting on a pile of smack and bleating, 'It's no' me ye're after but the fuckers wi' the big motors.' So they searched the Thompsons' abode and found the girlie magazine.

The laundry basket was empty apart from that magazine. This didn't surprise me since often enough I'd witnessed Rita Thompson's daily washing routine when anything left lying about was thrown into the machine. A page of the magazine had a corner ripped off and that corner was found wrapped round some smack in Jonah McKenzie's house. Very convenient. Too convenient and quite out of character for Arty.

I couldn't understand a few things, such as the magazine hidden in the laundry basket like some young kid with dirty photographs. Arty was as grown a man as he was ever going to be and his family were far from prudish. Young Thompson was well known for not carrying any dubious goods in his car, on his person or in his room. He just didn't do it, getting others to carry out the dirty work. Why did the police not raid Jonah's house when all three guys were in there? Why hightail after Arty on his own?

While they were on remand in Bar-L, Jonah made a confession, 'That magazine wis in ma place.'

'What are you telling us, Jonah?' I asked, needing to hear the guy spell it out.

'A'm saying the fuckin' magazine wis mine. Somebody lifted it and planted it oan Arty.'

Seemed clear enough to me. Arty went ballistic and leaned on Jonah to confess his ownership of the incriminating journal. When he refused, Arty offered him increasingly substantial sums of money to take the rap. Still Jonah refused. It was every man for himself.

By the time of the trial it was Arty and Jonah McKenzie in the dock with Bagan off the hook though charged with less serious firearms offences. Jonah was sentenced to seven years while Arty went down for eleven. No evidence on the drug charges had been presented against Tam Bagan who'd been seen in a house, with people and in a car implicated in the supply of heroin. He walked from the court while Arty and Jonah were driven away on the Bar-L special.

A short while later, Arty was moved into B Hall and we met up in the textile workshop. 'That fucking Bagan, man. He must've had something tae dae wi' the polis,' he fumed. 'Fuckin' walkin away like that wi' nae case tae answer. Fuck's sake.' Okay, Arty was upset at the prospect of eleven years but I dismissed his comments against Tam Bagan as a straightforward case of sour grapes.

In Bar-L you pick up all sorts of information about people and not just cons. At one point there were photographs in circulation of judges, politicians and well-known businessmen caught with their trousers down being entertained by hookers. A prominent member of the Conservative Party had also been so compromised, not naked but wearing women's clothing.

Nobody or nothing was sacred, especially not the players. Bar-L's specialist subject was the history of prisoners in prisons. The major figures of Scotland's crime world, the dirty protests, the cages at Inverness – all were catalogued and recounted like old-world folk entertaining each other with tales round the campfire at night. According to the prison gossip machine, Tam Bagan had got caught between two of the jail's most celebrated residents.

Jimmy Boyle is now a free man and a sculptor turned finger pointer but was once deemed the prisoner the system couldn't cope with. The razor king of the Gorbals, he'd fought with the screws from the first day of his murder sentence. Facing regular beatings from the hit squads, he stripped off his clothes and smeared himself in his own shite – the inventor of the dirty protest. Eventually, Boyle was given credit for the creation of the ultra therapeutic unit in Bar-L's Special Unit. But that wasn't accurate. There were other wild, uncontrollable men that the prison service couldn't manage. Then there were guys like Willie Bennett senior, a murderous gang leader who worked by the rules, his rules. Boyle and Bennett had a falling out.

While Bagan had been serving his eight years in Perth prison for the two shootings in Easterhouse, it was alleged he got caught up in this war and took Bennett's side. Jail gossip made a big deal of this choice since Bennett was renowned to be an aggressive homosexual – dangerous company in a prison if you're not of similar tastes. In the squabble, Bagan was severely scalded by having a bucket of boiling water thrown over him – then disgraced himself by grassing on his assailant, or so the rumour mill would have it. The gossipmongers marked him down as an all-round informer. I kept an open mind about Bagan and everyone else till I had the proof.

Arty was also on my mind. What had he been up to with the planting of guns then telephoning the police? It was beginning to sound like trade-offs, fitting up some known hood for what in return? Rothesay still haunted me. The timing of that police warrant when only the Thompsons knew I was there. Old Arthur was beyond my suspicion so I flashed the offending brown envelope to Arty one day in Bar-L. 'The old man will go mental if he finds oot about that,' he said, visibly shaking, and before I could stop him he ripped the paper to shreds.

Why was the warrant for drugs when the police had 14 allegations of attempted murder against me? What was that brown envelope with Arty's scribbles about? Would the most careful criminal family in Glasgow leave an order for drugs lying around their holiday home – by mistake? The police tried to get me to hold that envelope to examine the writing. They went on and on about it. But did they find it, was it left there for them or had they brought it along? The phantom gun felt very real pushed into my neck. What about the shooter? Did Arty want me taken out? Did the police turn on Arty because Rothesay went egg-shaped?

My scrapes with the screws resulted in me doing the full 18 months of my sentence in Bar-L. Once released, I was given little time to settle into my family life with my newborn son, Paul. Old Arthur was raging blaming the police for arresting his son and directed all *his anger at the lead officer Duff Idle. Idle was a fanatic, hated on the streets and disliked by his own colleagues. Word from other polis was that he was determined to get the biggest scores.*

So, I was asked to kill the policeman. Fix up a car with a trigger explosive device and park it on a quiet city street. Make an anonymous call to Duff Idle in person and tell him the whereabouts of the car with its boot stashed full of drugs. Idle was such a keen copper that he'd zoom down there on his own with a crowbar. From what I've heard since, that was an accurate description of the man. I was becoming increasingly concerned about Arty's conviction.

There are those who will believe Arty was guilty of other crimes so it doesn't matter about the accuracy of the charges used to jail him. So, where does that stop? Charge you with assault for all the times you've been speeding in your car undetected? Bust somebody for heroin because they're a regular dope smoker? What if they get it wrong, as they have so often? The Birmingham Six, the Guildford Four, the Glasgow Two, Ernest Barrie and all the others wrongly convicted – were any of them convicted through an error? Not one. All by the deliberate, wilful actions of the police. What if it was your partner, brother, son, daughter, friend or parent? How would you feel then?

In my world, setting somebody up was viewed as a form of unacceptable corruption. I was fast coming to the conclusion that those in positions of authority who strayed beyond their powers were as bad as corrupt gangsters and I would tolerate neither. I was convinced I knew who had set up young Arty. However, I still gave Idle the benefit of the doubt, accepting that he was basically an honest copper if somewhat over-enthusiastic.

The young man stands naked in front of the camera's gaze. A set of clothes is handed to him, while off screen a voice explains that these have been provided by Scottish Television (STV) and been checked as drug free. An older, unidentified man tapes a tiny remote transmitter to the young man's skin. Russell Stirton begins to dress, slowly and carefully, for his appointment with the police.

Earlier in the filming, Russell had explained on camera and tape that people had been leaning on him to fit up Paul Ferris with drugs. Russell had dealt with one policeman, Detective Sergeant Duff Idle of Strathclyde Police. As he dressed, he thought of an earlier taped meeting with DS Idle and his colleague Lonnie Smut.

'A'll only deal wi' you, Duff,' said Russell.

'Any time,' replied Idle.

Russell Stirton was arrested when a matchbox full of heroin was found underneath his car. The police admitted this was a plant carried out by a known criminal who had been allowed off with drug-dealing charges for his efforts. They were less forthcoming with the fit-up merchant's name. Russell's friend Terry was mentioned and the prospect angered and upset him.

'Can ye no' dae it tae Terry then?' DS Duff Idle had asked on tape.

Russell Stirton played along, 'See if A get a hundred per cent evidence it's Terry that's done it tae me.'

'Aye?' asked Idle.

'A could fit him up the morrow like that,' Stirton replied, snapping his fingers.

'You don't need a fucking hundred per cent evidence,' Idle leaned on him.

On tape, the policeman gloated about taking down Martin Ross

PAUL FERRIS & REG McKAY

and how the former associate of Arthur Thompson junior had been set up by someone hiding drugs in his car then informing the police. 'Martin Ross ended up fucking standing there greetin' an' sayin' A plead guilty,' Idle boasted. 'Now he was hard tae get but he got caught cause some o' his mates fitted him up.' It was that easy, according to Idle; Russell Stirton was a 'good ned' and he could fit up anyone he wanted.

They offered Russell inducements like pulling his case file. Still they returned to fitting up, and Wee Paul. They inducted him to the morals of their colleagues – a raid on a drug dealer where £13,600 was found in his house, but arresting officers handed in only £4,500. A policeman called Gillette featured large according to his mates. 'Fitting up is easy – just get in his car and slip the smack down the back seat.' Paul Ferris's name floats in and out of the conversation. Then they let slip that a detective we'll call Ernie Midden had been putting it around the streets that Russell was let off with charges for doing the police favours – a death sentence in Glasgow.

Russell Stirton was frightened for his life but decided to fight them back at their own game by telling me, and STV's crime reporter, Don Lindsay. From me he received support and gratitude: from Don Lindsay he received a starring role in a documentary of the police at their tricks. A meeting with DS Duff Idle had been set up at Lenzie railway station when the police would hand over the fit-up heroin. That morning, an STV crew knocked at the door of a Lenzie flat asking if the owners would consent to them filming from their back room – for **Taggart**, the TV detective series. The householders were chuffed, the cameras set up, the microphone tested.

Russell Stirton is on his way. The camera follows Russell across the car park and on to the platform where he stands alone. A minute or two later a woman with a small dog on a leash appears – Lenzie is full of women with lap dogs on a leash. Shortly thereafter a man approaches Russell and shakes his hand. The camera zooms in to a perfect shot of Russell Stirton and DS Duff Idle.

Idle has good news – Ernie Midden and all other police have been ordered to back off Russell. The two men are edgy and nervous. The Wee Man is mentioned time and again by Idle. Normally he calls him Wee Paul but today he is nervous, careful. The microphone records the conversation. 'Right. What we spoke about the other day,' says Idle. 'Russell, are you fucking wired up?'

'Fuck off,' replies Russell. 'Are you?' Both men stand on the platform and pat each other down. The woman with the dog studiously ignores their antics. Across the railway line, Don Lindsay and the STV camera crew tense and hold their breath. Why would a policeman be anxious about being recorded doing his job – if that is all he is doing? The two men are satisfied they're not being recorded. Idle is anxious to bring the meeting to a close. 'Right, here is a starter for ten,' he says and puts his hand in his pocket. A train rushes through the station and high above the track the camera man curses. Russell feels the wraps of heroin in his pocket.

'Okay,' he acknowledges receipt.

'When's this gonnae happen then?' Idle needs to be sure to have his team ready to arrest Paul Ferris.

'Friday,' replies Russell.

'A thought ye said Thursday?' and the two of them bicker and argue over the fit-up day. Idle has to settle for Friday.

'Right, get us the Wee Man and . . . '

'It's a bit tricky, you know,' Russell is trying to draw the policeman out.

'Aye, but you get us the Wee Man. You get us Ferris and don't let us down or I'll have to sort you out.' Idle returns to threatening the young man.

'Look, that number ye gave us,' says Russell.

'Whit, the office?' asks the policeman.

'Aye, gie me another one.'

'What for?'

'In case someone answers.'

'Oh, right,' Idle now understands Russell's fears about other cops with loose lips. He writes down another number and hands it across. 'Mind now what I said,' and nods in a curt, threatening manner.

'Okay,' replies Russell meekly and the two men part. Idle leaves the station while Stirton stands stock still in full and constant view of the camera. He is joined by Don Lindsay on the platform. Russell hands over the five wraps to Lindsay who commentates all that is happening, 'Here are the packages that have been given to Russell Stirton. I will now have these forensically examined.'

The film moves to a laboratory where a man in a white coat introduces himself as a forensic scientist. He demonstrates how he *conducted his experiments before declaring that all five wraps contained diamorphine of a high purity – enough top-grade heroin to convince any court of an intention to supply.*

The smack, worth tens of thousands of pounds, represented ten years in jail for the Wee Man, for me, for Paul Ferris, for something I didn't do.

23.

TAPES, VIDEOTAPES AND LIES

Heroin, Paul. They want me to fit you up with a load of smack.' Russell Stirton looked warily around as he spoke with the look of a haunted man expecting to be jumped at any time.

'Who does, Russell?' I asked, my mind overflowing with the possible options.

'The fucking polis, man,' he spluttered, looking me straight in the eye. My smile disconcerted Russell who didn't know that only weeks before I'd been asked to blow Duff Idle away. I'd declined to finish him off as too much, too extreme and unnecessary. The car bomb notion would've reduced us to the status of Colombians and all hell would have broken loose. Besides, I was sure another opportunity would come along, though not so soon or in the form of an own goal.

Russell Stirton had been fitted up with possession of large quantities of heroin and was looking at ten years in prison. Russell had already linked up with Don Lindsay, the chief crime reporter for Scottish Television, and the scenario at Lenzie railway station was in the can heading for public broadcast.

Russell and I met in the anonymity of a service station and he was telling me details of the meeting with DS Duff Idle. I thanked Russell profusely and said he had my entire support. What he was doing was entirely moral from my point of view and took guts. If the escapade didn't work out and the police got wind of it, he'd be in trouble for the rest of his life. We agreed to keep in touch and he drove away from the service station.

As I went to pay for the petrol for my car, I was tapped on the shoulder. 'Can I have a word, pal?' The questioner was a nondescript looking young man I vaguely recognised but couldn't place.

'Sure,' I replied, clueless as to what this bloke might want with me.

'Saw you with Stirton out in the forecourt,' he continued.

'Aye, so what?' and I wondered what exactly it had to do with him.

'Just wanted to warn you about him,' he continued.

'Tell me more,' I invited and he did.

He introduced himself by his real name but we'll call him Grady Midden, an off-duty uniformed cop based at Baird Street in Glasgow. He was no relative of the fanatical, bitter Ernie. This Grady Midden lived with his parents in Riddrie and thought I might have seen him about. He claimed to have met me once before when I was charged with some offence when younger. All this was very interesting but I wanted him to cut to the chase.

'Look, Paul, I'm jist markin' your cards about Stirton. He's been offering to land us a big fish and I think it might be you.' This was a first, being warned by the police, but I suspected there was something else coming my way. 'Why are you doing this?' I asked the perfectly reasonable question. 'I'm an honest cop and disagree with fit ups. That's what they've got planned for you.' Inside my head I fretted for the whole story but kept my mouth shut. 'I'll be your eyes and ears in Baird Street and maybe you can do a favour for me in return.'

I was expecting a request for a payment but none came. Playing along, I gave him a reminder that I wouldn't mind cooperating as long as no one was set up or arrested.

'Naw, naw. Like a said, I'm an honest cop,' he reassured before revealing the nature of the favour. 'I need a gun.' He had a friend who wanted a shotgun but didn't have a licence and he wondered if I could help. 'I'll owe you one and give ye the inside info, like.' I concluded that he was lying and decided to string him along while getting proof of what he was up to. The coincidence of Russell Stirton's news and this conversation happening in the same night at the same place had a less than subtle impact on my alarm bells. I was going to go along with it and see more.

'Okay, no problem,' I replied with a curt nod of my head. Midden told me to contact him through the guy behind the cash desk at the petrol station when I was ready to do business. With that we split, going our separate ways.

That night I couldn't sleep for excitement knowing I was on the verge of exposing the underhand police techniques publicly. Grady Midden seemed to me a second-rate small cheese and I'd no concerns he might be trying to have a go in the style of Greg Diddle in Rothesay. Rather he was handing the gun in to gain some brownie points at work.

Next day I hurried to contact Russell Stirton. A quick telephone call later and we were in the STV headquarters in the Cowcaddens area of the city in conference with Don Lindsay. The media man listened to my story aghast. In spite of his investigations so far and sitting on some red-hot footage of the bold Russell and DS Idle, he couldn't believe his luck. What I was offering him was proof that the police bartered in guns with known criminals, people like me. Don Lindsay didn't need persuasion. He already believed that our police were corrupt. I left the TV studios with a voice-activated tape recorder and a plan for that night.

The shotgun had a sawn-off barrel and cost me £100. Wrapping it in a black bin liner, I hid it under a box on the Three Hills near the rhubarb fields, territory I knew like the back of my hand. At home I practised on the tape recorder so all mistakes would be avoided. Stopping off at the petrol station I asked the young cashier to pass the message to Grady Midden to meet me that night.

Before we met up I recorded a brief summary of the events in case Midden's mates summarily lifted me. Loading a handgun, I stuffed it into the waistband of my trousers, determined not to be caught out by twitchy-fingered armed police. Rothesay had alerted me to the prospect of being taken out by the bizzies and recent events with Midden and Idle had done nothing but make me more convinced. I applied the same rules that had guided me through my life – face them up, striking faster and harder. The gun was not an ornament. This time there would be no Anne Marie to save me. I'd save myself and damage the polis in the process.

Midden kept me waiting till the early hours of the morning. The longer he took the more leery I became of whatever plot he might be hatching. He hadn't known tonight would be the night and maybe his colleagues were taking a little time to organise the surprise they planned for me. Eventually, around 2 a.m., he appeared, spinning me some line about Ernie Midden wanting to speak to him about Russell Stirton trying to find PC Sweeney Gilettte's house to sort him out. Total lies, given what I knew about Russell. But he kept rabbiting on and on, dropping names right and left.

He said I should tell him where the shotgun was so he could

arrange for someone else to pick it up. For a second, the whole night hung in the balance then Midden added, with the tape catching every word, 'Depends how near it is, of course.'

'Very near,' I replied. 'Three Hills.'

'If it's a set-up, Paul,' he warned.

'Naw, it's all right.'

'Right, A'll come wi' ye.' Game on and we were off in his car. As we drove the couple of miles to the Three Hills police constable Grady Midden simply wouldn't shut up. Russell Stirton and his police colleagues was a recurring theme. He confided, 'Somebody in the drugs squad is supposed to have given somebody who's been in Russell's car – some wee guy who's been in Russell's car – stuff tae plant.' Later I asked, 'How did he get out on bail?'

The answer came back without a hesitation, 'Ah well, the deal wis, right, that Russell had tae gie them something, right.'

'Aye?'

'What he told them was he'd gie them you.' Poor Russell had been under undue pressure as Midden went on to confirm, 'I know he took them an' gave them a sawn-off and an automatic.'

'Aye?'

'And a butcher's knife or something. He took them and told them where tae dig and they dug it up which they've still got. Right.' Midden revealed that the weapons had not been signed in by the police but held back – for what? If Russell pulled in somebody big, his outstanding charges would be dropped. I couldn't believe that the policeman was blabbing without much, if any, encouragement and hoped that the tape was picking up everything. It was.

PC Grady Midden chatted about who set Russell up with drugs, listing a range of possibilities and how the police rewarded such good citizenship, 'He's getting paid oot o' the tout fund for this.' So, it was a registered police informant who'd gone one stage further in planting the heroin – a dirty deed the police were aware of and happy to pay him out of the public purse for. Poor Russell had been well stitched up and he wasn't alone. This wasn't a one-off.

DCI Downer's name came into the frame. (His colleagues didn't hesitate to use his real name – unlike us). The street knew him as a man capable of torture, corruption and extortion. It was good to have the street view confirmed by PC Midden on my secret tape recorder, 'Downer said tae me that they were gonnae get a man oan oor patch wi' a kilo.' Then later, 'Downer widnae say who it wis, obviously. It wis your name, you know.'

'Aye?'

'Because, A mean, every cunt's been chasing you for some reason.'

We discussed the merits of a man we're calling DS Lonnie Smut of the drugs squad and whose acquaintance Russell had made. Apparently he was so keen he'd tried to enter a two-storey building by climbing a drainpipe that collapsed, sending him tumbling down onto spiked railings. According to PC Midden, DS Smut had special attributes, 'He's a fucking glory hunter that cunt. Kamikaze cunt!'

Grady Midden had yapped so much I was worried that the voice-activated recorder would run out of tape. When we pulled the car in at the site, I made the excuse that I needed to pee, walking away a distance and changing the tape. When he emerged with the plastic wrapped shotgun in his hand he'd an unexpected complaint, 'The boy says there's dog shite up here.' Through the night young kids wandered round the Three Hills doing their drugs, chasing a gang bang or just hiding.

'Where?' I asked, flabbergasted that this policeman with an illegal shotgun found time to complain about such trivialities.

'Here, smell,' he said, holding the bag out – he was right. As we drove away I enquired of the business at hand, 'Will you be able to dig up cartridges for that?'

'It's a standard size,' PC Grady Midden replied. 'Ye've nae bother. Ye can buy them.'

'Has he got a ticket for shotguns?' I asked playing along with his ruse.

'Naw, that's whit's wrong . . . anyway.'

One more time I said, 'They're fucking out and out fit ups, you know.'

He knew now I was talking about Arty as well as Russell and a score of other people he'd mentioned that night. 'Aye, obviously,' the policeman confirmed what he'd been telling me for the past few hours.

Parting, I watched him drive off in his car with the illegal shotgun stowed in the boot and wondered exactly how and when I'd see him again. I didn't reckon it would be a social call.

Earlier that same evening, Russell Stirton had been carrying out a little impromptu recording of his own. Russell had been openly angry with the coppers who fitted him up with drugs. Detective Sergeant

Ernie Midden had cornered him to warn him against making threats against their colleagues. Russell smiled ruefully and recalled what DS Idle had said of Ernie Midden, 'See, Ernie's wife or ex-wife hates his fucking guts.'

'Aye,' said Russell, hoping Idle would continue. He wasn't disappointed.

'She's trying tae have him blown away. Would suit her doon tae the ground, ye know.'

Russell had taken to hiding a tape recorder in the sun visor of his car, always prepared for just such an approach by the police and it was switched on. 'Just a wee word of friendly advice,' started Ernie Midden and proceeded to warn Russell that he couldn't go making threats against police. 'Right listen, Russell. We're all involved in a game here. A wee while ago you decided that you didn't want to be poor any more so you decided to make some money in some wee deals. That's fine, for I couldn't care less what those bastards shoot up their arms. If they want to do themselves in then that's up to them. But unfortunately there are some folks in this world who don't see why they should be allowed to do that. Every so often somebody is made an example of, otherwise they would all be at it.'

'I understand that,' said Russell, trying to appease the detective.

'You'll get the jail this time,' was Ernie Midden's reply.

'Oh, I understand that,' said Russell, keen to avoid making an enemy out of this policeman.

Midden continued, 'All I'm saying is we've got our job to do and you've got to accept that you're in a high-risk occupation. Every so often – you, Ferris, Baird – they'll all go. It's a high-risk occupation. You have to accept that you'll get the jail sometime. All right? But the one thing you do not do is to go about threatening the police.'

Midden was reaching his point. 'See Wee Paul made a threat to the polis in Rothesay. I can tell you here and now that Wee Paul was very nearly wasted. He was very nearly away up for a walk in the Campsie Hills one night. He was never nearer going.'

Russell couldn't believe what he'd heard – a confession by a ranking detective that the police had considered deliberately killing a member of the public. He tried to keep the conversation going, 'I'm going to jail. I know I'm going but I'm no grass. People can think what they want but I'm no taking anyone wi' me.'

The policeman sympathised and said that he only played by the *rules. Russell offered apologies all round the police force. The detective began to meet him halfway, 'If we go into court and put the mix in for you, you'll go to jail. If we go into court and don't put the mix in for you and you've got a decent lawyer, then you'll walk away from this.' The pressure was still on Russell but he expressed his gratitude and another round of apologies. Detective Sergeant Midden encouraged him by saying that a lot could happen before a trial date, then ended with a final warning, 'But don't start threatening police because, like I said, Wee Paul very nearly went for a walk up the Campsie's one night. If I thought you were going to start playing those games, I'd take you on a night fishing trip and you wouldn't be coming back.'*

Russell remonstrated one last time, 'I never threatened one police officer.'

'Well, word came back to us that you did. It's a big outfit to take on if you take on the police and, Russell, you cannot win.'

As the detective walked away, Russell Stirton was aware of the tape recorder whirring quietly away and thought, 'We'll see.'

The following day, Russell and I met up with Don Lindsay at the STV headquarters. Lindsay thought Christmas had arrived early as we handed over the tape recordings. The TV presenter was now sitting on film and audiotapes implicating four policemen directly as well as referring to numerous other coppers participating in the same lethal games. He had an admission that the police contemplated killing me back on Rothesay and a direct statement that the same fate would be dealt out to Russell or anyone else threatening the police. He had evidence of the police dealing in firearms, heroin and offering to barter outstanding charges in return for information. Planting evidence was the least of their sins.

Don Lindsay had an exclusive scoop. An exposé of official corruption. All that was left now was the standard practice of the television company's lawyers checking over the libel issues and he would be set to go public. Russell and I left our tapes in the safekeeping of the media man and hit the streets excited. We were taking enormous risks but felt as if we'd done a good deed. We didn't expect to be stabbed in the back.

They call them the M family in the newspapers. The code always comes up when some newspaper decides to write a piece on who exactly are the Mr Bigs of organised crime in the UK. Sometimes the journalists go as far as to put in a blanked-out profile next to mug-shots of the Krays, Arthur Thompson, Paul Ferris, the Adams family and others. The people on the streets know who the papers are getting at – Joe, Tommy, Tony and James McGovern of Springburn to the north of the Glasgow. Paul Ferris liked the McGoverns and so did Russell Stirton, which is just as well since he married their sister, Jackie.

By Reg McKay

Russell Stirton had been arrested and his wife Jackie was concerned about his recent contact with me. I met up with her and her sister Jean regularly over the next couple of weeks. I was impressed by how both of them were standing firmly behind Russell and would do anything to help him. Still, they were anxious times.

At an early stage after the recording session, I made a point of going to Arthur Thompson senior and giving him a full report. I expected him to welcome the chance to catch out DS Duff Idle, Lonnie Smut and other police likely to have been involved with young Arty. His response was quite strange,

'You might be turning over too many stones, son.' With that he wanted to know no more. Yet Arty was mounting an appeal against his conviction and surely exposing this material would be helpful, to say the least? The old man's warning bothered me and I began to ask what stone he didn't want turned over. One with his name on?

One of my frequent visits to my parents' house coincided with another group of visitors – the police. Not the usual faces from Strathclyde but a team from Lothian and Borders Police Force – well out of their territory and for good reason. The arresting officer, Detective Chief Inspector Charles Boulton, had been called in to investigate claims of corruption within Strathclyde – the first time this had happened in the force's history. Boulton assured me that all his men were totally impartial. One look at their long faces and I could tell they were relishing the task – not.

Possessing a firearm was to be the charge, or so I found out when they bundled me down to Stewart Street police station. The same shotgun I'd handed over to PC Grady Midden. The weeks had rolled by and we'd heard nothing from the previously enthusiastic Don Lindsay and I was intrigued as to how the police had been informed of the incident. At first I thought it was a straight set-up by Midden, but I was wrong. How did the police become involved? Certain information slowly began to make sense.

My lawyer, Peter Forbes, advised that I go to the court and tell the whole story at a judicial interview that day. So I did and made one of the longest judicial statements ever made, being determined to paint the full landscape of police corruption. When I was brought back to the police station I was placed in an American-style cell with steels bars on the front rather than a solid metal door. Through the bars I spotted PC Grady Midden escorted by two policemen, his puffy face and red eyes revealing a man who'd recently wept a great deal. When he saw me he wailed, 'Look what you've done to me.' I laughed out loud.

It transpired that Midden hadn't handed the gun into the police after all but kept it at home under his bed. Naughty but not so naughty as me, it would appear. Midden was freed on bail that day while yours truly was sent to what was fast becoming my second home, Bar-L, where I found myself in the company of Russell Stirton. For the next few months we concentrated on working on our respective cases till, out of the blue, we were driven back to the court one day. There we were both charged with 15 new allegations, all stemming from the tape recording and filming of the police. The long-winded list amounted to counter-allegations that we'd lied and tricked the police in a conspiracy to trap them. Don Lindsay's name was mentioned a number of times, as were all the bit-part actors

PAUL FERRIS & REG McKAY

from the police ranks. What I couldn't understand is how the procurator fiscal decided that we'd breached the law when we'd made the original claims against the police.

The independent police inquiry resulted in no action. Detective Inspector Downer – he of the reputation for getting his man at any cost and, of course, of Strathclyde Police – had been sent round all the officers asking, 'Do you know anything about police officers making deals with Stirton and Ferris and being taped doing so?'

'No, sir. Of course not, sir. Psst, lads, let's meet up in the pub later and get our story straight.' They were warned in big, bold capitals. What else can you expect from a system that allows the police to investigate themselves? We were charged with conspiring to bring Strathclyde Police into disrepute. Conspiracy? No need when they were managing to be disreputable all on their own.

I would've been happy to spend a few years in jail for possessing the shotgun if justice was handed out fairly all round. But Peter Forbes explained to me that if those charges went to court I could face 20 years behind bars while Idle, Smut, Midden, Downer and company walked free. What had DS Ernie Midden said to Russell? 'If you take on the police you cannot win.' Looks like they were determined to stack the odds against us by foul means or foul. I was facing this legal battle or going out to risk that 'long walk up the Campsies'.

A few weeks later we were rushed back to court and freed on bail. When I told Peter Forbes I intended to refuse release on the grounds I believed my life was at risk from the police, he said he understood but refusing bail might influence my case detrimentally. Peter persuaded me and I was on my way home to Anne Marie and Paul junior. We'd been going through a difficult phase which was entirely my fault. Too busy with business and jail time, I wasn't a regular husband or father, particularly in facing the problems all young couples have setting up home with a new baby. But I loved them both and would try and work at it. A detective we'll call Death and a UDA supergrass by the name of Andrew Robertson had different ideas.

Much like my father before me, I had discussed various possible enterprises with a fellow prisoner in Bar-L by the name of Rab Smith. I'd been released before Rab but met up with him soon after he *walked through the Big House's gates. It's an honourable tradition to help a friend released from prison – a little money, some practical help and that was all I'd planned.*

Rab had no car and asked if I could drive him to a meeting at the Little Chef in Baillieston. When we arrived, Rab introduced me to his friend, Andy, before I took my leave, going into the restaurant for something to eat. The two men sat in my car talking. When I noticed that Andy had left my car I returned to Rab and drove him home – a harmless courtesy.

A few days later I was fast asleep with Anne Marie when the front door came crashing in and armed police rushed in and upstairs to my room. At the time, we stayed with Anne Marie's mother and the old dame was in a terrible state, Anne Marie not much better and baby Paul frightened out of his wits. As I lay naked and handcuffed on the floor I asked why I was being arrested but they refused any information. I eyed the guns warily, expecting a mistake at any minute. When nothing happened I concluded it was just another police tactic to harass me. So much so that, on the way out, I said to Anne Marie, 'Won't be long. Put something on for me to eat please, hen.'

At London Road police station I was thrown into a cell and told I'd be going to court the next morning. Late at night, the man we're calling Detective Inspector Death unlocked my door, sneered at me and spat, 'You're in real trouble now, ye wee bastard.' Then he slammed the door shut.

Next morning I was led into the dock in handcuffs. The procurator fiscal asked the sheriff to revoke my bail since, 'We have received reliable information that Ferris is about to commit an offence.' Well, they're good, but reading the future? Peter Forbes pressed for more information. 'We cannot go any further on the matter for reasons of national security,' pronounced the procurator. I watched the sheriff glance at a document before agreeing and sending me off to Bar-L.

Back in prison I could only conclude the Midden tapes had turned political somehow. Then Joe the Jew came up to me and asked, 'Are you Paul John Ferris?'

'Aye.'

'There's something you better see.' Joe the Jew took me to his cell and handed me a sheaf of papers filled with close type. It was a

statement by Rab Smith's friend from the car park of the Little Chef – Andy Robertson by name but also known as Justice, an armourer for the UDA. Part of his statement related to that meeting, naming and incriminating Rab Smith and Paul Ferris. It read, 'Smith wanted to buy some guns for me to set up a new right-wing movement and had indicated that he has some contacts in South Africa/Brazil who wanted him (Rab Smith) to break into the African National Congress offices in London and steal some files from them.'

Now the little I knew of the ANC and Nelson Mandela was that my kind and me had more in common with them than any right-wing mob. In truth, back then I paid such political matters very little attention. As if that wasn't bad enough, I later found out that the security services had been taking photographs of the meeting in the car park.

Joe the Jew wasn't much happier. He was facing similar charges and had consistently pleaded his disinterest, his Judaism and his innocence. I couldn't think of anyone less likely to get caught up in the politics of Ireland, South Africa or fascism. 'Listen, Paul, you'd better watch out. Every time they've interviewed me they've asked countless questions about you. I keep telling them I've never met you. Next time they ask about you again.'

For whatever reasons, the security services were trying to implicate me in this whole sordid business. Though I'd never met Joe before he was obviously a solid guy, never once trading lies against me for an open gate, unlike Robertson, who was bandying names around like confetti. When asked, Joe pointed out Robertson in the canteen queue downstairs and sure enough I recognised the guy from the car park. Waiting till he came up the landing, I pulled the grass into an empty cell and gave him the most severe barehanded beating I could muster, making sure he knew who I was.

Minutes later the riot bell sounded. Robertson was in the hospital wing with a broken nose and other injuries. Breaking my cardinal rule, I'd been furious when I assaulted Robertson, hating the guy for wilfully, needlessly whisking away my bail and Christmas with my family. It was my one shot at him as he was placed on protection before turning Queen's Evidence. In the long run it did him no good. He was later found guilty of membership of the UDA and conspiring to get guns, ammunition and explosives for the Ulster mob and sentenced to 12 years.

Donald Findlay QC wanted this trial badly and I wanted him to be up there fighting for me. It was held in the High Court, Glasgow, with Lord Kincraig presiding. While the charges of conspiracy had faded off the scene, my co-accused, PC Grady Midden, and I were accused of illegal possession of a firearm. Good Lord Kincraig allowed all the tapes and film to be used as evidence, although the prosecution tried hard to prevent it. It gave me hope that my original aims to expose the police might be achieved in court rather than on the television screen.

During breaks in the staggered agenda of the early days, Grady Midden continued to moan. He told me that he'd failed his sergeant's exams and had hoped to win promotion by landing me. It was as if he was trying to win sympathy from me – the very man he was willing to trap into a lengthy jail sentence so he could gain a few stripes. He was pathetic, a view I haven't changed over the years.

My defence was based on the tapes and films. Midden claimed I'd offered him the gun and he had intended arresting me. When we'd left the petrol station that night, he said that he'd slipped into the kiosk and asked the young guy behind the desk to phone his colleague Rennie McDowd. I already knew all of this, courtesy of the young bloke whom I'd known for years. McDowd had been called away to deal with a burglary, leaving Midden on his own.

I've no idea what Midden had really planned for me that night. Reading the transcripts of the tapes I reckon McDowd was called on as back-up in case I turned nasty. Midden hid the shotgun in his locker at the police station for a few weeks before taking it home and hiding it under a bed in his mother's house. Donald Findlay was on fire, 'Constable Midden, can you tell the court why you moved the gun to your parents' home in Riddrie?'

'I thought it was safer,' he replied.

'Safer? Than a police station? Are you aware that housebreakers are at work at all times, even when people are asleep? That they can empty houses and sometimes even take the wallpaper? Yet you, as a serving police officer, couldn't trust his own police station. I find that very hard to believe.' Findlay left Midden a speechless, absurd figure.

Things were looking good when the jury were treated to the tape and video show. Trouble was that the passing train had obscured those crucial seconds. That still left the question of how the smack had fallen into Russell's possession since he'd been on camera all the time. The police suggested that I'd been disguised as the woman with the dog. In other words, I'd conspired to plant the drugs and incriminate the police. The absurd fantasy of me pulling off such a stunt was blown out of the water since Russell hadn't gone near the woman or her dog – he hadn't left DS Duff Idle's side – and it was all captured on film. When Don Lindsay stepped up to give evidence I couldn't believe the change in the previously robust, confident TV presenter. Physically he looked drained and had lost about three stone in weight. His voice was weak and hesitant. Lindsay gave a very good impression of a man nobbled big style.

Detective Sergeant Ernie Midden took the stand and was questioned over his taped comments to Russell about 'Wee Paul nearly being wasted' and the threats to Russell. Findlay made him define 'wasted' and without hesitating he answered 'Killed'.

'So you were talking about my client, Paul Ferris, nearly being killed?' Findlay asked.

'Look, I was speaking to Russell Stirton in a language that he would understand,' the policeman responded. Findlay sought more explanation of what he meant. Midden turned to the jury and said, 'It is all part of a police procedure called bluff and counter-bluff. I didn't mean what I said.' I almost fell from the dock in admiration. The tapes prevented him denying the statement so he grasped a semi-credible explanation. Looking back, we should have cited the police training manual and looked for that reference – still, you live and learn.

At the end of the trial Lord Kincraig instructed the jury to find me Guilty, a most unusual step in Scotland. My defence of conspiracy or entrapment was declared invalid in Scottish criminal law by the judge. The jury could ask for leniency if they believed what the judge described as my 'incredible story'. However, he waxed lyrical about the role of policemen, explaining how at times they may carry out actions in the course of their duty that would be unlawful for a member of the public. The example I remember most is that of stopping to pick up an unregistered, loaded pistol when giving chase to an armed robber. Yes, judge, but then taking it home and hiding it under your Mammy's bed? The steer was obvious and lengthy. The judge was on the side of the bluecoats and no doubt – aren't they always?

The jury did ask for leniency on my behalf and Kincraig

grudgingly sentenced me to three years' imprisonment. Grady Midden was found Not Guilty and for a second I thought his old red eyes were back. The independent inquiry into corruption in Strathclyde Police had simply fizzled out – planting drugs, trading charges, bartering guns and threatening to kill were obviously accepted as routine police practice. When Russell Stirton appeared in court he was found Not Guilty on all charges and went on to make a good, law-abiding life for himself and his wife Jackie. Don Lindsay was transferred to cover sport then disappeared off the scene altogether. A few years later I bumped into Grady Midden again – Sergeant Grady Midden based in Paisley. While I had gone to prison, Strathclyde Police had rewarded their boy with his much-coveted promotion.

At the end of the trial, Peter Forbes asked for the return of all our productions. Some months later we were advised that they'd been lost – the audiotapes and film. Convenient. Too convenient. Just as well we had kept copies and transcripts.

Lord Kincraig's pleasure converted me into a long-term prisoner, aged 23 years, and a sojourn in HMP Shotts, the biggest hovel of all Scotland's crumbling jails. Shotts was built in the middle of nowhere with only a smattering of prison warders' houses for company. When I arrived they were close to taking advantage of all that space by building a new showcase prison. In the meantime it was the pits.

The Sweat Shop was the main form of work, an apt name for a huge industrial laundry. The place hissed and buzzed with angry white noise, matched only by the temperature and dank, stinking humidity. The guys stripped to the waist yet within minutes were dripping and heaving. The main customer was nearby Law Hospital who sent all their shit-smeared sheets, blood-soaked gowns and vomit-encrusted blankets. The medical jokers would occasionally leave a severed finger in a pocket, a ruptured spleen in a cotton package or yards of intestines uncoiling all over the floor. It might have made the quacks laugh but led the cons to lose all trust in doctors.

I'd other plans and after a short spell in the laundry reported to the sick bay. My spiel on the Sweat Shop's effect on my psoriasis was unnecessary as I encountered prison officer Davie McCallum who'd saved my skin and mental health back in Glenochil. He consulted the doctor, spelling out the state I'd been in when transferred from Longriggend. Within the hour I was excused from the Sweat Shop.

Shotts housed many long-term prisoners, old lags and the usual quota of sweetie brigade who gossiped and bickered over every tiny institutional detail. Prison was their lives, poor sods. They quickly put it about that Arthur Thompson senior had bought off the Governor to get me out of the Sweat Shop. Myths in the making made me laugh but I stayed tight-lipped, letting them have their little fantasies. One furious hall governor threatened to have me transferred out of Shotts because I couldn't work in his beloved laundry.

When we all moved across to the model prison it was night and day. Plumbing abounded, the muted colour scheme was selected by psychologists to foster calm, and the heating was thermostatically controlled. It was too much too suddenly. Like starving men invited to a banquet, the prisoners couldn't appreciate it.

Four extra halls meant that prisoners were to be bussed in from other sites, especially Peterhead Prison. George Silver, an old and wise prison officer, puffed on his pipe and predicted trouble. The guys on reception had already warned me who was coming and I was ready for them. Like John Gallacher, close associate of Arty's and idle threat merchant.

For some time, I'd been seriously reviewing my work relationship with the Thompsons. In one short period, Tam Bagan and I had collected in over £500,000, taking all the risks and being paid buttons in return. We were no more than dispensable wage slaves. In Bar-L I'd met Martin Ross who confided in me that when he was set up with drugs planted in his car it had nothing to do with any Wattie Douglas but, he reckoned, was down to Arty. I was beginning to wonder. Worse were the stories I was being told about Arty's boastful threats against me from the distance of HMP Peterhead. He was going to have me beaten up, killed, dispensed with. I'd been loyal to his family throughout – why should he make such threats? I was beginning to hope that Arty was transferred to Shotts so he could say these things to my face.

James McLean, known as Jaimba, was one of the transfers from Peterhead. I'd met Jaimba in Longriggend when he was an under-age 15-year-old. A good close friend, he confirmed Arty's prison ranting against me. Arty was trying to run the jail by buying favours and hiring protection. Like one guy who was an ex-French Foreign Legionnaire who looked tough but was soon outed as someone who couldn't fight. Quickly he took refuge in born-again religion – a bit of a comedian, like his mate Arty.

John Gallacher was serving life for the armed robbery of a butcher's shop when he knifed the shopkeeper to death and stabbed a policeman. Normally I'd an affinity with lifers, like my brother

Billy, but I just didn't like Gallacher one bit. The older Peterhead mob and younger Shotts crew were in conflict. The new prison was tense with the edgy screws coming down hard on everyone.

One day Gallacher went for a visit to the family room and never returned. Rumours quickly spread that he'd been ambushed by the uniforms, huckled into a van and whisked off to the cages in Inverness. Created for the most unmanageable prisoners in Scotland – the men of the dirty protests refusing to succumb to daily beatings and extended torture – the cages were aptly named. As much as I disliked Gallacher, he was one of us and didn't deserve to be treated like an animal. This wouldn't do at all.

26

RIOTOUS BEHAVIOUR
by Reg McKay

A war summit was hurriedly convened. Zander, Jim Healy, McGroarty, Donaldson, Ferris all determined to make some protest, not just for Gallacher but against the regime. Dicey Cannon would also have been there but was serving the men their evening meal that nothing stopped. They quickly agreed that a hostage would be taken and set about devising a plan.

Jock Donaldson would be the hostage taker. He was serving a life sentence for killing a man in a bloody squabble in an Ayrshire pub. Only one year into a minimum 15-year stretch, he had little to lose, unlike the others on time-limited sentences. There were other volunteers like Dan Sweeney but he was too volatile. They needed someone with a cool head.

The strategy required careful planning. The Bar-L riots of several years before had been soured by a prisoner called Ronnie Garland, rampaging along with the rest then turning grass. Ten-year sentences were doled out on men due for release in months. Earlier riots in Peterhead saw many prisoners severely beaten by gangs of warders after the event. The Shotts crew wanted to make their point with minimum damage all round. So, they chose prison officer Hugh Lees as the hostage. Lees was a fair man, respected by the cons. If they had chosen one of the many bully boys the prisoners would wreak their revenge and death would be the outcome. The prisoners were that angry. It's no consolation to Lees but it was his decency that put him in the frame.

They stocked Jock Donaldson's cell with survival goods of food, water and tobacco then waited. Jock was to grab Hugh Lees and pull him into his cell in the full view of the prison staff, letting them know who was taking the action and exactly what was happening. All the other conspirators were to wear masks. As the appointed hour approached Jock became increasingly nervy and jumped the gun.

'Get the fuck back. Get back or he gets it.' Without warning Donaldson had grabbed Lees and held a knife at his throat. About 30 other prisoners up on the second landing began to howl.

'Out. Out. Out . . .' The ringleaders looked up and cursed. The retreating uniforms could identify every man-jack of them. Not a great start to the campaign.

With the screws out of the hall, the prisoners bundled chairs, beds and tables against the doors, dousing them in petrol. A man was posted there with a Molotov cocktail under strict instructions to set the whole pile blazing if the Riot Squad attempted to break through. These were specially trained staff equipped with crash helmets, body armour, shields and batons. Their retribution would be fierce. So the inmates decided to roast them.

27.

AN HONOURABLE HOSTAGE

The rioters went berserk, ripping out the toilets and sinks, smashing the furniture and breaking everything they could lay their hands on. A bundle of keys was taken from Hugh Lees, now guarded in the safety of a cell, and used to open secure cupboards. As I gathered together the screws' personal cache of cannabis and a camera, others were opening the cells of the sex offenders.

There followed a series of kangaroo courts, all resulting in the most terrible thrashings possible without killing. While, at that time, I agreed with their sentiments, I took no part in these beatings, being too busy plotting. I wandered round the jail taking holiday snaps of the deluge and of Hugh Lees, hostage. After the event, the authorities would explain away the riot in their own, inaccurate way. The media and the public would know the truth if I had anything to do with it.

Two days later numerous splinter groups were forming and there was mounting danger that anarchy and bedlam would rise with lethal consequences for our hostage or the sex offenders. Killing was out and remedial action required pronto. Jock Donaldson and Hugh Lees asked me to take over the negotiations. Riot leaders in Scotland had a habit of becoming scapegoats and falling foul of the uniformed boot boys alone in their cells or in court. So I accepted the responsibility but took precautions. I asked Hugh Lees to write a short statement and he did: 'I, Hugh Lees, personally asked Paul John Ferris to be a neutral body in the negotiations for a peaceful settlement to this situation. Signed: Hugh Lees.'

The man was badly shaken but unhurt. Under the circumstances we'd protected him and treated him well. I would have to trust my

PAUL FERRIS & REG McKAY

137

judgement that he was a man of honour and wouldn't change his story when released. Going immediately to the barricades I presented a list of demands written out by Hugh Lees.

1. No one is to leave the hall unless everyone leaves together.

2. Radio Clyde must be informed of the reasons for the riot and those stated reasons must be heard on our prison radios during subsequent news bulletins.

3. All prisoners leaving the hall must have their nominated solicitor present or have in their possession proof of their solicitor's knowledge regarding such matters.

4. All prisoners must be subject to a full medical examination immediately an agreed settlement is reached.

5. PO Davie McCallum and PO George Silver to witness medical inspections and to ensure that no brutalities are inflicted upon any prisoners after a settlement has been reached.

6. Once the radio broadcast has been made the current situation will immediately be resolved.

7. Hugh Lees and Jock Donaldson will be the last persons out of the hall and if any prisoners are to be heard screaming upon being beaten up by staff then the health and well being of our hostage, Hugh Lees, cannot be guaranteed.

We sat and waited as the Prison Negotiating Team weighed up the pros and cons of ignoring our terms and rushing the barricade. But I'd already taken other precautions. A well-known trusty who was allowed to work the gates had agreed to hide the letters and the film negatives in the back of his transistor radio. He was the prisoner who would fall under least scrutiny from the screws and could smuggle the goods outside. Even now I can't mention his name to protect him against the prison authorities' long, bitter memories. As we waited, the tension increased, knowing that it was victory or war – nothing else.

Radio Clyde made the broadcast. While it was a major breakthrough for a prison protest, it didn't feel like it at the time.

'Paul, what if they gie us a doing out there?'

'Dae ye think it's jist a trick?'

'It's a set-up, man. A can sense it.'

The withering doubts were understandable. Many of these guys

had been double-crossed plenty of times by the screws and management. But fretting wouldn't help anyone so I had to speak up: 'I give you my personal guarantee that you'll all be safe. To prove it, I'll go through the doors first on my own. If they grab me I'll howl like a demented banshee and you slam the shutters back down.'

My confidence drained as I walked through the doors. My precautions would serve well to finger treachery after the event but couldn't prevent me being beaten up first. The management kept to their agreement. So much so that a certain lawyer picked up the letters and the negatives from the trusted prisoner, taking them out through the gates where they might serve their purpose in the public domain.

At the High Court in Edinburgh some time later, Jock Donaldson pleaded guilty to taking a hostage and inciting a riot and was sentenced to an additional 11 years. John Graham, J.J. Johnstone, Jim Healy, Chas Crawford and Ronnie McGroarty were also charged, having been identified by the screws as running around shouting, deemed to be riotous behaviour. Hugh Lees was a man of honour. During his evidence he described events factually, avoiding temptation and, I'm sure, the encouragement of his bosses to gild the lily. Paraphrasing his words, he said, 'The situation was fast running out of control and I was fearful for my life. I asked Paul Ferris to negotiate on my behalf. He worked to end the riot. Without him I don't know what would've happened.' Many of the screws would've been spitting blood when they heard of Lees' statements in court. Imagine, one of them speaking up for a con – betrayal. No, just honesty.

I regret the mental anguish Hugh Lees faced after that ordeal. The prison system traps people together in an unholy union where the good and the bad are stuck with each other and hurt each other because there's no one else. He was in a uniform, paid to keep me behind bars – for that I resented him. But as a man I held him in high esteem. Hugh Lees gained a great deal of respect from me and from other prisoners – damn few screws have that claim to fame.

I was never charged but was cited as a defence and a Crown witness at the trial of my brothers-in-arms. Much as I balked at the prospect at giving evidence for the Crown, I'd little alternative, being a captive. Besides, I'd a plan to help my mates, not hinder them – an act always allowed, always honourable and always required of a decent human of the streets. Because of the hostage's evidence my position had been elevated from a con expected to lie to help out friends to the saviour of the peace. So, I told the truth, 'Shotts prison is full of murderers and violent men. There was no way I could control them by myself. The accused helped me.'

'But, Mr Ferris, the accused were seen running excitedly up and down stairs shouting and screaming.' The prosecutor thought that was riotous behaviour.

'Of course they were. I'd sent them to different parts of the prison to talk to the men and curb their activities. They took great risks.' Faced with increasing mayhem they'd stood firm, protected the hostage and worked to a peaceful resolution. Now they were gong to be singled out and punished for their pains.

All were found Not Guilty or Not Proven apart from Jock Donaldson, who pleaded guilty. The letters and the photographs were never needed, never shown. I have them still as a record of the most expensive prison riot in the UK at that time, perhaps still. The cost of repairing the damage stretched into millions of pounds – an expense which could've been avoided by more humanitarian management. All we asked was that they treat us as people and worked to their own rule book.

While I was waiting to appear at court at the Shotts trial, unexpected visitors arrived. Arty, Jaimba McLean and the bold John Gallacher had been bussed from Peterhead for a trial. All the way down Arty had boasted out loud of what he was going to do to me when we met. The ignorant screws put us together. The other Peterhead prisoners tensed and waited for Arty's promised violence.

'Paul, how you doing? Long time no see, mate.' The prisoners eyed each other quizzically. 'Why did ye no' pop in an' see the old man when ye were oot?'

'I'd no reason to go and see him,' I answered, watching his expression closely.

'Aw, he'd be disappointed, ye know. Always askin' for ye.'

Then my old pal Jaimba piped up, 'Whit's aw the chat for, Arty Farty? Thought ye wis gonnae gie Paul a right doin'.' Jaimba couldn't wait for an answer. 'Aw that crap about knifing him an' having him shot. Ye're jist a lying fat joking bastard, aren't ye?'

It wasn't a question but a statement. All the other men seemed *to agree. Arty blustered on about setting me up with a good car when I got out and playing to an old pal's act that had long since expired. Like a slow-punctured balloon his credibility fizzled out in front of my very eyes.*

I turned my attention to John Gallacher whose alleged forcible removal to the cages of Inverness had caused the riot. It emerged that Gallacher was forced nowhere. In the tinder-box atmosphere of Shotts he'd become convinced someone was planning to kill him. To my knowledge he was fantasising, simply not being important enough. Gallacher had requested a transfer to another prison. He was so paranoid that the screws agreed to tell no one and smuggled him out of Shotts to Peterhead. The whole affair had been a farce. We had rioted over a deadbeat neurotic.

28.

LUCK OF THE DRAW
by Reg McKay

In prison, Arty was trying to rule the roost by buying or bribing. To all and sundry he was the fat joker, a genuinely funny man with a gift for mimicry specialising in the sounds of gunfire. He was still Arthur Thompson's son, the heir apparent and, in his own opinion, important.

Arty never learned that in jail your father is not much help. When he started boasting of who he was going to have killed everyone knew he meant just that – paying someone else to pull the trigger. Through his money and his father anything was possible. When Arty threatened to kill Bagan, Ferris, McLean, Ross, McGraw, Healy and every other named player, some laughed. Others took him seriously and asked what his father might do. When Arty's threats were believed the targets looked warily at old Arthur Thompson.

Most days, Arthur Thompson could be found sitting behind his desk at his timber yard. It was a habit he'd formed many years ago when still a young man and Thompson liked his routines. The casual passer-by would see a run-of-the-mill wood merchant's and not pay a second glance. But Thompson conducted a great deal of his other business from behind that cheap, scarred desk. Those who knew the streets also knew where they were likely to find Thompson – behind that desk.

The man entering the yard attracted no attention. Single callers were a common sight and, besides, he knew where he was going. When the visitor walked through the doorway, Thompson looked up with a dour face but said nothing. He didn't even call out when the young man drew his pistol, pointing it straight at the old gangster's head.

The shot sounded lethal but the powder was damp, sending the bullet spiralling downwards, landing on the table with a pathetic dull clonk. The gunman went to fire again, aiming straight at that stern face. Thompson still said nothing but fear drove him to his feet as the second bullet came winging towards him. Yet again the shot curved and drooped. Thompson clutched between his legs as the bullet pierced his groin. The gunman turned and fled cursing, 'Probably blown his cock off. Fucking useless tae the old bastard anyway.' As he walked quickly out and down the pavement he knew Arthur Thompson had cheated death once more.

At the hospital, Thompson declared he had injured himself with a drill bit when carrying out some work at his home. He mentioned no names and made no complaint. He wondered who could want him dead now. Up in Peterhead prison Arty was flapping a piece of paper, 'Ma hit list. Youse better make sure yer name's no oan it.'

Whit's this aw about, son?' It was one of the longest sentences old Arthur had said to me. I would've been honoured, especially since he'd bothered to visit me in prison. I would've been, except that he was looking after his own interests and he'd called me son. Every time someone did that I wanted to stand up and shout, grab them by the throat and give them a nose-to-nose lecture on Willie Ferris, my Da, half their size and twice as big. Still I suppose it wasn't every day you were shot in the groin, even if your name was Arthur Thompson.

So, I told him straight about the growing list of people claiming young Arty had fitted them up and that they weren't best pleased. That Arty had been threatening everyone that moved. If any of them had taken him half seriously then most of the street life would be looking to get the Thompsons. Those of us who knew Arty Farty just shook our heads and laughed, but everyone had friends and relatives who might take any threat from any Thompson seriously. Old Arthur listened, stood up, shook his head and left. I watched him walk away with the hint of a limp and thought, 'Well, he got what he came for – why should he hang around?' It was my parting of the ways with Arthur Thompson.

Apart from family, my other visitor in Shotts was Tam Bagan. Before my spell in Shotts I recall warning him that the word was out that the Thompsons would like to see him on a slab. He just laughed and asked, 'Have you jist worked that oot?' This was a strange world of mine where someone brought up by a family could laugh at the notion of being killed by them. I should've listened to my father and Bertie Connor but it was too late. The gangsters and the police wouldn't allow me to walk away. I'd have to earn my passage, but the question was how?

The day I walked out of Shotts I congratulated myself for avoiding any added days in the pokey though, God knows, the temptations ran high. The millions of pounds spent on the new Shotts Prison were wasted by their continued employment of too many narrow-minded thugs in uniform. I could count on the fingers of one hand the times I'd pursued violence for my gratification – namely the Welsh bros. Most of the screws were into thuggery and cruelty for their own pleasure. I often wondered what their sex lives were like – if they had any.

Out of Shotts to freedom and I proposed a new start. Back with Anne Marie and Paul. In prison I carried a murmuring, low-level ache that was their absence. It was the type of feeling you have to play down and deny or it will get to you more effectively than any torture. But walking through those gates is like starting all over again. A prisoner holds a notion of his wife and child as unchanging but nothing stays the same for three years. Jail life is designed to end prisoners' relationships by stealth. Most don't notice at first, being seduced by the soft skin of his woman and the smile of his boy.

A living I must earn and I knew only one way. My mind was made up and I split from Arthur Thompson but couldn't leave crime. What would I turn to – van boy? Tam Bagan had already walked and I teamed up with him and a guy I'd known for most of my life, Bobby Glover. Bobby was a few years older than me and a highly respected street fighter. An old-fashioned square-go guy. His fighting style summed up his character – open, honest and direct. Bobby was no one's fool but he was fun. Always with a wry joke or a song. I took to Bobby right away.

The three of us decided to try our hands at making a legitimate living and joined Cottage Conservatories, a small company installing double-glazing and conservatories. The two company directors were Barnie McCrae and Jimmy Johnstone, known as JJ and, unlike his better-known Celtic namesake, a Rangers footballer who managed only a few first-team games. Later these two would head to London and make a good life converting old churches into designer flats. At one time, Barnie was the only outsider to lecture the Bank of Scotland – on capital investment, as it happened. At that point, though, I was made company secretary for Cottage Conservatories.

It was a tough business to make a dime in but I reckoned I could cope with anything. Then I learned fast that sales people were the most vicious, uncaring, focused beings in the human race. They'd cheat their grannies with a smile, making it sound like a good deal. They made the hardmen of Bar-L look like limp-wristed wimps and, boy, could they gab. Some of the women amazed me. All flashing eyes, short skirts, soft laughs, gliding in a waft of sensuous perfume. When their targets were lulled into a soporific daze they went for the jugular. They were like beautifully bloomed Venus fly-traps. And I thought I was hard.

The police hadn't forgotten my name or my record. As soon as I was back on the streets they came on to my trail. Baird Street, the local nick, made a point of hassling me at every turn. So I simply moved outwith their area – to Barlanark. Only a couple of miles east within Glasgow, I might as well have emigrated. Anne Marie, Paul junior and myself took up residence in Pendeen Road in an ordinary council house in a quiet little street. A few hundred yards down the street from us lived a young fellow by the name of Joe Hanlon. This was the same Joe Hanlon who had lived above young Arty's garage, Maryhill Autos. Whose father, Shoulders Hanlon, had been a close associate of Arthur Thompson till choked to death with his fish supper.

Joe was as keen as mustard. Not yet 20 years old, he'd built up a reputation as a bare-knuckle street-fighter, like Bobby. Joe had spent most of his early adulthood in prisons and during one sentence battered a guy severely for bad-mouthing me. He hadn't even known me then but still saw fit to stand against unfair comments. Brave, strong and loyal – you couldn't help but love Joe Hanlon. At first I got to know Joe's brother but before long it would be Joe I would count as a very special friend.

At the time we all had our separate business interests. I was still making an income from certain illegal activities of which the police remain ignorant to this day, so let's leave it that way. Officially, Bobby became manager of the Cottage Bar and I was trying to make the double-glazing firm pay. While he wasn't hanging around with us at the time, it's important to know that Joe was doorman at the Caravel Bar, owned by Margaret McGraw but backed up by her husband Thomas McGraw, better known on the streets as The Licensee. The pub had nothing to do with McGraw's nickname, in fact his name was never over the door. McGraw seemed to get off with every crime, every financial irregularity and every breach of every law. McGraw had a licence to do as he pleased. More of him later.

Looking back, that year was one of the most reassuring years of my adult life. But trouble was never far away.

I watched the large man in the tuxedo come striding across the *road and reminded myself he was carrying a knife. Checking the loaded pistol in my jacket as the car doors sprung open, I turned round, 'Hi, Drew. All right?'*

'Been better, Paul.'

Bobby Glover slipped into the front seat and the bulk of Drew Drummond sat uneasily in the back. Drummond was a violent sod but that wasn't the point. He ran a nightclub called McKinlay's and had an association with McGraw, The Licensee.

Earlier that night Anne Marie, Tam Bagan's wife and Bobby Glover's sister had gone there. Instead of the normal courtesies expected in our world, a fracas had erupted at the front door and the three women had been assaulted by the hefty bouncers. Not on. Violence against women, children and oldies was never acceptable and when it arrived at your own family you were obliged to seek revenge. We were taking Drummond to Tam Bagan's house to discuss the matter. Unknown to the others I'd decided that if abject apologies were not forthcoming I was going to shoot Drummond.

As we drove, Bobby described the cause of our grief. Bagan's house was nearby but I steered the car on to the motorway, hit the accelerator and headed out of town fast. Loud music was blaring from the radio but my ears were tuned into the mutterings between Bobby and Drummond.

'It's simply not on, Drew.'

'Bobby, I didnae know, man. I'd heard there was a bit o' trouble at the door like but no names were mentioned.'

'Those guys knew who they were slapping, Drew.'

'You sure . . . '

'You calling me a fucking liar?'

'Naw, man, naw. Jist checking like, Bobby. Jist being sure, man.'

'Be sure that they knew. Right?'

'Of course, I'll take yer word for it.'

'So what ye doing about it?'

'That big bouncer's pure trouble, man. I'll bet it was him. Fight wi' his fuckin' shadow like.'

'Is that no' why ye hired him?'

'Aye, but he jist disnae think. I'll bet it wis him.'

'So?'

'I'll hand him his jotters the night and any o' the rest that were involved.'

'Is that it?'

'Of course, I'll gie the arsehole a right kicking. Maybe worse.'

'Okay . . . '

'And, Bobby. Paul. I'm really sorry, ye know. We have nae trouble between us. You and yer people are welcome in the club any time. Fuck's sake, man, if A knew yer womenfolk were at the door it would've been a free night a wis dishing oot.'

'Right, Drew, sounds okay but it was still a serious insult.'

'Bobby, A know, man.' By this time the car is speeding at 90 miles an hour out of the city and heading towards the vast expanse of Strathclyde Park. At night the park was full of hookers with their johns, flashers, gay guys looking for a pick-up in the bushes, prowling kids out for a rumble.

'Where we going, lads?' Drummond was sweating, tugging at his bow tie.

Slowly I turned the music down, glanced over my shoulder and asked, 'How far do you want to go?' I watched carefully for that knife, then relented. After all, he had apologised. 'Nothing is going to happen.'

Too late. Drummond pushed his bulk between the front seats, yanked at the handbrake and sent the car spinning round at high speed. Wedging my left shoulder under his arm, I braked hard. The car shimmied all over the road, Drummond reached across Bobby, sprung the front door and clambered out. Thump, thud, bump – he bounced across the motorway and tumbled down the steep grass embankment. As the car screeched to a halt, the mud-smeared, dishevelled Drummond crawled up on to the road and sprinted across six lanes of fast-moving traffic. As he ran he screamed, 'Bastards. Bastards. Ya bastard, Glover. I'd never have thought you'd set me up. Bastards,' then he disappeared into the darkness. In truth I was heading for a roundabout intending to steer back into the city towards Bagan's house. Drummond had been as safe as houses when he threw himself from the car.

'We'll have to go and see McGraw, Bobby,' I said as I watched the dishevelled Drummond limp off into the shadows.

'The Licensee? What for?' Bobby took the view that the problem had been with Drummond and it was sorted.

'The matter's not finished. He either apologises or we see to him as well.' McGraw would be at the Caravel Bar but as we drove *through the city he suddenly appeared along with his doorman, Joe Hanlon. Drummond had telephoned him for a pick-up.*

When McGraw saw us he flipped and tried to back away wittering on and on, 'Whit's goin' oan here?'

'Whit's going down, boys?'

'It's got fuck all tae dae wi' me.'

I moved near to him and touched him, 'If I can get this close, McGraw, it would've happened already.'

Appeased but still jumpy, he listened and twitched as I explained the cause of our unhappiness. He apologised and we agreed to leave the matter as it stood. I invited him back to Tam Bagan's house. McGraw leapt a foot and refused but young Joe offered to come along. Joe knew my style, was aware I was armed and still was willing. I refused, but how could I not admire the man?

When I returned to my own home late at night, I told Anne Marie of the night's events and warned her of repercussions. In the near distance I heard the unmistakable crack of a shot. Waiting for trouble has always irritated me so I slipped out of the house to sniff around the area. Before long I spied McGraw, Drummond and Joe coming out of the local cemetery and heading into Tam Bagan's house. Was this curtains for Bagan? Standing in the shadows of a school playground, I watched the events inside the house, gun drawn and cocked at the ready. McGraw and Joe departed the house, leaving Drummond alone with Bagan – exactly when danger is most likely. Edging closer, I tensed and waited.

When Drummond left the house all was peaceful and I strolled home and to bed with a bitter taste in my mouth. Overreacting? Playing at gangsters? Later I learned that the shot had been McGraw testing out a .45 automatic. McGraw then handed the gun to Joe telling him to, 'Go and deal with this,' meaning shoot Bagan.

'Fuck off,' said Joe. 'I'm no dealing wi' anything like that.' The gun was then handed to Drew Drummond with the same order. In Bagan's front room, McGraw sat watching and waiting for Drummond to pull the gun and execute their host. Fed up and disgusted at the lack of a show, McGraw stormed out of the house with Joe in tow. Drummond had had a cup of tea and chatted with Bagan rather than shooting him dead. Smart move, since I would've blasted him in the process. In the meantime I'd gone to bed with a very bad feeling about Thomas McGraw, The Licensee.

LICENSED
by Reg McKay

Thomas McGraw was a mediocre crook. He couldn't fight and his only skill was an ability to disable alarms, one of the easiest jobs in the robber's repertoire. As a youth he was a gang member and never a leader, making up the numbers. Tolerated but not respected, all his life he has displayed an aptitude for nervy, incessant chat and an insatiable appetite for knowing other people's business.

Graduating through the usual juvenile penal establishments McGraw teamed up with Margaret and married her. They called Margaret McGraw, the Jeweller, because of the amount of gold she wore. Some on the streets say that was the point when he changed, when brains and cunning entered his life. Others say that he was always willing to sell his comrades, to cheat anyone as long as he gained.

As an adult in the 1970s, McGraw was involved on raids on post offices all over Scotland. So successful were the hits that the police ran a national campaign trying to catch them. TC Campbell was an occasional member of that team and one of the rare ones to survive. After every job, the proceeds were hidden and the robbers left empty-handed, very careful not to show any signs of sudden wealth, a sure way to attract police attention. Every so often one of the gang would be arrested on his way home. Never McGraw.

Street life was beginning to buzz about McGraw and his charmed existence. It seemed he could get away with anything and accordingly he was given the name The Licensee. His powers extended to other enterprises such as taxis, ice-cream vans, pubs – he would jump queues and obtain certificates where others were refused.

McGraw had several houses but kept his council flat in Barlanark for contact with his favoured policemen. He couldn't stop himself from boasting about the coppers on his payroll. One night, a policeman pal telephoned the flat warning McGraw that the Scottish Crime Squad were on the way with fit-up material. They arrived and arrested McGraw but before they could get him into their car, DI Jakey Waddle, as we'll call him, and his Strathclyde team sped up. In the street the police argued over the custody of McGraw and a tug of war ensued, deteriorating into a punch-up between the detectives. McGraw drove away to freedom.

A short while later, Waddle and a policeman we'll call Geordie Crowdie faced internal investigations for hanging around too often at McGraw's house. They were let off and returned to work. McGraw invited them round for a celebration drink which rolled on for hours. Some local youths took exception to the police car and turned it over on its roof. Still they were not sacked.

In the early 1980s, the police were trading in heroin. The dealers down south were moving large quantities towards Glasgow. If the police picked up four kilos they would hand in only half a kilo, redistributing the rest. McGraw thought he would try his hand as a drugs baron and contacted his police friends. Trouble was he used his usual contacts as dealers and none had a clue about smack. The pure heroin was sold directly on to the streets. Junkies overdosed and died like flies.

On one occasion McGraw's car full of stolen goods was cut off by a police barricade. Determined to escape, he rushed it, smashing through but overturning. His detective friends picked him up, dusted him down and gave him a lift home. The loot was lost, other team members advised by the police to lie low and McGraw went home to Margaret and a cup of tea.

Margaret was a good friend to the police. One time when McGraw was serving a short sentence she went on holiday to Spain. Rather than have her husband fret she didn't tell him and left a series of letters with her sister which were posted to the prison every day. When the pasty-faced McGraw was released, two lightly tanned detectives took pleasure in telling him what his wife liked for breakfast, the little blemish in that intimate place, the noises she made when excited and much, much more. Visibly upset, he shrugged. It was a price worth paying. It wasn't to be a one-off.

In 1984, an ice-cream van driver, Andrew Doyle, and his family were slaughtered when their house was deliberately set on fire. The six deaths horrified the public and the tabloids screamed ICE CREAM

WARS. The police picked up everybody who moved. Threats were made, beatings dished out, dustbin lids banged on unsuspecting skulls. Some were arrested every day for a week, a week off then it would start again. Twelve-hour repeat interviews ensued and the net was thrown wide but most often in the east end of Glasgow. One name was always on the police lips – interview rooms screamed TC CAMPBELL. The streets howled THOMAS McGRAW. There were no witnesses, no forensics, nothing to corroborate. An overheard conversation in a pub by a man named William Love – that would do nicely, thank you. TC Campbell and Joe Steele were jailed for life. McGraw was never went to trial.

McGraw was fast running out of new territory to buy his way into. He didn't care. He could do what he wanted. He was The Licensee.

Joe, Bobby and I became close socially. As the oldest, we looked up to Bobby as the boss, the leader. He'd an easy-going manner and a sharp brain – the ideal deterrent to Joe's occasional over-enthusiasm. Our wives and partners were strong women all – Eileen Glover, Sharon Hanlon and Anne Marie. These were the kind of women we couldn't go home to with an open pay packet and we knew it. It used to unnerve us when the three of them got together – a prospect which soon came to an end when Anne Marie and I separated.

One day I telephoned up this woman I'd met and asked if she was interested in a load of designer clothes, mentioning a price I knew she couldn't resist. Soon we were an item. Karen Owens was another strong woman – all slim good looks and as assertive as hell. She'd recently separated from her husband, Mick Edwards, who came from money. Karen had standards and she intended to maintain them. Her three young daughters – Natalie, Clare and Carly – were a new experience for me entirely. The girls were better able to handle the changes and welcomed me with open arms.

Joe and Bobby Glover had taken a recent interest in skiing – a most unlikely hobby for a pair of ragamuffins from the shitty schemes of Glasgow. But the world was our oyster and bugger anybody who stood in our way. Eventually I agreed to try out a day's skiing at Glenshee in the Grampian Mountains.

We whizzed up the mountain roads in my new 4x4 jeep, aware that we were all fur coat and no knickers, having no skiing clothes or gear. Hiring the lot from a shop, it was all the same bright colour, very tatty and marked with huge numbers to deter those thieving rascals. You can take the boy out of Blackhill but you can't take Blackhill out of the boy. I loved the skiing but hated looking cheap.

It was as if everyone was pointing at us and whispering, 'Poor Boy.'

On the way back down the road we made a date for another trip on my insistence that we went out and got all our own flash gear. The following Saturday, Joe Hanlon and I drove into the city centre to splash out big style. Before we arrived I warned him, 'Right, Joe. No lifting anything.'

Joe, looking hurt, promised, 'Naw, naw, Paul. I'll behave.' He was one of the most skilled kleptomaniacs I'd ever met. In spite of having more money than he could hope to spend sometimes, Joe just couldn't help himself.

We were in the shop for over an hour, waiting to have the blocks fitted on our new skis and trying on all the latest gear. During that time we got chatting with the staff, finding out that one of the guys was in a mountain rescue team, and meeting another's girlfriend – a real looker. They treated us well but, mind you, we paid £1,500 in cash for the goods. The next day we spent a much more enjoyable day's skiing on the piste at Glenshee.

A short while later, Joe telephoned me at Karen Owens' house in Monteith Row near the famous Barrowland market area of Glasgow. McGraw had just told him that one of his police contacts had spotted an arrest warrant with my name on it. Apparently I was wanted for stealing a car, something I'd refrained from since a teenager. There was one other Paul Ferris in Glasgow who was no relation. Maybe it was him. I went back to bed thinking that McGraw was trying to make me feel I owed him something.

When the thumping rattled the door in the early hours of the morning, I knew exactly who it was. As I opened the door the police were trying keys in the lock. The Cinderella Syndrome – if the keys fitted the lock I was in serious trouble. They'd been found in a stolen car and I'd been identified as the driver. Impossible. The funny thing was the keys almost worked.

The car was a red Astra, stolen with changed number plates. Down at London Road police station they eventually revealed that £20,000 of speed had been found in it. Now I grasped the gist. They had three witnesses, all bizzies. A beat cop had spotted the car outside a house close to Karen's. Identical to hers in every way just at the opposite far end of the street, it was the home of Jonah McKenzie's girlfriend, Jacqui Urquhart. I mentioned sweet FA to the police. The other two witnesses were traffic cops who had chased the red Astra into a dead-end before the men abandoned the car, running off.

I refused to undergo an ID parade. There was no need for any one-way mirror palaver when it was a simple matter of paid officers of the law checking it was me they'd seen. Get the cops into the room to eyeball me and the mistake would be cleared up. Eventually they agreed and the beat cop came in first.

'Naw, that's no' the guy I saw,' he said almost immediately and left the room. Then one of the traffic bizzies came in and proclaimed, 'That's the driver,' before shooting the crow sharpish. As the interview tape recorder wound on I made a point of making a long, angry statement about the young cop having made a mistake. This was beginning to feel like a set-up and I'd make them all regret it. Fine, but now I had go on to an ID parade.

Six is my lucky number and that's the position I chose in the line-up. It feels surreal standing among strangers all looking at a mirror, knowing that behind it is someone looking at you.

'Number six. He's the driver,' I heard called out and I lost the place – rushing at the mirror and kicking it, shouting and screaming till overpowered by a bunch of polis. One of the traffic cops was based in Paisley, the very posting of Grady Midden, ex-PC, now sergeant and a bitter man. Midden would never forget what I looked like.

The alleged incident had happened when I was in the ski shop. Before long Peter Forbes had gone there to interview the staff only to be told that the police had beaten him to it. They had been advised 'not to become involved in the case – in any way'. The car had shown evidence of having been used by the culprit for a long time and was bound to be covered in his fingerprints, not mine. Still they were coming at me and two traffic cops who'd never seen me before could recognise me from the back of my head during a frantic car chase.

Peter obtained a dated and timed till roll of all sales that had been made that day at the ski shop. All we had to do was identify our purchases. Having been slung into Bar-L on remand I asked Joe up for a visit. 'Be straight with me, Joe, did you steal anything that day?'

He blushed and looked shamefaced at my query. 'Well, aye. No' much, just a couple things – gloves, goggles and two ski poles.'

This was too serious to admire his stealth in lifting the awkward sticks. Still I had to spend some time reassuring Joe who was very worried that people would think of him as a shoplifter. Eventually he laughed when I pointed out, 'Right then. I'll just do the ten-year stretch to save you a red face.'

The new, accurate information was enough to secure my bail. We weren't finished. Peter Forbes had arranged a most unusual step – a privately commissioned ID parade. Under the official procedures at Shettleston police station, I stood at number six again as the ski shop staff traipsed behind the one-way mirror. Five times out of five I was identified as the guy who'd been in the ski shop that day.

While waiting to learn of the police's next step I made my own inquiries, discovering the red Astra had been chased again by traffic cops at the very time I was being held at the local police station. The driver of the red Astra had been Jonah McKenzie's cousin, James Kinnon, a tall, burly bloke with thick, jet-black hair. The police had already contacted him to say that his fingerprints were all over the car. They knew it was him, the police admitted, but wee Paul Ferris was going to go down for it.

Nothing was ever heard of the red Astra again. No charges were raised, no notification given, no apology issued for wrongful arrest. Peter Forbes plagued the procurator fiscal and Strathclyde Police for an explanation and received none. Years later he would advise me never to cooperate with the police again but to make this statement, 'I am not prepared to answer any question put to me by any police officer until I have had satisfactory explanation for the red Astra charges and the evidence allegedly available against me.'

I appreciated Peter's style but had another statement I should've sent to the police: 'I wish to thank the officers who pursued charges against me in connection with the red Astra. In doing so they completed my education in the methods of the force.'

32.

DOG DIRT ON MY SHOE

Okay, I confess – I used to do dope. As in smoke it, not deal it, and it seemed to me that the whole world did. By now I was splitting my time between London's Finsbury Park area and Karen Owens' house in the Barrowland area of Glasgow. When I was in the city, Karen and I would share some joints, our habit costing around £25 per week. One night, there was no cannabis in the house and I left with the aim of buying some. In my style of the time I was easily diverted, meeting a few people and eventually deciding to go to Anne Marie's to sleep the night on the sofa so I could see my son Paul the next morning. Only Joe Hanlon knew where I was heading.

Karen and the three girls were fast asleep when the police burst in the door at 7 a.m. She awoke terrified and startled, sitting up in bed just in time to see three burly policemen run into her bedroom. In their formal report they would claim that they knocked on the front door and when they heard someone screaming decided to break it down. Karen had been fast asleep but was now wide awake and in the company of one Detective Sergeant Greg Diddle.

Seven houses had been raided that night – my parents', Bobby Glover's houses in Cambuslang and Springboig, Joe Hanlon's, Tam Bagan's and my own flat in the Merchant City. Karen's was last on the list and they were looking for me.

'Where's the Wee Man?' growled Greg Diddle as Karen tried to grasp what was happening. 'Get the fuck out o' that bed, you.' Karen was only too happy to get out, wanting to go and comfort her crying kids and a young female babysitter who had stayed over. They wouldn't let her. 'Where's the Wee Man?' Diddle and his colleagues, we'll call Trumper and Belt, kept asking. At every other house they'd visited that night they had asked the same question. So far no one

PAUL FERRIS & REG McKAY

157

had been shown a warrant or given any reason why they were searching for me.

'You the Wee Man's burd then?' one policeman grunted as if that was a crime. Of course she was. 'Where is the Wee Man, then?' Karen kept telling the same story, the truth. She had no experience of this before, was frightened and unsure. Confused and bewildered, looking from one to the other as they spoke to her – burly, threatening men standing uninvited in her bedroom – turning and speaking, trying to be helpful, scared witless.

'Whit's this then?' DS Belt asked as he pulled the mattress up. Karen thought it was a hardback book and wondered to herself how it had managed to get stuck under there and why she hadn't felt the bulge.

'You smoke dope, hen?' Diddle asked.

'Aye, I smoke a bit of hash now and then.' Karen wasn't a liar.

But it wasn't a book under the bed, it was a half-pound block of cannabis resin. So I'd gone on a search for some dope when according to the police's testimony there was enough cannabis under my bed to roll 2,470 joints.

It was the start of a day of hell for Karen. Taken down to London Road police station and held in for one day and one night, she was formally interviewed 16 hours after the raid. Tired, hungry, thirsty, anxious, she sat down and they turned on the tape. It wasn't the first chat they'd had with her, without the tape. All day little jibes and queries about how she was in serious trouble and they knew that the drugs had nothing to do with her. Who else could have brought them in – her young kids, the babysitter, her boyfriend? Her boyfriend – it must have been her boyfriend. Karen just kept telling the truth.

The police never revealed why they raided seven houses searching for me that night. Detective Sergeant Greg Diddle retired one month later to take up employment in a private company. No one was ever prosecuted for the drugs. Who provided that block of cannabis resin? Not me.

33.

SHOWDOWN
by Reg McKay

Billy Thompson scrambled up on the roof, poured petrol down through a break in the tiles and lit a match. It was unusual for the hapless Billy to be trusted with anything, but the Thompsons were in dire straits. Ferris and Bagan had left them and Arty was in prison. It was in prison that Arty and Jonah McKenzie had planned this little piece of action. Billy and his young colleagues fled giggling at their handiwork. The fire brigade arrived soon after and doused the blazing Caravel Bar, saving it from destruction, but they were helpless to deal with another problem. Painted big and bold on the road outside the pub were the words McGRAW IS A GRASS.

Everybody could read the message for months on end. Being called a grass is bad for business and The Licensee called in favours from the police. For weeks people were being arrested on trumped-up charges, hassled off the streets and beaten up on McGraw's behalf. Jonah McKenzie's girlfriend's flat was found to contain the same paint used for the graffiti. People were being singled out for special treatment and soon they were bleating, 'It wisnae us, Tam. Big Arthur sent us in. Honest, Tam.'

McGraw had bought the Caravel Bar from the brewers who were glad to ditch it as the scene of a great deal of violence and dealing in all sorts. The profit wasn't worth the trouble and Margaret McGraw's name went over the door. Tam Bagan and Arthur Thompson both had ambitions to take over the bar but The Licensee had beaten them by stealth, bribery and corrupt officials. That was not the main problem but strife was coming big style.

McGraw wanted all his enemies off the streets. He had succeeded in having TC Campbell jailed for life for a murder he didn't commit. TC and Joe Steele drew attention to their fight for justice by bold escapes, hunger strikes and much more. McGraw didn't brood. He wanted Tam Bagan and Jonah McKenzie out of it and increasingly Arthur Thompson was caught in the crossfire. Arthur Thompson suspected that Tam Bagan had been behind his recent bullet in the groin. None of them trusted Bagan.

In prison, young Arty continued to stir trouble. Recently he had taken to having knives smuggled in for both sides of a stir-crazy war then sit back, watch the bloodshed and laugh. They weren't smiling on the streets of Glasgow – it was their friends who were being stabbed. Arty was issuing threats right, left and centre – Ferris, Bagan, Jaimba McLean. Paul Ferris was working away quietly with Bobby Glover and, increasingly, Joe Hanlon. Arthur and the tabloid press reckoned he had made contacts with the powerful London gangs. His reputation was sound and old Arthur Thompson thought he posed the biggest threat. In the meantime a range war with McGraw had to be diverted and a meeting was called.

Arthur Thompson offered to pay for the fire damage to the Caravel Bar and McGraw accepted immediately. It was uncharacteristic generosity by Thompson and McGraw treated it as a sign of weakness. It would never be paid. As Thompson, McGraw and their backers emerged from the Caravel blinking in the daylight, a car screeched up and out jumped Tam Bagan with a team. It was a showdown no one had planned but no one was turning away.

As the two groups faced each other, old Arthur pulled a gun from his jacket, shoving it against Bagan's head before lashing out and cracking him on the skull. Thompson stood over Bagan, pressing the gun against his temple. Bagan's cousin tackled Thompson who swivelled and pushed the gun into his face. It was a Mexican stand-off and someone was going to get hurt. Seizing the moment, Bagan jumped Arthur Thompson, smashing him repeatedly on the face with his fists then boots. The old man crumpled and lay unconscious on the ground. Straddling Thompson, Bagan went to shoot him with his own pistol.

'Don't kill him,' pleaded McGraw, knowing that such an act would bring Glasgow to a state of conflict that would burn for years. 'Don't kill him, for Christ's sake.' Poised over the prone old gangster, Bagan hesitated before pocketing the gun and calmly walking away. As he climbed into his car, his crew smashed the front of Arthur Thompson's car – a Glasgow calling card.

While McGraw saved his life that day, Arthur Thompson believed that he had been set up by The Licensee. A series of meetings were arranged where both men agreed Bagan was out of control, though the thoughtful Ferris was the serious, long-term risk. In the meantime, the Godfather and The Licensee increased an old business – trading in flesh.

34.

TRADING IN FLESH

Bobby and I had split with Tam Bagan and there was a great deal of bad blood hanging over many matters. McGraw, always keen to know others' business, heard about the dispute and asked for a meeting with me via Joe Hanlon who still worked for him at the Caravel. By this time I viewed McGraw as the most slippery snake in the pit and took along some insurance, a loaded pistol.

'I can have Bagan put out the road for you,' McGraw offered in the backroom of his pub.

'The trouble I have with Tam Bagan won't need to go as far as killing him,' I replied, amazed at his nerve.

'Naw, Paul, I didnae mean that. I'll have him put in prison – get people tae see tae it,' he explained in hurt tones.

I couldn't believe the guy's stupidity.

'What do you mean exactly?' I wanted him to tell me as much as possible.

'I've got police contacts like Bradman or Handless who can put a little smack in his car. Bagan gets stopped and he's offski.'

Well, that was plain enough. He'd confirmed all the street talk of The Licensee, the police and trading in flesh. Bradman and Handless were two cops forever hanging around McGraw, often pissed and always obnoxious. McGraw needed telling straight, 'Don't know about you but I don't work that way. If I've got a problem I sort it.'

As I turned to leave I looked straight at Joe Hanlon, the only other man in the room. Later that night I contacted Joe and warned him to watch his back working for someone as unscrupulous as McGraw. Before long Joe split from McGraw, joining myself and Bobby. The team was now together. McGraw was spitting blood but he'd a few other things to worry about.

Young Arty's grasp of reality had finally been melted by too many

Mafia movies. The wee fat joker thought he was running some kind of crime empire from his prison cell. Everybody knew about his hit list and his money. Trouble was Arty's reputation was keech and nobody half-decent took him seriously. But there are always loudmouthed jokers around talking a bigger game than they can deliver and Arty didn't have the nous to suss them out. Add to that the increasing number of wired-out junkies on the street and Arty had turned into a pay cheque with little required in return. What was he going to do, send another smackhead after them?

Anne Marie was making her way to the pub when the grenade was tossed into the Caravel Bar, rolling along the floor and ignored by the drinkers. Then someone sober enough spotted it, recognised it and promptly kicked it out the door right into a group of guys having a smoke and a chat – Tam McGraw, his brother-in-law Snaz Adams, Joe Hanlon and Tam Bagan, the very dudes the grenade was aimed for. They weren't so slow as the boozers and someone promptly hiked it up, ran down the road and chucked it as far as they could – into the local cemetery. The explosive device lay there for a while, close to a freshly dug grave, and nothing happened. Respect for the dead is a good value but can be taken too far. The group of heroes decided against desecration of the hallowed ground. It wasn't McGraw who now lifted the bomb – he was too frightened to come out of his home after 10 p.m. – but Tam Bagan. Over the wall, grabbed the grenade, ran like hell and lob – right on to a disused railway line.

When the Bomb Disposal Unit arrived they detonated the device, its explosion rattling the windows and blasting a gaping crater. It was identified as a NATO issue fragmentation device capable of shredding the Caravel's customers – lethal, but only when primed. Whoever junkie Arty had hired had forgotten to pull the grenade's pin before tossing it. Arty had to start hiring some decent help.

A guy called Danny Lorimer informed me that he'd been asked by Arty to do me harm, along with a Kenny Kelly and Martin Hamilton, known unkindly as Hammy the Poof. The plan was that the three musketeers were to kidnap me and inject me with heroin, thereby rendering me an addict. This was a typical far-fetched notion. Arty was infamous for borrowing from film plots. Why bother? Why not just shoot me? Danny revealed that it wasn't just Arty who was in on the act but Arthur Thompson himself. The old man welcomed the would-be hit squad into his home, providing £20,000 and two guns. The message was clear – ignore Arty's fantasies and take Ferris out permanently. Danny thought twice about the risks and scampered with the dosh, body-swerving Thompson territory for as long as it took.

McGraw had a falling out with his only son William, known as Winky, over the boy's heroin addiction and threw the youngster out on to the streets to fend for himself. As much as I hated The Licensee, I bore no grudge against his lad who was living in a derelict house and looked unkempt, tired, worn out. I invited him in to my house for something to eat, a wash and clean-up. I just hope that if my child ended up on the streets then someone, anyone – friend or enemy – would take him in.

'Paul, see if anybody ever found out what ma Da had been up tae he'd be a dead man.' Winky McGraw's comments came out of the blue as we were finishing some food and chatting about the football. The kid obviously had something he needed to get off his chest. He was shaking, withdrawing, jittery, but here was an outburst of anger. 'Because he's a grass. Has been a grass for years. He's shopped nearly every bloody person that knows him.' Watching his friends' older brothers and fathers betrayed hurt the young guy. He carried the responsibility heavily and I hoped he wouldn't end up paying the price of his father's sins.

Snaz Adams, McGraw's brother-in-law, turned against him and spoke bitterly about The Licensee's police handlers we'll have to disguise. Bradman, Handless and a whole stack of collaborators were the day-to-day police contacts always hanging around. Geordie Crowdie had a mutual convenience arrangement going with McGraw for years. Jakey Waddle, a violent, bullish man, had rescued McGraw from the mitts of the Scottish Crime Squad and provided other favours. Why?

A policeman investigating the Doyle murders handcuffed TC Campbell to a desk while he'd screamed, 'A fit up yer Da and I'm gonnae fit you up,' punching, kicking and throttling TC till other policemen tore him off, scared that their suspect might die before he could be tried. McGraw was arrested in connection with the Doyle murders and held on remand in Bar-L close to TC Campbell and Joe Steele. After some weeks, McGraw was released and never went to trial. People spoke openly of his role as a police plant, *eavesdropping on their main target and his main target – TC Campbell.*

McGraw and his police allies had resorted to an old business – trading in flesh. Meanwhile, the murderer of the Doyle family walks the street while Campbell and Steele spend their lives behind bars, unjustly convicted.

PAUL FERRIS & REG McKAY

35.

NO SINGER, NO SONG
by Reg McKay

Arthur Thompson had a few drinks more than his usual quota but not enough to get drunk. He had got over the death of his daughter, Margaret, a couple of years before. They all said she was a junkie but he wouldn't allow that. After all, he had an image to uphold. When she and that waster of a boyfriend were allocated the council house directly across from his own home, old Arthur sensed trouble and embarrassment. He hadn't spoken to her for years but got her mother to look her up and offer her money to go anywhere else. She'd taken the cash and the house. For two pins he would have given her a hiding and finished off that excuse of a man of hers. But folk were watching.

The day she died in that unfurnished hovel he'd set the family line straight. 'She choked oan her vomit. Right. Pissed like.' In Glasgow drunks suffocated that way every day. Margaret's mouth was full of her own vomit – she'd messed herself in every way. But first she had mainlined heroin like she mainlined every day. Weeks before she died she said, 'I'm taking the house in spite of what he says.' Local people were fond of the young woman. Within hours of her death her boyfriend was down on the motorway hard shoulder hitching a lift south and out of Glasgow forever. He might be a junkie but he wanted to live.

But tonight Thompson had a couple of drinks and was in his own territory a few hundred yards up Provanmill Road to his home and safety. He'd had a few but not enough to make him sing the old Scottish songs he enjoyed.

As the car approached he recognised the driver and passenger. Often enough he'd expressed the view, 'One's trouble, the other's fucking mental.' He wished them both dead. He paid to have them both killed. Arty tried to fit them up at different times. Even McGraw,

THE FERRIS CONSPIRACY

no friend to Thompson, had done his best. They should've been taken out years ago. No time like the present.

When the car mounted the pavement Arthur Thompson reached inside his jacket and found no gun. The last thing he remembered was the driver's smile. The pain hit him in the legs, the wind was knocked from his lungs and Arthur Thompson blacked out, sprawled on the ground.

The car bumped over his body, hit a fence then swerved out on to the road accelerating all the way. Fifty yards down it pulled in with a squeal of brakes.

'He wis gonnae have us, man. Did ye see him goin' for his . . .' One man was upset, anxious, angry.

'No point leavin' it at that, is there?' The other man was cool, thinking.

'Naw, man, might as well finish the old bastard.'

'Fuckin' piece o' luck, eh? Bumping in tae him like that.'

'Bumping into him. Like it . . . bumping into him.'

The driver reversed fast up the street till he felt the jolt of the body under the wheels. A screech of tyres and forward over the body again. Once more for luck. Bump. Bump. 'That should sort the old cunt.'

'Aye, but we need tae cover ourselves. The bizzies will be straight up tae our doors.'

'I have jist the thing right here in my very pocket.'

The two men left the car, stood back a few paces and fired two bullets through the windscreen scattering crystal shards into the car. The gunman wiped the pistol all over, lifted the hand of the battered, bloody body and clasped it round the grip.

'Heh, heh, heh . . . '

'Whit's so fucking humorous?'

'The shooter used tae belong tae the old fucker.'

'He'll be well pleased tae have his property back.'

'Aye, tight-fisted bastard.'

'Ha. Tight-fisted. Fisted. Get it?'

As they drove away they congratulated themselves on getting rid of a dangerous man.

'Fucking grass so he was.'

'Police informer.'

'Aye, and the rest.'

The assailants were in high spirits driving through the busy city-centre traffic when there was a stirring back in Provanmill Road. Arthur Thompson was trying to edge his way across the pavement, inch by agonising inch, dragging his legs, the pistol in his fist. He had done this before and knew to hold the gun by the tip of its barrel and to spin it through the air. Legs trapped under a fence, he couldn't make it and was going to pass out. A shadow crossed his body and peering down at him was a familiar shape, a man in dark glasses.

'Christ almighty, whit happened tae ye?'

'Ditch the gun, son. Here.' The newcomer lifted the gun and ran over the wasteland, moving awkwardly and staggering in the rutted ground. By the time he had returned to the road, old Arthur was being helped by a local man, James Roarty. Pushing his dark glasses up the ridge of his nose, he said to Roarty, 'Away ye go now. Away home, I'll take him frae here.' The good Samaritan must have wondered what sort of man goes wearing sunglasses in Scotland late at night.

'Help us home, son,' Arthur mumbled. 'It's jist up the road,' as if the man in the shades needed directions. As if. When the ambulance and police arrived Arthur Thompson insisted that it had been an accident. When, fully recovered, he was interviewed by the press he said that he'd been drunk, walking home alone and singing a song. 'Somebody must never have liked my singing,' he stated in a typical Glasgow put-down. Arthur Thompson wasn't drunk and hadn't been singing. There was business to do – he had two men to kill.

36.

CUCKOO IN THE NEST

As the flick knives opened all around me I laughed out loud and said to my friends sitting around me, 'Here we go. Custer's last stand.'

London was full of interesting people and opportunities. For a couple of years in the early 1990s I kept a flat there in the Finsbury Park area. Wherever I went I met faces who knew or knew of Arthur Thompson. For these guys the name Thompson meant Glasgow like the Krays meant London. Then there were others who made their way in life, respecting what had gone before but respecting themselves more. Guys, such as the A brothers, who lived to a code of honour as ancient and as binding as any and as familiar to me as the nose on my face. At that time the A's were the most respected family in the capital. Londoners are so like Glaswegians with their sense of humour, toughness and thick accents – I felt at home.

A London friend pulled a black guy up over an unpaid debt and slapped him. Two seconds later we were surrounded by his team. Flick. Whirp. Flump, Snick, as the flick knives opened. It made me feel at home and I laughed out loud. A couple of the black giants looked down at this little whippet of a Scotsman with expressions of curiosity mixed with contempt. With no reputation I'd nothing to defend and everything to prove. I liked it in London.

I was still floating in and out of Glasgow keeping business alive and doing the odd job. Now Bobby, Joe and I were recognised as partners and we associated with a range of guys like JJ, Jaimba McLean, the Rollo brothers and others. The newspapers at the time and since were full of talk of the so-called Barlanark Team and would muse about Arty being part of it, me taking it over, how we ran the biggest drugs cartel in the country and other scams. All crap

– not that I'm denying we were a bunch of rogues making a living out of crime but we were never a team.

The Barlanark Team did exist, emerging in the 1970s to rob post offices, banks and the like. By the time I came along in the late 1980s they were jailed, dead or operating as individuals. That's how it was, small groupings who needed to relate to the others but were not part of a unified organisation. It probably suited the police and sold newspapers to say that this big, sinister gang existed. We might have been sinister but we weren't a mob.

Bobby and Joe were my main partners and friends. In spite of what people thought, we looked up to Bobby, the oldest, as a leader if we needed to look up to anyone, though we worked as equals, contributing our own strengths and listening to each other's points of view. When it came down to it Bobby Glover was the man.

We had the same philosophy in life and sense of humour. It used to break us up when we saw somebody acting the gangster, talking a big game. That was for kids who couldn't cut it. Donnie McMillan was a bit like that, always dressing up in suits, long coats and the black leather gloves. Donnie's ambition was to play the Glasgow gangster in a soap series and he practised his acting every day. We tolerated him as a joke.

Bobby had taken over the Cottage Bar and had interests in other pubs. Joe made a living out of ice-cream vans he owned. My legitimate concern at the time was dealing in cars with some other friends. The gossip machine had Joe dealing drugs from his vans, an absolute myth – can you imagine out-speeding the bizzies in one of those vans? Unlike McGraw and the Thompsons, neither Bobby nor Joe dealt in drugs. The police couldn't let us be and were investigating allegations that we robbed a couple of banks, netting £250,000. For all I know they're still investigating those robberies.

One day a young guy, William Lobban, turned up. He was an escapee from prison and was looking for help. I didn't know the man but was always happy to help those evading the law. So, I did the honourable thing and made arrangements for him to have a flat in London, a change of identity and money to support him. It was no big deal, we helped people we didn't know all the time. All we expected in return was respect and that they should do us no ill.

Lobban was a strange young man. With a pleasant, almost feminine face he had a large, bulging forehead reminding me of *someone out of a sci-fi film. He was incredibly fit without trying. I mean, he was surrounded by men who had to be strong to pursue their business but he outstretched them all – though he was the laziest pig I've come across. At one point he was so determined to avoid the police that for a long time he dressed and lived like a woman, earning him the inevitable nickname Tootsie from the media. Some reckoned he enjoyed cross-dressing though I saw no evidence to that effect.*

Lobban was an ungrateful moaner who started turning up in Glasgow saying he was unhappy with being out of the scene in London. So we got him a place in Glasgow. Soon he was complaining about that and hanging around Bobby's house. Bobby and his wife Eileen took pity on the young guy and took him in for meals and sometimes he would stay over. On occasions he would even baby-sit their children. At the time we didn't know that a cuckoo's egg had just landed in the nest.

37.

BLOOD ON THE STREETS
by Reg McKay

The Apprentice is known and not known. Players of the streets are familiar with his particular talents. The media and the public have read of his actions yet remain clueless of his identity. He is called The Apprentice since he was so good so young.

By the advent of the 1990s The Apprentice was in his late twenties. Small-built with a taste for fashions of the day, he would be anonymous in any crowd anywhere. He has been injured though not often or so that you would notice. He speaks quietly, in an accent stuck somewhere between the slums and the suburbs of Glasgow, a voice trusted by everyone everywhere. The Apprentice is good at what he does – killing people. There was a time he was none too fussy who hired him.

Life had been difficult for Joe Hanlon – shot through the penis in a street confrontation only to be thrown out by the nuns of the Bon Secours Hospital. 'Have ye any money?' they squealed, throwing a bucket of water over him. Joe had not recovered from his wounds when his enemies petrol-bombed his ice-cream van. Nor was he walking without a limp when they blew up his XR2 sports car. Whoever was after Joe it wasn't The Apprentice who liked Joe as well as Glover and Ferris and, besides, he wouldn't have missed.

The likely culprits would be the Thompsons and their supporters like Jonah McKenzie, who had been jailed with Arty for drug dealing and was back on the streets. He was known as Blind Jonah ever since one night in the Palaceum Bar in Shettleston a drunk called Rab Craig lobbed a pint tumbler and it smashed into his face, piercing one eye. It could have been anybody but it was Jonah's luck that the glass hit him. People who knew Jonah before his troubles remember a happy-go-lucky man, always making jokes against himself and doing pathetic Shakin' Stevens impersonations. Jonah left McGraw to work for the Thompsons, making himself doubly dangerous. When Joe Hanlon was accused of attacking Jonah, stabbing him repeatedly and removing his other eye, they should have looked closer.

A guy called Edward Barnes, known as Barney, a friend of Jonah's, was asked to visit him in hospital in the middle of the night. His task – to check that Jonah was really blind. Terrified, Blind Jonah expected to be murdered at any minute and took a long time to relax. Still, Barney had to check out his blindness and led him down the ward standing, watching and wincing as the severely wounded man walked into a wall. One more message, 'Tell the bizzies it was a Pakistani bloke that jumped you on the street, right.'

Blind Jonah had been lifted off the street and taken to a flat where Thomas McGraw and others tortured and stabbed him for hours. When he was flung out on to the street he was blind and lucky to be alive. He intended to stay that way and would tell any story McGraw wanted.

Stephen Guy, known as Guydo, was next. An associate of Arty's, he had been charged and acquitted with setting fire to Joe Hanlon's ice-cream van. If he were killed now who would the police look for? – Hanlon, Glover and, of course, Ferris. One night in his flat in Rutherglen he told the men he lived with that a bunch of guys with a gun had been hanging around outside hassling him about Hanlon's van. The next night, three men stood out on the street throwing stones up at a window. When the shape of a man peering out appeared at the window, The Apprentice took aim and fired, the bullet piercing his target's neck. The Apprentice was good. He walked away with a bloke called Billy McPhee and Thomas McGraw, not knowing that his victim was not Guydo but an innocent by the name of Robert Johnstone.

William Gillen was desperate for cash and work. When Blind Jonah disappeared off the scene Gillen told McGraw that he could locate him in Ayrshire about 30 miles outside Glasgow.

'It's worth 50 quid and some pills,' said McGraw.

'Whit pills?' asked Gillen, not unreasonably.

'A don't fucking know but they're meant tae be Ecstasy. Get yer jacket.' Gillen knew the deal was miserly but he had no choice given the company he was in. The Apprentice joined them on the short trip towards the coast. When they searched and searched and found no sign of Blind Jonah, they turned around and headed back towards Glasgow.

'The fella swore that Jonah was there. I'm right pissed off wi' him,' harped Gillen all the way up the road.

McGraw complained in his typical manner, 'Ye've let me down badly, man. I'm really disappointed in you.'

The Apprentice was silent until he growled, 'Pull the motor in here.'

'Sure it's quiet enough?' asked McGraw.

'It'll no' take long,' the grim-faced man replied.

In the quiet country road near Loganswell, The Apprentice pulled Gillen from the back seat and threw him to the ground. 'You've been wasting ma time, ye wee cunt,' spat McGraw and then nodded at The Apprentice. Leaning over the cowering Gillen, The Apprentice shot into his knees. As the car drove away the howls of the writhing man could be heard over the noise of the car engine.

Evidence would emerge that the same gun was used in the shooting of both Robert Johnstone and William Gillen. The gun had once belonged to Arthur Thompson senior. It had been a busy weapon but had one more serious task to perform.

Down in London, Paul Ferris was going about his business oblivious to events that were ready to catch up with him.

I 'd been living off and on in London for several months, considering moving permanently, but my head was still in Glasgow. Then there were the telephone calls. Information is like an extra weapon in the crime world so the lines buzz with little snippets about everyone else. The tension between the groups was strained so everyone worried about everything anyone else was doing or might be doing. It's how I imagine war – constantly collecting and analysing information on enemies and would-be foes. Trouble is a lot of it is gossip and much of the rest myths.

For weeks I'd been hearing of the grief dished out to Joe and tales of Thompson and The Licensee on the warpath. Much as I considered McGraw a poor show of a man, he was licensed by the police and had the means to pay all sorts of people to do whatever he wanted. Things were rapidly spinning out of control. Returning to Glasgow was a risk and I knew only too well the bizzies would pay me undue attention. But I wanted to visit my son, Paul, and it had been too long since I'd seen my folks. A short while before, my father had been run over by an articulated lorry, crushing both of his legs. The doctors said he'd never walk again but Willie Ferris showed them otherwise. He used two sticks and was shaky on his feet but he was walking and getting about.

Karen had been down visiting me and for the last couple of weeks I'd been socialising with Barnie McCrae's son, Gary. The three of us decided to return to Glasgow together. On the flight the drinks flow was furious as it usually was with Gary. Arriving at Glasgow Airport about 6 p.m., we caught a cab together. As we dropped the young guy off in the city centre I stepped out of the cab and Karen's hearing and told Gary I'd meet up with him in town later.

Early in the evening I went over to catch up with Bobby Glover but

PAUL FERRIS & REG McKAY

175

he was out at a christening. Then I met up with Gary and we went on a Glasgow stroll – a pub-crawl around the city centre. It was a great night with Gary always in a good mood, always the same way. Later I visited Bobby again and on the way to Anne Marie's house in Balornock passed the Caravel Bar. The place was swathed in the flashing blue lights of trouble. I stopped the cab and asked the bundle of guys hanging around what had happened.

'Guy's been killed – a soldier,' was the reply. He was a soldier and Falklands veteran by the name of Robert Mills who'd been stabbed to death. He was a soldier not a player, just another victim of Glasgow's streets. Then other news came my way, 'Arthur Thompson's dead.'

'Whaaat?'

'Arthur's dead.' Poor Robert Mills was being ignored as the crowd murmured about reprisal killings and war. I thought old Arthur had been killed since, as far as I knew, young Arty was still in jail. Suddenly the polis-crawling Caravel wasn't the place for me and I left pronto, going on to Anne Marie's, a night on the sofa and time with Paul the next morning.

The following day I flew back to London. By then I'd heard, as had the whole world, that Arty was the dead man and the old man was on the loose. I could smell blood in the air.

39.

FETTESGATE UNCUT

Derek Donaldson was one of the smoothest con merchants I've come across but in prison he was being bashed regularly, suspected of being a closet queen. I don't care how grown-ups make the double-backed monster and I despise bullying. So I put the word about the other cons to back off and demonstrated I was serious by being seen chatting with Derek. He was an interesting and capable bloke with some good scams but I was surprised when he contacted me in 1992 out of the blue. We met up in my car and he spilled the beans.

Derek was gay and had had an affair with a high-ranking police officer from the Lothian and Borders force. The married detective called it off and Derek was hurt and jealous – so hurt he broke into the force's HQ at Fettes in Edinburgh. Climbing through an open window, he strolled freely about the building, removing whatever took his interest. Daubing the walls with Animal Liberation slogans as a diversion, he escaped with his spoils. He wanted my advice on what to do next. Sitting in my car in an Edinburgh back street he opened this hefty briefcase and out spilled a goldmine.

There was a file on a well-known Edinburgh family called Deacon, naming an informant who had grassed them up on a huge list of issues. There was a file on an Operation Ulysses targeting IRA sympathisers in Scotland, including named lawyers involved in fund raising. There were surveillance records of known UDA sympathisers from London and Edinburgh with photographs of some visiting Belfast. The batch included what looked like surveillance listening devices. The haul was dynamite and dangerous.

Donaldson offered me my pick but I didn't want to be found with any of that lot on me. I advised him to photocopy what he thought might be of value and get rid of the originals. He copied the lot. The police offered him immunity if he returned the entire collection and Derek was all for accepting. The Chief Constable, Sir William Sutherland, learned of the deal and the two cops responsible, Detective Chief Superintendent Hiddleston and Sergeant Peter Brown, were carpeted, with one retiring and the other being put back into uniform.

The trouble is that the bizzies weren't too sure exactly what had been taken and got all confused with another investigation into an alleged secret circle of homosexual judges suspected of giving preferential treatment to gays accused of crimes. Just before Derek had burgled their HQ, a senior detective had investigated the allegations, concluding they were true. The bold Sir William was having none of that and buried the report – or did he? All those bizzies fretted that the burglar had got his mitts on a copy.

As the publicity blazed on what had become known as Fettesgate, Sir William appointed William Nimmo Smith QC and James Friel, a regional procurator fiscal, to investigate the gay judges rumours. Nimmo Smith was duped by a bogus journalist into revealing the highly confidential report's conclusions – that the gay conspiracy didn't exist. Well, there was a surprise. The bogus journalist was none other than Derek Donaldson who promptly contacted The Sun.

But all that was in the future. In 1992, Derek Donaldson copied all the records. Some friends of mine, who cannot be named, got their hands on some of the documents and went on to use them to their advantage in trading with the police. But Derek Donaldson is a very astute man and, I'm sure, didn't stop at one or two copies. Some are still out there in private houses. In the meantime, I understand that Derek and his detective lover got back together. All that fuss over a lover's tiff.

40.

I KNEW YOUR FATHER
by Reg McKay

The Apprentice made a telephone call for assistance. Usually he worked alone but this hit was too important, too sensitive and the target's family too wary to take any risks. The man had to be killed on the first strike.

The help would have to come from out of town. Where better to go than London? The Apprentice was well connected, having slipped down on contracts when they needed an unknown face. He liked the reliable and efficient young guys, professionals like him. Two for back-up while he carried out the job himself. They would watch and only move if he was shot or caught out by a team response. He would use a .22 pistol with a silencer. Accurate and powerful enough from close quarters to do the work. It had to be quiet. If he was caught out on this job he would have to flee the country but nowhere would be far enough away. The back-up men needed higher calibre, rapid-fire pistols and a rifle for long-range shots. If they became involved it would be a street battle and the need for secrecy blown out of the sky.

Two cars would be needed and stolen for the night. The Apprentice hadn't stolen cars since he was a young teenager and now considered the act beneath his dignity. He thought of those who specialised in the trade. Like David Logue, a local guy in Blackhill, but considered too unreliable, too desperate. He thought of William Lobban, Tootsie, who had been moaning and pestering anyone for work. But Lobban's uncle, Billy Manson, was a close associate of the target's family. Needs must when the devil drives – The Apprentice stole the cars himself. Now he was ready.

Arty was enjoying his first time out from prison in six years. Having first torn up his early release application papers he eventually relented. Moving to Noranside Prison in Angus marked the official start of his training for freedom, including a couple of days at home.

He'd had a good day – a couple of pints in the pub in the afternoon and a meal at the Café India that night. Glasgow curries – you couldn't beat them. It was like he had never been away.

But Arty had been away and life in the city had changed. He was The Godfather's son and couldn't see beyond the old man's reputation. So he had stood in the pub talking loudly about his hit list – Ferris, Glover, Hanlon, McLean, McGraw, Bagan – as if joking with paid lackeys back in his cell. He bought some weaponry, stocking up his arsenal for his imminent release. Around the pub cold eyes, faked smiles and thin lips grimaced. There was going to be more trouble.

The Apprentice stepped quickly from the bushes and headed directly across the road when he saw the rotund shape of Arty leave his father's house. He was heading the 70 yards to his own home and, no doubt, bed. This was the opportunity. Two-handed, the long snouted pistol was pointed directly at the startled fat man's head as The Apprentice stepped closer and closer.

'You'd better get your father to bail you out of this, you fat bastard,' The Apprentice broke his own rules of silence. Thirty yards up the street the two Londoners watched, guns at the ready.

'Just you wait here,' blurted Arty. 'A'm gonnae get ma faither.'

But The Apprentice's contract was for the son, not the old man. He shot at young Thompson's head. The first bullet caught Arty on the cheek, spinning him around and dumping him on the ground. Arty whimpered, scrambling on his hands and knees towards his own house. The second bullet shattered his rib cage, puncturing a lung. The third pierced his anus, travelling through his stomach and into his heart. The Apprentice paused for a second, considering a close-range headshot. The man was dying and the silencer hadn't been that silent. Time to go.

The hit squad drove to two different scrap dealers where the cars were immediately wrecked and squashed into two-foot cubes of metal. By the time The Apprentice sat in a taxi the Londoners had been paid and were on their way home. His car was waiting for him, a tank full of petrol and a packed case in the boot. He would drive south, maybe Newcastle, maybe Manchester. Tomorrow it would be Amsterdam, his favourite city for loose women and good quality hash. In Amsterdam he would lose himself and chill out for months as the streets of Glasgow were set ablaze.

When Tracy Thompson ran into the street, her brother lay

crumpled in a pool of blood, but was conscious. 'What's happened?' she shrieked.

'I've been shot, hen,' gasped her brother. 'I think I'm going tae collapse.' His mother, Rita, rushed to kneel at his side while old Arthur scoured the street, a loaded gun in his fist. They carried Arty's bleeding body into his brother Billy's car and sped him to the Royal. No one telephoned the police, of course. Forty-three minutes after his arrival Arthur Thompson junior was certified dead. Outside the Royal stood Arthur Thompson and his son, Billy, smoking and talking.

'It must've been Paul Ferris,' said Billy. As usual Arthur Thompson said nothing. Two policemen overheard the comment.

It was 0018 hours on 18 August 1991, the minute war was declared in Glasgow.

he tom-toms were working overtime from the instant of Arty's death. When I was told it didn't come as a surprise and, to be honest, I hardly felt anything for him though I was sorry for his wife and his sister. Arty had lived in a fantasyland of his own making. He'd shopped and traded bodies for years. His father's street credibility had pay-rolled the havoc Arty continued to create from his prison cell. If I felt anything it was relief that a nuisance was gone.

Back in London, a couple of weeks after Arty's killing, I received word that I was due at Hamilton Sheriff Court on a road traffic offence. That's not what irked me but the whispers that the police were searching for Bobby Glover and me in connection with several shooting incidents. After a telephone consultation with my lawyer, Peter Forbes, it was agreed that I should come back and hand myself in. First I should write a detailed account of my movements covering the time of Arty's death – good advice and I completed it promptly. Totally against the grain I telephoned the police advising them of my return and availability for interview with my lawyer.

'Here we go again,' I thought. 'The end of peace.'

My court appearance at Hamilton had been conveniently postponed at the last minute and replaced by a posse of police arresting myself and Bobby. We'll call the arresting officer DI Paddy Death – a fanatical bull of a man and well known to me. In the police car he demanded unnecessarily, 'Whit's yer name?' Like it was a bit late for introductions. 'Whit's yer name?' The guy had to be joking given he'd just arrested me on a warrant in a court where I'd been cited and that I had so many dealings with him I was almost sending him Christmas hate mail. But he insisted.

'Your fucking name's Paddy Death and you can call me Nostradamus,' I eventually replied.

He went berserk. Spitting and huffing, lifting his fist, desperate to shove it into my face but just managing to restrain himself. It was a rule, albeit petty, that he had to ascertain my identity. Just like the rule that in a section two arrest he was meant to take me to the nearest police station. We were in Hamilton, 20 miles from Glasgow, yet they drove past six or seven police stations to take me into their own gaff at Baird Street.

For the statutory six hours they questioned us about Arty's murder but ended up charging us with the kneecapping of Gillen. With that we were whisked to Barlinnie Prison's segregation unit, the Wendy House, and given the status of Category A prisoners – most unusual for untried men. The Wendy House comes with extras – guards wearing riot gear watching you 24 hours a day.

Seven days later we were bussed down to Kilmarnock Sheriff Court. In the holding dungeon, directly underneath the courtroom, we were slung into separate cells and had our cigarettes confiscated as a fire risk. You can fester for hours in holding and are usually allowed a few basic comforts such as a cup of tea and a smoke. After all, we were innocent men. I took grave exception to their health and safety rules and started howling and kicking the cell door in protest. Bobby was laughing at me and telling me to cool it. 'These guys are just taking a rise, Paul.' Bobby was one of the few people who could always make me see sense and I started laughing at myself. 'Tell ye what – I'll sing you a song,' he offered and did. Bobby was a great fan of big band music and could hold a tune. He treated me to his favourite:

> For the shark has
> Pretty teeth, dear
> Which show up
> Pearly white . . .

The strains of 'Mack the Knife' floated upstairs into the well of the court, infiltrating the sombre proceedings. Twice the sheriff sent officials down to ask us to be quiet and then to threaten us with contempt of court. We just laughed and sang louder:

On a side walk
One Sunday morning
Lies a body oozing life
There's someone
Shaking round the corner
Bet that someone's Mack the Knife

When Bobby was called I was still laughing and he was still singing as he was led out of the cell. He was released immediately on the Procurator Fiscal's decision – an extremely unusual and totally unexplained move for someone who has been held under Category A. By the time I arrived in front of the sheriff Bobby had been whisked away. I was to be held on remand and returned to the Wendy House under strict security in spite of them having exactly the same case against each of us. Bobby hadn't even asked to be released by applying for bail – the PF simply decided to let him go. The decision is usually based on information from the police but the PF wasn't obliged to explain. At the time I thought they were getting at me and not my pal. Bobby's release delighted me. All the way back to Glasgow I was still smiling at his rendition of 'Mack the Knife.'

Oh, the shark has
Pretty teeth, dear
Which show up
Pearly white

I didn't know then they were to be the last words I would hear my friend say.

The Wendy House was no game. Isolation was the main aim with prisoners being forbidden contact with each other. Built on a single floor you could call out to those in adjoining cells but everyone else would hear your conversation and the effort required made for brief chats at best. Most of the men in the segregation unit were too preoccupied by their plight to have the will for idle banter.

Contact with staff was a joke. All day, every day, they dressed in full riot gear – helmets, body armour, shields and batons drawn. They only ever opened one cell at a time and always team-handed. In the mornings when they opened my cell for slopping out, showers and so on, I was forced to step into the corridor surrounded by the Riot Squad – two at the front, two at the back. Playing them at their own absurd game I dubbed them the Motorcycle Display Team, making appropriate engine revving noises during our wanders. I'd make a point of needing to repeat the trek several times and always opened the lid to my chamber pot allowing the fetid stink of my night's piss and shit to waft all around me. Small rebellions kept me sane.

The night was a different matter. Every 15 minutes they opened my peephole with a grating and clanging noise and shouted out, 'Ferris, are you okay?' A fluorescent tube with a harsh white glow was kept on in my cell for 24 hours a day. Repeatedly I asked them to switch it off but they refused. Eventually I took matters into my own hands and smashed it, relieving my aching eyes and pounding head. That was me on report, as if they could treat me much worse. They kept peering through the spy-hole but in the pitch darkness they had to call out, 'Are ye in there, Ferris?' I'd sit silently till they opened the door. Another report. I added to the device and placed a piece of paper over the peephole on which I'd written, 'I'M NO IN'. They didn't get the joke and sent the wing governor down to give me a bad time. As he opened the door he shone a torch into the cell to find me sitting on my bunk pretending to read a book. 'Could you hold that light steady for a while, I'm almost finished.' They lacked a sense of humour and I was put on another report. In Bar-L I was wising them up, playing them at their own big boys' silliness but outside life was far from funny.

Bobby and Joe were under 24-hour surveillance by the police. Cool customers the pair of them, they just went about their business. One night outside the Cottage Bar Joe and McGraw had a very public falling out. 'You'll no' treat people like that,' shouted Joe, grabbing McGraw by the throat. 'You're nothing but a fucking grass – always have been. I'll fucking see to you.' Joe stormed away, leaving The Licensee shaking.

Joe turned to him once more and said, 'You're finished. You're fucking finished.'

Almost a month to the day from Arty's killing the telephone rang in the Glover household. Eileen Glover answered and listened to a familiar voice ask for Bobby. It was William Lobban doing the usual – moaning about a lack of money and asking for help. Bobby being Bobby agreed, even when Lobban asked to meet him elsewhere, away from the safety of his home. The man was still on the run from prison and everyone knew the Glovers' house was watched by the police. Coming off the telephone, Bobby Glover made a call to Joe Hanlon. Bobby's car had been impounded in connection with the Gillen investigation. Could Joe give him a lift? Joe being Joe agreed to help his friend.

The two men drove off for the last time.

43.

I WAS GIVEN IT BUT . . .
by Reg McKay

Joe lay in the front and Bobby in the back of the car. There was blood everywhere. Early in the morning a passer-by had spotted the bodies lying in Joe's blue Ford Orion car in Darleith Street and ran to the nearest building for help – the Cottage Bar, Bobby's pub. Alan Cross, the barman, ran out on to the street and heaved at the sight of the two familiar men. Cross would be the man to notify the police. It was early in the morning of Arthur Thompson junior's funeral. The cortège would pass by the murder scene. Street talk had it as a mark of respect to the Thompsons. But was it?

Eileen Glover was frantic about Bobby's failure to return. She'd hardly slept a minute all night listening for his footsteps. She telephoned the font of all local information – Thomas McGraw. Margaret McGraw answered and said her husband was not at home. A short while later, McGraw appeared at the Glover house and told Eileen bluntly that Bobby had been shot dead. Eileen rushed from the house to Darleith Street, pushing her way through the police cordon. 'That's my man in there. Let me past. That's Bobby,' she screamed. The police asked her husband's name. 'Bobby Glover,' she cried.

Eileen was immediately detained and taken to Shettleston police station. For nine hours they grilled her on one question, 'How did you know your husband had been murdered before we had identified him?' Thomas McGraw, The Licensee, knew that Bobby Glover and Joe Hanlon had been shot dead hours before the police. How?

The night before the murders, Edward Barnes had been drinking at the home of Snaz Adams, McGraw's brother-in-law and associate. The next morning, Barney returned to Snaz's house for a hair-of-the-dog. As Barney was putting the kettle on Snaz answered the telephone in the hall squealing, 'Oh no! He shouldn't have been there.' Snaz came into the room and told Barney that Bobby and Joe had been murdered. Barney forgot the overheard comment till shortly later and then it became clear. Joe Hanlon should not have been there that night. The bullets were intended for Bobby alone.

The police were struggling to unravel the events of the night. A blue Transit van was reported being parked in Darleith Street during the night but gone by daybreak. The police surmised that the two men had been shot elsewhere and driven to Darleith Street in the blue Ford Orion. There the driver had abandoned the car and the bodies and driven away in the van. The investigation and trial would be full of reported sightings of that blue van. For many on the streets it was a red herring avoiding the main questions. The men were under 24-hour surveillance so where were the police? Who would risk driving through Glasgow even at night with two bloody bodies slumped on the floor? Unless they knew they were safe from detection? The police had tracked the car every minute since Arty's murder only to lose it for nine hours on the fateful night.

Locals would say that they had seen a policeman in mourning at the Thompson house and they would be watching him carefully from now on. Rumours spread about a rogue cop acting as an executioner and everyone named their favourite suspect based on beatings received, fit-ups and known associations with powerful police informers – Thompson and McGraw. If it wasn't the police – they did turn a blind eye.

It didn't take The Apprentice long to find out what had been going on. 'William Lobban was paid £10,000 and a gun for setting up Bobby – giving the Judas kiss. Joe was there by accident but he was there. Both were shot by contract outsiders and taken into a back room of the Caravel Bar. McGraw then telephoned Arthur Thompson who sent over a delegation to check they were dead. I liked Bobby and Joe – they were good, honourable men.' When the murder investigation had ground to a halt but was suddenly reopened by the police, McGraw would demolish the Caravel Bar late one night without warning or planning consent. How did McGraw know detectives were due to investigate the bar the next day?

When asked about the killings of Bobby Glover and Joe Hanlon, Arthur Thompson senior is alleged to have said, 'I was given it but it didn't suit me.'

When the tears started I thought they'd never stop. I'd been told of Bobby and Joe's murders by Peter Forbes and was glad it was that calm, gentle man who passed on the bad news. I've no idea what he said for some time afterwards. My grief kept gripping me and shaking me in my seat. Pictures and memories of those two – us three – together flit through my mind as vivid and as real as the first time. Darker pictures of their broken, bloody bodies slumped and crumpled on the floor of that car. I wept more than I can remember weeping, ever. Horror snaps of the instant they knew they were about to die, the pistol pushed hard into the backs of their heads. Did they kill one first, then the other? Did one hear his mate shot and wait his own turn? Unashamedly, I howled.

I was grateful it had been a legal visit and no grim-faced screw had been peering over me in my state. As the meeting drew to a close I knew I'd have to pull myself together and not appear weak in front of the Riot Squad. Through their visors they watched for the tiniest crack in your veneer and they went for it tooth and nail. I had to buck up and face up for my sake and for the memory of my dead comrades. There were three and now there was one.

The next few days were a lost blur. Gradually the details of their deaths were percolating through and registering in my brain. With the information came questions and anger and fury and I wished ill on all men. Bad enough if they'd died by accident, but someone slaughtered them. Who?

'Was it my fault?' I kept asking myself. 'If they'd never met me would they still be alive?' Self-searching that broke my heart and tortured my soul. And self-pity, wallowing in it I was, as if making up for all the years of never running away, never telling, always fighting back. All the hardmen who'd tried to break me failed. My *pals' deaths splintered me into a million morsels and scattered me to the winds. Those days in that cell I changed and have never been the same since.*

Every time a screw turned up I bucked up. For a while I gave them peace but knew I had to act like my old self, at least when they were around, or they would try to take advantage. So back to my old routines of the triple journeys up and down the corridor, complaints about the lights and a refusal to lay my plates down as specified. Smashing the plastic plate and glass when they made a fuss. Going on hunger strike. The constant light and 15-minute checks were driving me to distraction – I couldn't even shelter my grief in the privacy of darkness. I complained and griped and got nowhere so I smashed it again. This time they let it be and added a distraction. Pushing newspapers under the door.

Bobby and Joe's death was front page news every day. The police had carried out a highly orchestrated and pre-publicised armed raid on the Thompsons' house. Scores of marksmen, helicopters, newspaper reporters and photographers turned up at dawn. Old Arthur made a song and dance about it, ably represented by his long-time lawyer, Joe Beltrami. The whole escapade smacked of farce and a set-up. The only dubious item found in the house was a bulletproof vest. Rita must have been doing extra cleaning that week.

Mick Healy, an escaped bank robber and at one time listed as Scotland's most wanted man, wrote to the tabloids declaring, 'I'm not an assassin. You couldn't pay me in gold to shoot a man in the back. Bobby Glover and Joe Hanlon never had any reason to do me no harm.'

John Masterton, a Londoner and a campaigner for the release of the Kray twins, was allegedly kidnapped by two gunmen and driven to Glasgow in the back of a van. As the vehicle sped up the motorway he was held out of an open door before having a gun barrel pushed in his mouth and the trigger pulled. All the way he was asked only one question, 'Who killed Glover and Hanlon?' The gun was empty. When they arrived in Glasgow, apparently the men continued to torture him for hours, asking the same question, dangling him by his ankles out of the window of a high flat, drenching him in petrol and playing with a box of matches. Eventually he was dumped on the road outside the Royal Infirmary.

Every day with every headline, Bobby and Joe's murders were rehashed. Somebody even suggested that I had ordered their murders. The stories were sensational and hysterical but never failed to get to me. I took solace in thinking how bad it must be for Eileen Glover, Sharon Hanlon and the kids – I felt angry for them. Rumours were rife and printed as fact.

When the screws saw that they were not reaching me, they pushed burning newspapers under my cell door and growled, 'You'll get what your pals got, Ferris,' then wandered away laughing gleefully. I'd scream at them and demand they lifted their visors and show me their faces. They never did.

After three months in the Wendy House I won an appeal for bail. People warned me that Thompson and a pack of bounty hunters were out to get me but I wasn't going to run away. This was my place and I had to find out who killed my friends. Going about my business I was constantly followed by several police cars – the same treatment which had been handed out to Karen Owens while I was in jail. They would park by the kerb and stare in the lounge window. She'd been lifted several times for questioning and her home raided just as often.

After a few days of this I stomped down into Baillieston police station to make a formal complaint. As soon as they eyed me I was surrounded by a platoon of blue uniforms and advised I was under arrest. I thought they hadn't realised that I'd been released and were arresting me as an escapee. When we hit the road driving the few miles to London Road police station there were motorbike outriders front and rear, a convoy of cars, armed police and the helicopter hovering above. Within an hour I was advised that I'd been charged with the murder of Arthur Thompson Junior and was heading back to the Wendy House. I was innocent but the police, aided and abetted by a helper, had other plans.

DENNIS WHO?
by Reg McKay

The young man was naked and spreadeagled, his wrists and ankles securely tied to the corners of his bed. Two older men, Reeves and Wilkinson, had been holding him captive for days, leaving the house one at a time to withdraw large sums of money from his bank account and buy food and drink.

Reeves was an escaped patient from the state secure hospital in Broadmoor that housed some of the most dangerous, unstable people in England. But Reeves was in good company, his sadistic imagination being matched by Wilkinson. A few days into the ordeal the kidnappers became bored and their hostage became the entertainment.

First they lashed him with a car aerial, slicing the flesh of his back, buttocks and legs, rubbing table salt hard into the 122 weals, enjoying his pleas for mercy. Next the long handle of a frying pan was forced all the way up his anus to prepare him. As the young man lay bleeding and sobbing into the soiled mattress, one by one they buggered him. Not finished, Reeves held a knife at his neck and grunted, 'Lick the shit off and if you retch I'll cut your throat,' thrusting his limp penis at his captive's mouth. Wilkinson was aroused by the man's suffering. Laughing, he pulled the man's head back and shoved his faeces-smeared erection down his victim's throat again and again.

More days of the same treatment followed till the young man threw himself through a plate-glass window and escaped. Reeves and Wilkinson fled to the Netherlands. When Wilkinson returned to England he was arrested for attempted murder, indecent assault, extortion and robbery. Back in the Netherlands Reeves was jailed for the murder of a policeman. Facing all of the charges himself and a possible 20-year sentence, Wilkinson traded. He swore under oath that Danny Vaughan and John Hass had confessed in the prison exercise yard to robbery as members of the infamous Transit Gang who plagued England in the late '80s. The two men denied the confession but were convicted on Wilkinson's evidence alone.

Superintendent Mervyn Davies appeared at Wilkinson's trial telling the court how helpful he had been in assisting the police in convicting dangerous armed criminals and that his help was ongoing. For the repeated sexual assault of the young man, attempted murder and all the rest, Dennis Wilkinson was given a very lenient eight-year sentence.

Dennis Wilkinson had found a role in life. Over a period of four years he appeared in 12 different English courts giving evidence against 15 men. All had voluntarily confessed to him, according to Wilkinson. But life was difficult and he wrote to the *Sunday People* confessing he had lied about Vaughan and claiming that a policeman, we'll call him Sergeant Ryder, had passed him Vaughan's confidential investigation record. There was bad blood between the policeman and Danny Vaughan.

Wilkinson also wrote to the high-ranking police officers involved in the cases he had perjured and asked for help. Wilkinson was given a new name and a new National Insurance number and was moved to Dumfries in Scotland. But old habits die hard and soon he found himself on remand in Dumfries Prison charged with extortion and kidnap of a farmer called Charlie Stewart. He was a low-risk prisoner but mysteriously was moved to Bar-L overnight. Not just the prison but the segregation unit. According to Donald Findlay QC, 'This was a most unusual move which would have required authorisation by the prison service, the police and the government.'

Within a few days of the move, Wilkinson was spotted by another prisoner, Mark Leech, a veteran of some 60 British prisons who knew all about this man. But he was no longer known as Wilkinson. Now he was called Dennis Woodman. Whatever his name, the prison authorities, the police, the prosecution and the government all knew his background. He was a serial perjurer, Scotland's first supergrass, and he was moved to Bar-L for one reason – Paul Ferris.

The code of the streets dictates that no women, children, elderly people or innocent parties be assaulted. If they are present, then the action should be postponed to another day. They should never be targeted as a way to get to an enemy. Many of the public and the commentators would have us believe this code is just a myth and quote the rising tide of seemingly mindless violence and brutal muggings in support of their viewpoint. Some of this behaviour has been caused by drugs. A violent junkie is not a gangster but simply a desperate addict. Yet the code does exist and is upheld by a surprising number of gangsters who have to be encouraged to speak of such incidences, modesty coming high on their list of personal values.

During the days of the famous post office raids by the Barlanark Team, TC Campbell recalls aborting a raid on a shop after weeks of preparation in order to rescue a woman being raped. The names of his associates that night are well known in the annals of crime yet none grumbled at the diversion. Another time, the same gang were confronted by a typically tiny, vociferous Glasgow woman who threatened to batter the strapping, heavily armed crooks with her handbag. They left the scene. When TC Campbell was charged with the horrendous murder of the Doyle family, those on the streets knew he was not guilty – TC Campbell would never knowingly hurt the innocent.

On the other hand, the Welsh brothers were despised in the city precisely because they applied no rules, no limits. They were deemed to be low animal life compared to the established leaders of organised crime such as the Thompsons. Paul's father, Willie Ferris, was about to find out otherwise.

By Reg McKay

The media was so full of rumours of revenge contracts and killings I couldn't blame Anne Marie for becoming scared and worried. It seemed that the investigation and trial were conducted in the tabloids long before the first court session. Apparently the city was at war and the teams were stockpiling firearms for the final battle. If they could ceremoniously kill my two friends, why not my son? Anne Marie made a public plea to leave young Paul out of it.

My old man, Willie Ferris, visited me in prison and he was angry. 'You shouldn't be locked up in here, son,' he insisted. 'That fucking grass should get you out.' He meant Arthur Thompson and I pleaded with my old man to leave it be.

Willie Ferris knew his own mind. 'You're a fucking grass,' he spat, looking up into Thompson's face. 'My boy shouldn't be in prison and you know it.'

My father's pride and joy had always been his car. Since his accident he'd qualified for the government's Motability scheme in buying a new car – a small Vauxhall Nova. My mother would nag at him to take care, but still he found a sneaky way to wash and polish it till it was gleaming. Willie also needed the car to get about, as his legs were barely able to support him.

It started with the slashing of tyres – not one but four at a time for maximum inconvenience and expense. After a few goes at that they upped the ante and poured acid over the bodywork. My old man knew who was behind it – there are no secrets in Blackhill. With his two sticks he went round to the Thompsons, knocked on the door and asked to speak to big Arthur. When the door was slammed in his face my father gave Thompson a Glasgow sherricking – shouting, bawling and decrying him in the street. His reward was a severe beating from a bunch of young guys.

My old man had the heart of a lion and went back to that door every time something happened to his car. My mother, Jenny, begged him to let it go but she knew it was a hopeless argument. The old man was scared of no one and fought his own battles. One night coming back from the pub, hobbling slowly up the road with his walking sticks, he decided he'd had enough and was going to take Thompson to task again. Standing outside the heavily fortified house, my small, 63-year-old father invited Arthur Thompson out for a square go to settle the trouble once and for all. To encourage the battle he used his walking sticks to smash some windows.

A bunch of young guys came streaming out of the Thompsons' house battering my father with baseball bats and hammers. He fought fiercely but his legs wouldn't hold him and he hit the deck. Still they thumped into him. As he lay bruised and bloody on the pavement someone leaned over him and slowly slashed the full length of his face. He was found an hour later trying to get to his feet, trying to get home.

The harassment didn't stop there, with Willie Ferris's car being torched one night. Still he fought back. My mother and sisters suggested he move from Blackhill. 'This is my place,' he said. 'I'm moving for nobody.' People who met my father loved him for his character as I did, but it would be the death of him eventually. Dying as he lived, with his self-respect intact.

The assaults on my father were front-page news and often the first I'd hear of them would be as the papers were pushed under my cell door in the Wendy House. I knew this was being done to get at me. I knew if I were free they wouldn't dare harm a hair on his head. I knew all that and couldn't do a thing about it. My brother Billy was still languishing behind bars after 18 years. It was clear the prison and police service were giving him special treatment by holding him in. The lawyers' view was that his release was delayed because of me. After all, he'd been a young man when jailed and had spent a great deal of his prison time doing good works – raising funds for charities, designing and building toys and equipment for children with disabilities. The trouble our father was facing was driving Billy spare and tempting him to escape. Our old man told Billy, 'If you get out, Billy, that's all they need to bury Paul and that's just what they want.' He was right. We were tormented and helpless.

Willie Ferris never made a complaint to the police or named his attackers. His code was to deal with these problems himself. Now that he is sadly dead it can be revealed by me and not by the Ferris family it was Arthur Thompson senior who leaned over the old man's battered body and slashed his face from forehead to chin. The Godfather did not live up to his benign public image.

By Reg McKay

PAUL FERRIS & REG McKAY

47.

A GALLERY OF ROGUES

The display of might was impressive for a country not at war or ruled by a fascist dictatorship. A convoy of police cars, armed officers, motorcycle outriders and a helicopter flying overhead with me shackled in the middle. It was 23 March 1992 and the first of my journeys from Bar-L to Glasgow High Court where, in the famous North Courthouse, Lord McCluskey and a jury would decide my fate. We didn't know it then but the proceedings would last for 54 days, the longest trial in the history of Scottish criminal law.

I now faced 12 charges, including Arty's murder, Gillen's kneecapping, the attempted murder of Arthur Thompson Snr by running him over, the attempted murder of Robert Johnstone by shooting him through the neck, assault and a stack of related charges. A throng gathered outside the court while hard-faced men of the streets, scribblers of the press and full-time trial watchers competed for seats. In the public gallery the first two rows of seats were cordoned off. The court building was sealed and everyone entering was questioned and searched by the police, a metal detector checking for concealed weapons.

The inimitable Donald Findlay QC had a stage to match his style, prowess and brilliance. In the other corner, prosecuting, was the Advocate-depute, Roderick McDonald QC. Even as I sat there, my freedom dangling by a thread, I could understand the public's curiosity at what this circus was all about and how it would end. It must have been like this at public hangings.

When they called the charges, Bobby and Joe were listed as my co-accused for the murder of Arty. Dead men, long gone, yet they were charged. My emotional wounds reopened as their names were read out. Bobby was also accused of being my accomplice in kneecapping Gillen. An ideal opportunity had raised itself – to blame Bobby and Joe for the murder of Arty – but I couldn't go down that road. They were two innocent, honourable men and I refused to sully their memory. Anyway, they were innocent. I was innocent but I had a cast of rogues to deal with first.

The list of witnesses on both sides was a who's who of crime in Glasgow. Many so-called associates had been expressing their worries at what was to happen, declaring themselves useless as defence witnesses. Our code requires that if asked to stand as a defence witness you do so – no questions asked – but many men I considered allies were backing off. Who did and didn't turn up was intriguing.

Charles Glackin and Gordon Ross, two prime examples, had been sworn friends to Bobby and Joe and were cited by me. Their evidence wasn't crucial to my case, thank God, though it might well have been. Days into my trial they were spotted sitting in the public benches. A legal ruling was immediately made that they had to be debarred as witnesses. Years later Gordon Ross was telling me about being called as a witness at the forthcoming trial of Tam Bagan and how he didn't want to appear. 'I'll just sit in the gallery,' he said, explaining his strategy to be excluded.

'Haven't you done that once before?' I asked and he had the good grace to blush.

Thomas McGraw had been implicated in the Gillen kneecapping. Gillen claimed I shot him under orders from McGraw who'd also attended the event. My defence said I was elsewhere with McGraw that night helping a wounded man, Alex Kerr, get treatment at the Victoria Infirmary. Not only was McGraw not charged but, as a listed prosecution witness, he never appeared. Yet the only way the prosecution could ruin my alibi was to get The Licensee in the box. He failed to turn up and no warrant was ever issued for his arrest. They couldn't afford to put McGraw up for questioning – he knew too much about too many policemen and prosecution agents. Even at the end of the trial Lord McCluskey commented that the jury would have to make their own minds up about why so many witnesses failed to appear and not been pursued by the prosecution. It was clear to me that the list dripped with deals.

In contrast to that lot, young Gary McCrae, an honest and non-violent man, was absolutely solid. He detailed the time he and I had spent together on the night Arty was murdered and made himself available. He was a non-player risking a bullet to tell the truth, because, before and during the trial, Arthur Thompson was laying serious threats against all my defence witnesses. Bullets were being delivered, anonymous letters, children were being threatened, beatings handed out. You might ask how he knew who my witnesses were since the list was privileged to the officials and the accused. His many police friends would know, of course.

Arthur Thompson gave evidence against me and another cardinal rule bit the dust. There are only two reasons why he should've given evidence for the prosecution – to ruin their case or because he had no alternative, being in custody. He walked freely into the witness box. Given I was charged with his own attempted murder he'd obviously made a complaint to the police. So, overnight he wasn't run over because of his poor singing. If he believed it was me, he should have stayed silent and taken care of me himself.

In the witness box he put on a charade of The Godfather mythology. He was meant to be tough, gruff, condescending and full of one-liner put-downs, so Arthur played the role as he never did in real life. Old Arthur dismissed his involvement in crime and refuted the claim that he earned £100,000 per week from loan sharking alone. 'It's just the press,' he said. His son had nothing to do with drugs or guns, ever. Denying his possible involvement in the killing of Bobby and Joe, he came out with a line that brought me back to that first meeting between us, 'The boy Hanlon I've known since he was three years old. I knew his father well.' I sat in the dock and fumed at how he'd claimed to know and respect my father before it became more convenient to torture the old man then, for the first time, asked myself who killed Joe's father.

Many of the press entourage claim that Arthur Thompson came out of the trial with his reputation intact but they made the mistake of reporting only the words. I scribbled a note to Donald Findlay suggesting he ask Thompson who he thought killed his son. A lawyer will never ask a question unless he knows the answer. This was a risk, but Findlay took it. I was inviting Thompson to protect his reputation by declaring that it had not been me. It was also my chance to get the final measure of the man. Thompson turned in the witness box, moved his bullish neck forward and glaring directly at me, in full view of the jury, said, 'We all know who shot him. We *think so.' Thompson held my stare for about a minute, a long interval in court time, showing the jury who he wanted found guilty. Years later I shared this scenario with Charlie Kray, older brother of the twins. The old-time gangster was disgusted by Arthur Thompson's behaviour. But there was more to come.*

When Thompson left the box there was a file of 300 witnesses ranging from the coerced to the bribed to the honest and the loyal. Many claimed they'd been bullied and threatened by the police to attend. One woman said the police had reminded her of the Ice Cream Wars and the Doyle murders and we all knew they meant that innocent people could get killed, be jailed. I just prayed that the jury knew. One self-confessed drug addict and perjurer, Bernard Docherty, came out with a cock-and-bull story about me offering him £30,000 to assist in the murder of Arty.

At the time Docherty sounded convincing, but after the trial he told another story. Two detectives had hassled him for ages. Picking him up on outstanding charges, they kept him in the cells long enough for his withdrawal from heroin and Temgesics to kick in. Stripped naked and sick, Docherty was punched by the policemen who told him they wanted Ferris off the streets for a long time. They told him his own life was in danger and that of his wife, Sharon. The policemen told him that he hadn't really been in my house trying to sell me jewellery but to organise the murder of Arthur Thompson junior and he'd better agree. They had his statements prepared for him and watched him sign each one, his hand shaking, his stomach cramped, his whole system writhing with the descending gloom of cold turkey. Docherty was put under police protection but ran away several times, only to be caught and given the same treatment. He was promised a lot of money, a new identity and a house in another city if he gave the evidence they wanted. He had a choice – a long stretch in prison on trumped-up charges of police assault if he survived that long. The police threatened they would let it be known that Bernard Docherty had been involved in the murder of Arthur Thompson junior – a certain death sentence on the streets.

Finally, Docherty was dragged in front of a court official we'll call Bitter to sign his statements. As Docherty read over the papers, the official promised several times that all his outstanding charges would be dropped but only if he gave the evidence as written. Docherty signed the statement, gave the evidence and was promptly dumped by the police. No money, no new life, no house. He ended up sleeping in abandoned cars with his wife and baby and was taken to court on all his outstanding charges.

David Logue was a Blackhill guy and well known as a car thief. His evidence centred on a Nissan Bluebird he'd stolen then destroyed for a bloke called Gary, later revealed as William Lobban. The prosecution linked that car with the shooting of Arty, yet it was me in the dock and not Lobban. I can never forgive David Logue for appearing as a Crown witness but later he would explain his motivation as best he could.

Every street in Blackhill was being patrolled by two coppers. In the middle of the night they would batter doors and drag people away for interview. Failing to find Logue, they left the message that he was wanted in connection with Arty's murder – the black cap message. Logue was attacked on the streets a number of times and panicked. The police warned him he was the next person to be shot. Before long he was on the witness protection programme from November 1991 all the way through to his court appearance in April 1992. When it was all over for him he staggered on the brink of a mental breakdown, contemplating suicide. The police just abandoned him like that, his usefulness over.

Back in the Wendy House one night I was passed a copy of a letter that had been circulated in Glasgow pubs and delivered to the houses of some of my defence witnesses. On Crown Office headed paper, dated 12 February 1992 and addressed to me at Barlinnie, it read:

> Dear Sir,
> I refer to your letter of 12 January 1992 (sent on your behalf) which was passed to the Lord Advocate who acknowledge's [sic] the assistance given by you to the Stathclyde [sic] Serious Crime Squad over several years.
> However, inquires [sic] have shown that your prior assistance was for 'Monetary Consideration' and not 'Public Spirited'. Accordingly the Lord Advocate feels unable to intervene in the matters outstanding against you.
> Yours faithfully,
> Mr A. Vannet, Deputy Crown Agent.

I was pole-axed. The letter bluntly stated I'd been a paid grass for years. It was designed to discredit me, kill off the loyalty of my defence witnesses and serve as my death warrant. I hadn't a clue who Mr A. Vannet was, had never received the letter from him and wondered who had gone to all this trouble.

The spelling errors in the letter were the first chink, soon followed through by A. Vannet himself who testified that the letter was an obvious forgery. He always signed his name A.D. Vannet and Crown Office paper was light blue, not white. The letter had been presented to the court by Donald Findlay and went some way to proving there was an orchestrated conspiracy to discredit me and weaken my case. While the good Mr Vannet helped establish my innocence I was left with an outstanding problem – give a dog a bad name and it'll stick. I would have to make sure that the letter would be dismissed entirely in the views of my associates and other players. Such a message had a lethal effect and would come back to haunt me in future years.

Then came the Crown's top witness – Dennis Woodman. Ever since Mark Leech had tipped us off about Woodman's history, Peter Forbes had been doing his sleuth work and confirming everything we'd been told. Sure enough, Woodman claimed I'd confessed to murdering Arty while I was playing him at chess in the Wendy House. Let me put the record straight on that one. I've played chess since I was about 12 years old when taught the rules at one of those summer camps for kids from deprived areas. I've loved the game ever since and take it seriously. In the segregation unit you can play other prisoners by having a full board each and shouting out your moves to your unseen opponent. Before Woodman arrived, I'd played another prisoner and beaten him every time. That same prisoner played Woodman and beat him easily. I didn't play Dennis Woodman at chess because he was useless, no challenge and a waste of my time.

Woodman's claims that I confessed to him were laughable to anyone who knew me. For years I'd been recording all events with the police, I was that suspicious. But the Crown believed I confessed to a complete stranger whom they knew to be a serial perjurer. Nearing the end of the marathon trial it was clear that the prosecution were basing their entire case on Woodman's evidence.

Prior to the perjurer's testimony another prisoner had slipped me the wink that Woodman was spending hours at a time out of his cell in the company of Grant Kidd of Barlinnie's staff. Segregation unit prisoners are meant to be in isolation all the time. I challenged Kidd about his sweeteners for Woodman and he denied them, cursing. A day later a wad of papers was stuck under my cell door. It was a photocopy of the log for the segregation unit, clearly showing that Woodman and Kidd were spending long periods together in the screw's office. I have the papers still and they must have been a gift from an anonymous prison warden – one with a sense of justice. There are good men in the prison service but too often their efforts are negated by the actions of their corrupt and violent colleagues.

When word hit the grapevine that Woodman was giving evidence against me, those who knew him started alerting me. His brother-in-law and co-accused was one surprising source of assistance. Mark Irvine warned me of Woodman's record as supergrass and his intention to barter his evidence for early release. All prisoners' mail in the Wendy House is opened. Someone at Barlinnie held Irvine's letter back from me. What they didn't know was that the industrious Peter Forbes had visited Mark Irvine and been given a hand-written copy of the letter. Now why would they do that?

Peter Forbes was soon to become a target himself. Woodman claimed Peter had offered him £60,000 and £20,000 per year for the rest of his life to withdraw his evidence against me. The honourable and honest lawyer was dumbstruck. Such an accusation could lead to his professional and personal ruin. We eventually discovered that Woodman had tried the same scam years before. He had a well practised, destructive modus operandi. Forbes was totally exonerated from these accusations.

When Woodman took to the stand I could almost hear Donald Findlay crack his knuckles preparing to give him his best shot. For five days Woodman was questioned and with each passing hour his evidence became more hysterical and more absurd. His claims had upped a gear to include my confession to Arty's murder, kneecapping Gillen, dealing in drugs and almost everything else under the sun. If the man's claims were outrageous his appearance was bizarre. He wore a long shabby coat and a shirt five times too big, giving his neck a scrawny-turkey look. Everything he wore was old, ill-fitting, scruffy. At one point Findlay was driven to ask him about his outfit. It transpired that the police had given him the clothes to smarten him up for court. Smarten him up? He looked like a scruffy, shrunken man. An animated scarecrow. Were we dealing with someone so far beyond the pale he didn't have at least one set of clothes better than the rags he was wearing?

But Woodman was arrogant and many times he insulted Findlay directly in a high-pitched, squealing voice verging on insane gibbering. He admitted to giving evidence against others in England but claimed he did so only because his wife and family were being held hostage. His aliases had been necessary because of the contracts out on his life. He was terrified of me, apparently, then smiled and jabbed his finger accusingly at me throughout. Lord McCluskey let him rant on and Woodman showed his real colours to the jury.

A senior policeman thought otherwise. Superintendent Mervyn Davies, who had given a character reference on behalf of Dennis Woodman (then Wilkinson) at his sentencing for the sexual assault, attempted murder and robbery of the young man, turned up again. By this time Davies would have been fully aware of Woodman's capacity for hearing false confessions as well as his taste for sleazy, low-life crime. Yet Davies appeared at my trial describing Woodman as 'a credible and truthful witness'. This was the same Woodman who'd claimed that he had kidnapped and raped the young man as revenge for sexually assaulting his six-year-old son – only to admit this had been a lie three weeks later. The police knew all of these details.

At one point Findlay asked Woodman if he was being honest in his account. 'I swear on my two kids' dead ashes I'm telling the truth,' he answered, oozing sincerity.

That night in my cell as usual I worked over the day's events in my head and tried to make my way through the piles of documents in connection with the next day's proceedings. The intensity of the work, the tension of the trial and the sparse isolation of the cell combined to create great concentration, an almost spiritual focus. It's as I imagine a monk's life to be. But that night I couldn't deal with the papers and couldn't settle. I paced the short cell and worried at passing, seemingly irrelevant, thoughts. The name Peter Sutcliffe returned again and again to my thoughts. Sutcliffe, the Yorkshire Ripper, responsible for the slaughter of 13 women, mainly prostitutes. Sutcliffe? What did he have to do with anything? Sutcliffe? Sutcliffe?

I tried to distract myself in my books. Picking up the Bible, I played a childish game. Thinking of a number I looked up the related section. It was the Book of Proverbs and scanning the page the first sentence that caught my eye said something like, 'Fear not the serpent that bears false witness against you.' I was back worrying again. Sutcliffe? Peter Sutcliffe? Eventually, in the early hours of the morning, something clicked. Sutcliffe had murdered all those women but didn't harm his wife. Why? Woodman might be an evil snake but would he desecrate his kids' ashes? No. Were his kids still alive? His kids were still alive, weren't they?

Next morning at court Donald Findlay had reached the same conclusion as me but presumably from a different route. A few telephone calls later and Woodman's kids were confirmed as alive and well. In my view it was the final nail in his fantasy-laden, self-seeking evidence. Glaswegians don't like to be suckered. No woman or man in that jury could believe a word Woodman had said.

When it was my time to give evidence I was relaxed and confident. All along I had declared my innocence and belief I would be found innocent. Donald Findlay played me like a well-worn fiddle, an old partnership that gave me even more confidence. Yet the newspapers raged with stories of my imminent doom. In the course of the trial the judge had censured the BBC and Scotland on Sunday. Andrew Jaspan, Scotland on Sunday's editor, was fined £5,000 and Ron McKay, a journalist, £1,000 for an article mainly about Arthur Thompson. The BBC had shown footage of the daily security circus and me in handcuffs being led into court. The whole charade declared, 'Look, here is a dangerous and guilty man.' McCluskey was having none of it.

Throughout the trial, Donald Findlay and I had passed notes to each other. While most of these concerned the case some showed a human edge. Findlay was then a director of Rangers football club while I was a lifelong supporter of their rivals, Celtic. We would have a little scribbled banter about results. One Saturday, nearing the end of the trial, Rangers had won the league, making two of that season's major trophies. On the following Monday, a note was passed to me which read,' All we need is to have you found innocent and that'll be three out of three.' This from a man regularly accosted on the street by wild-eyed Celtic supporters – like I could be on occasion. The irony and humanity of the situation struck me. For once I was almost glad Rangers were doing well – almost.

As Donald Findlay stood up to make his closing speech, he strode away from the table leaving all notes and paperwork behind. He'd passed me a note that morning stating that we'd worked hard and well but now it was all down to the jury. He spoke for the better part of a day without props or prompts. Findlay watched the jury carefully, played to them skilfully. When he finished on 11 June 1992, 53 days after the trial had started, Lord McCluskey summed up and sent the jury off to decide. My future was now in the hands of those honest men and women of Glasgow.

As the jury deliberated I thought. All the threads of information were woven into an intricate and complex pattern in my head, like an optical illusion showing one thing one minute and something different the next. Arthur Thompson's treachery was bile in my stomach. Woodman's antics would have been hilarious if not so poisonous. The witnesses who had failed to turn up, particularly McGraw. The lies which had been told and Lord McCluskey making a point in his charge to the jury of saying, 'Even liars tell the truth sometime.' Well, Woodman was the obvious, blatant liar of the event – was McCluskey steering the jury to believe him?

I thought of TC Campbell and Joe Steele's trial years ago in the same court. Convicted on the word of another serial perjurer. Was that the fate that awaited me? And the fake Crown Office letter – how many people out there had a copy? How many had heard the alleged author discredit it?

What of the hundreds of people who had written me messages of support? Good friends out there who had proven their loyalty. One was from the staff of the dermatology ward in Stobhill Hospital. Some of the cards were from people I didn't even know. People going out of their way to stand alongside me. I wanted to write to all of those people and tell them how their messages helped. I'd learned about human nature these past months.

Was Glasgow going to burn the way the media predicted it would? Were there really all these contracts out on my life? The media had played me up, calling me 'the next gangster king of Glasgow', all rot as far as I was concerned. But in Scotland the most dangerous possession is a reputation, earned or otherwise. There were plenty of people out there who might want to have a go, to make a name.

One full day after retiring, the jury made their decision. Over the three months I'd grown fond of that group. Some of them would smile across at me and others say good morning. As I watched the familiar faces file in I studied their expressions. Grim faces, sad faces, tired faces, some were in tears. For the first time I doubted the outcome. The tears were on the cheeks of those who'd displayed the greatest courtesy and kindness to me. By the time they sat down, my heart was in my feet, my body shaking with dread and I waited for the guilty verdicts.

Waiting out the verdicts took the longest minutes of my life. I was listening so hard I almost went deaf.

'Not Guilty.' The court went into uproar.

'Not Guilty.'

From behind someone shouted, 'Well done, the wee man.'

'Not Guilty.'

'Good on you, wee Paul.'

'Not Guilty.'

'That's showing them, Paul.'

'Not Guilty.'

The smile on Donald Findlay and Peter Forbes's faces were the brightest, most childlike I'd ever seen.

'Not Guilty.'

Somebody started singing though God knows what.

'Not Guilty.'

The doors at the back swung open and feet rushed out into the corridor – probably media people.

'Not Guilty.'

I could listen to those words all day. Part of my defence was to establish that Bobby and Joe were innocent of Arty's murder. While my two friends' names were read out as accused they weren't mentioned in the verdicts. The court should have said that Bobby and Joe were Not Guilty but I know they were innocent.

I was found Not Guilty on all charges. Glasgow High Court was in a state of pandemonium. Donald Findlay broke with tradition and invited me to his room to shelter from the hordes swarming about the place. Away from the fuss he explained that Glasgow Green in front of the court was heaving with people and he worried for my well-being. The front rows, of course, were occupied with the media who would demand a statement. I just wanted to get away as soon as I could. In the corridors of the court I spotted a journalist from the Sun called Stevie Wilkie, someone who'd been very fair to me in the past. I asked him if he had a car nearby and would he give me lift in return for an exclusive interview? Of course he would. In the following weeks certain editors would gripe about my big money deal with The Sun yet they got their scoop for a lift home.

When I stepped out of the Court I was dumbstruck for the first time in my life. From the elevated steps all I could see were people stretching way back into the park all shouting words of congratulations and support. They were the people of the schemes, the deprived and despised areas of Glasgow, they were the people I belonged to. Somehow they'd understood and identified with my struggle. Perhaps they recognised a little of themselves in me. Or maybe it was a case of wanting the minnow, the wee guy standing on his own, to win over the big boys. Flanked by a row of stern-faced polis, cameras whirring, flash-guns exploding, long-stemmed microphones pushed at my face, I almost wept. Turning on my heel I sprinted to big Steve Wilkie's car and off.

As Paul Ferris was driven away with an unfamiliar lump wedged in his throat, back on the steps of the courthouse stood ashen-faced policemen. Shortly after the trial the BBC recorded a feature on the role of Dennis Woodman, supergrass. They interviewed Chief Superintendent Pat Connor, head of Strathclyde CID, who said, 'The witnesses did come forward in this case. I commend each and every one of them.' He paused, 'I commend EACH and EVERY one of them. Because without them we would never have been able to take HIM to court.' The police had not forgotten or forgiven Paul Ferris.

By Reg McKay

49.

AFTERMATH

They expected me to flee so I stayed put. I hadn't survived the attentions of the Welsh bros for all those years just to run away now. After a few days at a friend's house in the village of Aberfoyle I returned to Glasgow and went about my business. I moved in with Karen Owens to Jagger Gardens, Baillieston, in the heart of the east end.

My first calls were on Eileen Glover and Sharon Hanlon. It was my first real opportunity to grieve with those good women. Both were experiencing financial difficulties from people who should've known better and taken care of them. Apart from his interest in pubs, Bobby had owned a couple of ice-cream vans operated by a partner who wasn't paying. I made sure they were returned to Eileen. Sharon's difficulties were more complex since McGraw owed Joe money but neither of us knew how much. When I looked for the cash to be repaid, McGraw became paranoid and evasive – right in character. He'd expected me to be in jail for a long time and thought he would keep Joe's money.

I set up Jagger Autos taking advantage of certain loopholes in the law. We would buy wrecked cars covered by third-party insurance only, so they weren't certified as write-offs. Building them up from scratch for a few thousand pounds, we sold them on throughout the country at a very healthy profit. I was going to stay around and give no one, including the police, any excuses for hassle.

All around me things continued to happen. Billy Manson, a long-time associate of the Thompsons and the uncle of William Lobban, was thought by some people to have been the one to get him to act as Judas. Some said Billy Manson was Lobban's natural father. Yet Lobban's mother was supposed to be Sylvia, Manson's sister. His origins are unclear is the best we could say. One day, Manson was

PAUL FERRIS & REG McKAY

stopped in his car with his partner, Graham Scott. Two men attacked Manson with baseball bats and knives, stabbing him more than 20 times while Scott escaped without a scratch. Manson survived the attack but was never strong again.

Blind Jonah McKenzie had fallen into a terrible state. He was a guy whom I'd liked in spite of him being part of the Thompsons' team. Jonah couldn't cope with his blindness, fearing he was going to be jumped at any time. He'd said to Edward Barnes that he'd give it a year and then end his life. Sure enough, almost exactly a year later Jonah was found dead of a heroin overdose. He didn't deserve that. One day a guy said to me, 'That was a smart move, Paul. Giving Jonah a lethal dose of smack.' Smartish, I put the bloke right but wondered again at the creation of urban myths and how many other people actually believed I had murdered poor Jonah.

Paul Hamilton had been boasting about driving the blue Transit van that allegedly carried Bobby and Joe's dead bodies. Every time he got drunk, which was often, he'd add to the story though he never got as far as suggesting he was the gunman. It came as no surprise when Hamilton was found shot dead. By that time I'd become close to Stephen McLaren, Bobby's nephew, a keen, bright spark of a young man who had looked up to his uncle. The imaginative Strathclyde Police picked us up, interviewing us for six hours on Hamilton's murder before releasing us, never to bother us again. I'm pleased to say that Stephen avoided all bitterness and has gone on to make an honest, trouble-free life for himself.

Judas, William Lobban, was not free for long. He was arrested on outstanding and new charges and ended up in Perth prison where someone promptly coshed him with an iron bar. He knew worse was to come and took a screw hostage, pretending a Parker pen was a weapon. This ensured his protection for a while till he was transferred to Shotts Prison. In the lovely Shotts they sussed that someone had been paid to put strychnine in his food. At that they tried to hide him in the English prison system – as if England was a different planet. He soon crossed paths with Mick Healy.

Mick, now jailed for an armed bank robbery in Torquay and once deemed to be the most dangerous man in Britain, was wary of Lobban. The Judas had let someone into Mick's flat to kill him at one point. That person had been me, chasing after Mick after having heard that he was spreading the word that I was a police informer.

What I found out years later was that Arthur Thompson senior had shown Mick the fake letter from the Crown Office and asked him if it would pass as genuine. Mick had showed it to an academic friend who immediately spotted the spelling errors. Nevertheless, Thompson had the letter produced and distributed. At the time I knew nothing of this and Mick Healy thought I had to be a grass if Thompson said so. Accordingly, I'd planned to shoot him though, thankfully, didn't. Mick and I have had our differences but now I think him to be a good man.

While Mick Healy and William Lobban were in Full Sutton prison together young Judas revealed a great deal. He confessed to making that telephone call to Bobby and being paid for the kiss. He moaned to Mick that all he had left of the payment was a wristwatch. Appearing as a witness in an Old Bailey trial involving Mick, Lobban appeared as Witness A, being under protection, and claimed to have found God. I think he'll need to do more than that. If Lobban had been charged and brought to trial in connection with the murders of Bobby and Joe, as much as I despise him, I would've been prepared to go to court as a defence witness to ensure he was on the streets where he belonged, where he would be judged and punished for his actions. He must be one of the most despised men in the UK, little more than a friendless low life.

In the middle of all this my brother, Billy, was allowed to visit my father who was in failing health. As the prison officer watched from the corner of the bedroom, Billy leaned over my old man and whispered, 'Da, I need some money.'

Willie Ferris gripped his oldest son's hand and told him there was a thousand pounds stashed for him, 'Son, just ask if ye need more.'

Father and son refused to let go and stared speechlessly into each other's eyes. Willie knew his oldest boy had been locked up for over 20 years and needed a taste of freedom. He'd been in prison and knew how hard it was. My old man believed Billy had been kept in prison simply because his name was Ferris. My father was proud of Billy for sticking through it and keeping his honour intact. He couldn't have been prouder of his son. Billy knew my father was dying – they both knew. Billy slipped away to spend months in Blackpool – months which helped him keep his sanity and survive. My father knew he needed that.

Five months later, when Willie Ferris died in his own bed, it was a time for tears again. Sadness, of course, but comfort in the memory of a life well lived. Willie Ferris was a lion of a man who died with his self-respect intact. What better eulogy can you have?

Billy Thompson used to drink at the Open Arms pub in Riddrie, a strange choice since it was a regular haunt of the off-duty screws from nearby Bar-L. One busy night a group of strangers grabbed young Thompson, declaring they were police and arresting him. When they handcuffed Billy Thompson he screamed the rafters down, shouting out that the men weren't real cops. The prison staff moseyed in and followed the group out to the car park. There a tug of war took place with the skinny nyaff of a Thompson stuck in the middle. The bogus polis were outnumbered and gave up, driving off in their car. Some people tied that in with the murders of Bobby and Joe but not so. It was a team owed money by Arthur Thompson who planned to kidnap Billy and worse till the old man coughed up.

Another incident was to do with Bobby and Joe, however. A group of Joe Hanlon's cousins came over from Ireland and asked to meet me at Baird's Bar in the Barrowland. As soon as I walked in I could tell these guys weren't tourists or over for the Celtic game. They warned me to be somewhere else in sober, trustworthy company on a certain night. They also let slip that they knew that Arthur Thompson senior drank in a particular pub in Bridgeton on the same night every week. These men were professionals who'd sussed Thompson's responsibility in Joe's death and knew if anything happened to him the finger would point at me. I booked a table at a city centre restaurant under my own name and took along Karen, Jaimba McLean and his wife, Elaine all oblivious to events elsewhere.

On the night in question I enjoyed a pleasant meal while Arthur Thompson was driven to the pub in a red Cavalier. Joe's cousins were primed at their posts and the old man was destined never to reach the pub door. On that particular night Thompson was escorted there by his daughter, Tracy. The deal was suddenly off – there was a woman and a non-combatant present. Joe's cousins returned to Ireland the following day but I'd no doubt they intended to visit again.

Life was getting too much for Arthur Thompson and he took off, ironically, to his house in Rothesay where he and his son had set me up with the cranky rozzer, Greg Diddle. While he was in hiding, two men were arrested in Euston Station with firearms, £50,000 in cash *and a few photos of the old man Thompson with circles drawn round his head. The tabloids put it about that there was a £50,000 contract out on his life and it became the talk of the streets. Thompson knew he had a credibility problem so returned to Glasgow to show face, but it wasn't to last long.*

50.

DEATH OF A GUNSLINGER
by Reg McKay

In the Provanmill Inn Arthur Thompson always sat in the gunslinger's seat – his back against the far wall, at the end of the bar where he could watch everyone. When he returned from Rothesay to show face that's where he could be found, yet something had changed, something was missing.

The locals noticed it first, being so used to that grim countenance and gruff manner. The old Arthur would cover a room without a flicker of his eyeballs. He could tell who was sitting where and what they were talking about. He could tell the difference between loud banter and a fight brewing – in his sleep. The man had a calm control about him, a sense of power that made people take notice. The locals noticed it had deserted him.

A banging door, dominoes being slammed on a table, a drunk shouting in mock affront and the old man would twitch and jump. He was drinking more than usual and would grip his glass as if his life depended on it. Old Arthur tagged on with people to walk the few hundred yards to his home. Arthur Thompson gave a good impersonation of a scared man.

The media would have it that he had started donating money to good causes, associating with politicians, football stars and attending fund-raising events. All true, probably, since the death of Arty and the 1992 trial had cast him in the role of benign old gangster and celebrity. But there was another problem – the lack of respect shown by men and women who had looked up to Arthur Thompson for decades. Questions were being asked about his relationship with the police and how many people he had traded over the years, how many good people were now in jail or dead because of him. They asked the questions in private, of course.

Was Arthur Thompson ill? Was he guilty? Was he frightened?

When he died in his bed of a heart attack on 13 March 1992 the media surprise wasn't matched by many local folk. They knew he was a spent force. Arthur Thompson had lived with and dealt with danger and violence all his life. Was he now unable to live with being frightened for the first time ever? Was he unable to live with himself? Did he take his own life?

At his funeral the press made a song and dance about the 600 mourners, many of whom were allegedly well-known faces from show business, sport and politics. They also filled a couple of headlines about a mock bomb planted in Riddrie Cemetery the night before. The Apprentice wasn't normally so childish but he felt he needed to make a point. He had considered calling the police an hour before the funeral, but relented. A shoebox, some wire and thread and they had the bomb disposal squad crawling all over the place. The Apprentice had sent his wreath.

While the press were fussing over those details locals were observing someone else – the Strathcylde policeman who the public blamed for losing Bobby Glover and Joe Hanlon on the night of their murders. Wearing a black tie, he dropped by to pay his condolences to Rita Thompson. In spite of his lowly status as a basic constable his influence and power were far reaching. Curious locals hung around and watched. As the police officer left the Thompson household he was wiping tears from his face.

Arthur Thompson was buried in the cemetery at the back of his house next to the daughter he had disowned and his son, Arty, who had brought the empire down. From the 1960s to the 1990s, Thompson was the leading figure in organised crime in Glasgow and one of the major players in Britain. His eulogies read like a film script entitled *The Death of the Godfather*. He was never The Godfather on the streets of Blackhill and if people thought his influence died in the grave they were to be sadly mistaken.

A can get it sorted for a few guns, Paul.' Edward Barnes' statement didn't seem to tie in with our discussion about his driving licence. I was running Jagger Autos and Barney was working for me as a driver. He was good at work but no way was I going to risk using him without a driving licence – that's all the excuse the polis would need to shut me down. 'I've been tae McGraw and he reckons a few guns handed in tae his police contacts and they'll withhold the file. Paul, he does it aw the time, man.'

Barney had done this kind of work for McGraw before, delivering guns to a cop we'll call DC Muddy at a Glasgow police station in return for all sorts of favours – charges dropped, bail allowed, anything you want. Police officers by the name of Bradman, Crowdie, Fritter and Handless were all keen to help. As much as I hated the idea of cooperating with the bizzies, I wanted to help Barney and went along with the idea, buying a few handguns which were hidden at a named grave in the cemetery at the back of the Caravel Bar. The police picked the guns up, McGraw had a word with a detective and hey presto, Barney heard no more about it.

Some time later I moved down to Manchester linking up with my good pal, Rab Carruthers. Rab was one of the old Glasgow gang members and long-time friend of Bobby Dempster out of a similar mould. Rab had been well established in Manchester since the early 1970s. Through Rab I met a group known as the Salford Gang, in particular Paul Massey. These guys were the tightest, most self-supporting characters you could meet and their reputation was second to none in our world. I took to the group immediately and they've stood by me ever since.

A guy from Liverpool visited Rab on behalf of John Hasse, one of Woodman the grass's earlier victims. Hasse was on remand accused of dealing in a large quantity of heroin and set to go down for a very long time if found guilty. His friend reckoned he could have his sentence reduced in return for a consignment of illegal weapons. Rab and I debated the implications. I pointed out to him that McGraw had been running this trade for years. The people selling the guns would get paid top dollar, the police could kid the public they were getting guns off the street, no one was arrested or jailed and Hass would get better treatment. It didn't resolve all the dilemmas but on balance it was reckoned to be within the code.

Hasse's friends bought £20,000 worth of weapons, including 50-calibre tripod-mounted machine-guns, machine-pistols, handguns, a rocket launcher and some plastic explosives. This bundle was handed in to the police. Hasse was originally jailed for 18 years – not a great result. After eighteen months, Michael Howard, the Home Secretary, announced that Hasse was to be released immediately for helping Customs and Excise smash a Turkish drugs ring. Hasse claimed that the early release was for the weapons, the Turkish story being the official cover-up.

Jaimba McLean had encountered a little local difficulty and was being hunted for shooting three men in Glasgow. I hid my old friend in Manchester and after a few weeks Barney telephoned me with an interesting offer from McGraw. Back in Glasgow I met up with The Licensee in the Caravel Bar. An offer of help from a snake is usually inviting venom so I packed a loaded pistol. The offer was simple – McGraw could get the attempted charges waived in return for a load of weapons.

Jaimba was facing a 20-year stretch and I was keen to help him but the final word had to be his. The deal was on. Barney phoned with the details – a load of firearms to be left at a named grave at the cemetery behind the Caravel Bar but I had to see McGraw in person. That night I was in the Caravel, a loaded pistol down the back of my waistband and, unknown to McGraw, two armed associates posted in the pub.

We would pass the guns to the police via Barney and the usual route, then Jaimba would hand himself in. The Licensee said Jaimba would be held on remand for seven days then released – end of story. I warned McGraw exactly what would happen if anything went wrong with Jaimba. It rattled The Licensee and he started blurting out that he knew all about Jaimba's case from his police contacts like Crowdie and Fritter. Only then was I convinced that the deal could be pulled off.

A machine-gun, two handguns and two shotguns were delivered via the cemetery. Without any hesitation or delay Jaimba attended a police station. Jaimba served his week remand, was released and heard no more about it. Why had McGraw helped a very good friend of mine? Simple – Jaimba McLean was and remains one of the most feared men in Glasgow. The Licensee hoped that by doing him a favour he would get into Jaimba's good books. That is all it took but McGraw wasn't always so generous.

Around that time one of McGraw's team, Gordon Ross, was arrested for shooting a bloke and given bail but never went to trial. The man Ross shot then went as a Crown witness against a friend of mine, Stevie Moffat, accused of stabbing a man in Victoria's nightclub during some fracas in the bogs. Stevie was a martial arts expert capable of killing a man barehanded and never needed to carry a weapon. He knew who had stabbed the bloke but refused to say a word. So the same guy shot by Gordon Ross but who refused to give evidence against him was persuaded to give false testimony against Stevie. McGraw had access to the Crown witness and Stevie hated McGraw. The Licensee was very discerning about using his contacts – if it benefited him, then fine. If not, stuff it. Good business strategy? Perhaps, but being surrounded by paid lackeys and no friends is a very lonely place.

The street tom-toms were telling me that McGraw was buying up guns like they were going out of fashion. As ever the gossip got talking about stockpiling for a range war so I paid attention and learned the real reasons. Charlie Glackin, a good friend of mine and of Bobby, was on the run in Spain for possessing 5,000 Ecstasy tablets. Word was he was returning to Scotland, not to hand himself in, but to spend time with his family over Christmas. The guns were a token gift to the police for turning a blind eye during his festive visit. Now Charlie is a very careful guy, very careful indeed, yet during his stay he made no effort to hide and could be found holding the bar up in the Town Tavern on Shettleston Road. The bartering of guns had bought Charlie total immunity and he knew it.

It seemed that the whole country was trading arms with the police. Leslie Sharp, the chief bummer of Strathclyde Police, ran a high-profile guns armistice. Most of the street fraternity laughed at *the guy's pompous showmanship. Who did he think he was kidding? Yet there he was on the TV news declaring what a roaring success the armistice had been and how much safer the streets were. Stretching his arms wide, the camera panned back showing a stack of machine-guns, handguns, shotguns. I recognised some of the guns as part of the trade for Jaimba's freedom. Chief Constable Sharp made a big fuss over the assault rifles as being particularly lethal dudes. Such weapons were rarely used on the streets of Glasgow. In fact, the only time I could recall a Kalashnikov rifle being used was Noel Ruddle's meaningless slaughter of a neighbour in his Gorbals flat, ending up in pot-shots at passers-by and a police siege. Ruddle was promptly declared insane and sent to the State Secure hospital in Carstairs. Interesting but most uncommon.*

The guns Chief Constable Leslie Sharp displayed had never been intended for use in crime. They'd all been purchased to buy a trade-off from the police. The guys doing the trading kept their own weapons. The illegal arms dealers were getting richer and the police had useful propaganda. Thomas McGraw was the main trader. He was licensed by the police.

THE GHOST LETTER

During this period I was convicted of two minor offences – not exactly a crime wave. I'd made a point of regularly going to London to show gratitude to my many friends there for sticking with me through my long trial. The A brothers were spot on, making me welcome and looking out for me. One day a friend told me about a letter that was circulating London saying I was a police informant. Jim Fraser, a relative of Mad Frankie Fraser, had been passing it about.

We went to Jim Fraser's pub, Tin Pan Alley. Ahead of me, my friends strolled in one by one at different times, standing alone spread around the bar. We were ready for a stramash and didn't want to give the game away. Old Arthur Thompson used to visit Mad Frankie Fraser when in prison – a sure sign of a close bond. I'd been in the pub years earlier with Thompson and eventually Jim Fraser recognised me. 'A round here for Arthur's boy,' he shouted and I cut him short. 'Not a social call,' I said, glowering up at him.

I had his attention and his expression changed. When I asked about the letter he replied, 'Oh, don't think I believed a word of that, mate.' I wanted to grab him by the throat and ask why the fuck he was circulating it then. But I kept my cool and asked who'd brought it in. It turned out to be a bloke called Gary Dennis, the son of Ginger Dennis and good friend of Arthur Thompson. I left the pub and Jim Fraser in no doubt as to the letter's status. 'It's shite. What's more, it's fake shite put about to get me in the deep shite. Get the drift?'

Fraser swore that he did and would tell anyone who raised the subject. As I left my friends filed out behind me with Fraser watching, realising just how serious we were.

I've always believed that most coincidences occur for a reason. A few months after my visit to Tin Pan Alley I was in Spain visiting another London friend, Neal Robertson, who sadly died a few years later of a suspected suicide. We drank most nights in a pub called the Queen Vic in Malaga – a kind of home from home for the many east-end Londoners living there. Sometimes we met up with Jamie Foreman, the actor son of Freddie Foreman. I was always impressed by how close father and son were.

Gary Dennis strolled into the bar. Spotting me, he turned on his heels and sprinted into the street with me right after him. When I caught him I pulled him into a dark alleyway and started to grill him. Gary hadn't inherited his father's toughness. Soon he was crying and gibbering. Arthur Thompson senior had asked him to circulate a thick wad of these letters around the key London pubs where the main firms hung out. Old Thompson wasn't content with trying to discredit me with my defence witnesses but wanted my credibility ruined in London, trying to dig my grave. I asked Dennis why he distributed the letters. 'Fuck, Paul, I was just doing what I was told to. You know the score.'

I should've belted Gary Dennis right there and then but felt sorry for him and the state he was in. He was just another wannabe gangster with a big mouth and no bottle. When he realised he was safe he tried to give me something back. 'The night you were in Tin Pan Alley – soon as you left Jim Fraser telephoned me to tell old Thompson you'd been in but not to tell anyone else.' Arthur Thompson had been alive at that time and, in a way, was living still. Jim Fraser was just another posing hoodlum – too scared to front up but sneaking behind people's backs. I wondered what the old man, Mad Frankie, would think of his behaviour.

That night I felt a weird mixture of emotions. I was satisfied that my suspicions about Thompson had been proven accurate. I was sad that a man I'd looked up to, risked my life and freedom for and respected, could treat me like this. My old father had been right. Why the hell do youngsters not listen to their caring elders? Why can't we accept the benefit of their experience? Tell me, why is that?

Edward Barnes had been bribed to set me up with heroin. When he told me at the time I was living on my own in a Clydeside flat loaned to me by Eileen Glover, Karen and I having split up. Barney went out of his way to visit me there one night rather than at work. I'd grown very fond of Barney but reminded myself that he'd worked with McGraw for years. In fact, during my trial for Arty's murder, McGraw paid Barney a daily rate for sitting in the public benches and reporting events to him at night. Barney had no intention of planting the gear but was scared I'd find out from someone else. I'd no choice but to test his loyalty.

Barney was wired up and met McGraw's two police helpers in a crowded bar near Glasgow's Buchanan Street bus station. According to Barney they confirmed the deal and mentioned Fritter's name. Barney drove my car at work, taking it for valets and the like, and was ideally placed to plant smack. Trouble was the bar was too noisy and the tape recorder picked up none of the conversation.

So I confronted McGraw. Poor Barney was petrified but, true man that he was, came right along. Gordon Ross opened the door and Snaz Adams was in the house. On the way there I'd stopped off and bought fish and chips, not having eaten for about two days. At first I went into The Licensee's house alone. As the meeting unfolded I sat cross-legged on the floor. I must have looked casual but had a loaded pistol on me and nearby a friend was parked, armed and poised.

McGraw denied there was any problem between us, while getting paler by the minute. For someone who arranged such grief for others he had a very weak stomach. When I was bored with McGraw's denials I went out and fetched Barney from my car. I thought McGraw was going to pass out. I sat down and continued eating my *fish supper and told Barney to say his piece. He did, leaving nothing out. McGraw was chain-smoking and bawling at Barney. Sitting on the floor staring at him, I watched his eyes straying nervously back to me. Finally, I butted in, offering McGraw a chip. He swallowed hard and dry.*

I'd heard and seen enough. In all his panic, McGraw had yet again mentioned Fritter's name. Standing up, I gave McGraw a message for all his police friends. If they persisted in trying to fit me up they were declaring war and had better watch themselves when leaving their homes in the morning. That night I left, feeling McGraw and his corrupt police friends were a stink I'd never get rid of whatever I did, wherever I went.

But Barney had proven to be a good friend. He told me once that he respected me because I respected him. McGraw used to treat him as Barney the Junkie who'd do anything for a few quid. Barney the Junkie was a stranger to me but Edward Barnes, decent man, I knew very well indeed.

Sometime in 1996, I was sitting in the office of GRO Recovery, a debt-collecting firm I ran. Two policemen, acting Detective Chief Inspector Robertson and DI Les Darling, called to see me with a strange message. Darling said they were there on two accounts, the first being a report I'd held a gun to the head of a Kenny Faulds in a pub in Rutherglen. I said nothing and waited for the second purpose of their visit, 'We have reasonable grounds to believe your life is at risk,' said po-faced Darling.

It reminded me of a couple of years before, returning from holiday in Gran Canaria. On the package flight back we noticed two rather pale guys sitting together and smoking Kensitas Club cigarettes, a particular favourite among Glaswegians. We'd searched the resort for Club king-size over the previous few days and failed to find the genuine article. Then across from us were two pale-faced blokes smoking them as if their lives depended on it. We crashed a couple of cigarettes and got chatting. Something wasn't quite right. When we hit Glasgow Airport we found out why.

We were apprehended by the police right away and they informed me that an attempt was going to be made on my life. They cautioned me on the risks and handed me a useful booklet – on how to protect myself against attack. I passed this Teach-Yourself-How-To manual right back and started laughing, but the police didn't get

PAUL FERRIS & REG McKAY

the joke. Instead we were escorted from the terminal building and I reckon there must have been around 50 rozzers involved. Outside they'd cordoned off the road and we were bundled into a taxi that zoomed off in a convoy of cars, motorbikes and the helicopter overhead. I knew they'd really flipped when we passed the roadblocks and drove down a traffic-free M8 motorway. Even royalty don't get that treatment. It transpired that the farce had resulted from a hoax call to the TV programme **Crimewatch**. A practical joke that must have cost the state a fortune.

Back in my small office DI Darling wasn't joking. I asked him to be reasonable and explain. He said they were deadly serious adding, 'No, we're not going to give you any daft book either.' How the hell did he know about the Protect-Yourself-Against-Assassins booklet? He worked for the largest police force in Europe. Was this police harassment? Sticking to the point I asked a direct question, 'Who?' Darling didn't hesitate, replying, 'Thomas McGraw of 36 Carrick Drive, Mount Vernon, Glasgow.'

To avoid warfare, it is most unusual for the police to name the supposed plotter in such issues. What were they trying to do – rile me up to have a go at McGraw? Watch me make a move then take me out themselves? Since Rothesay I viewed the police as the ones most likely to shoot me. Was I being too quiet for them? Were they trying to create the opportunity?

They'd hardly left when I contacted my current solicitor, John Macaulay. He arranged for us both to attend a meeting with the policemen. In the meantime, I wrote down not only what those coppers had told me but a whole heap of information about McGraw's contacts with police and passed the information to Macaulay. Too often they'd try to set me up and I knew part of my defence strategy had to be preparation. If they were going to get me, Macaulay would have an unpleasant surprise for them. When John Macaulay accompanied me to the police station again DI Les Darling repeated that my life was at risk from Thomas McGraw. They were definitely at it.

It was clear that I wasn't going to be allowed to get on with my life in peace. Businesses I was involved with were managing a healthy and legitimate profit. I was trying to walk away from the crime scene yet they wouldn't let me. A couple of years earlier Tam Bagan had been abandoned by McGraw and went to jail for a long

THE FERRIS CONSPIRACY

time. Furious, he blew the whistle on McGraw. The information went to the powers that be in Glasgow who decided that an external investigation wasn't necessary. No one could afford an independent review that could've resulted in the downfall of a host of senior coppers and, most likely, some others as well. The internal investigation resulted in no action against anybody whatsoever. The unholy alliance between The Licensee and the police was well protected and still on my tail.

I'd been in the hotel room minutes when the police knocked at the door. It was one of the grander London hotels, down by the Thames, and the receptionist had told me that Vincent Price and Christopher Lee stayed there when shooting horror movies. But I didn't expect my own horror – I was there on business.

I'd gradually involved myself in business enterprises like Premier Security, run by Harry Young and William Walker. Who could be better at preventing robberies or violence in a club than someone who'd done it all and then some? So many police moved into the security business, but they didn't know the inside form, how it really worked. To start with I think Harry was a bit sceptical, only knowing about me from newspaper headlines and expecting some rabid psychopath. But he gave it a go and soon I found myself on a building site in Clydebank where the local kids were stripping the goodies, like fitted kitchens, before they could be installed.

All the previous security firm had done was employ guards to scream at the kids. I wandered over to the group of gangly teenage boys, sussed out their leader, a young guy called Jamie, and made him a business proposition. The kids could collect all the lemonade bottles on the site for the cash back and I'd pay them £500 for the return of everything they'd stolen recently. Soon the place was crawling with tiny kids humping oversized flat-packs on their backs. They just kept coming and coming. They were absolutely true to their word so I used to throw Jamie a few quid every week to make sure the place stayed safe and it did. Jamie was an industrious kid, working at four or five jobs at a time – a businessman of the future. A newspaper ran a story about me employing underage kids as security guards. Tosh! I was just taking care of my kind of people and preventing a lot of thieving at the same time. Good kids of the schemes just needed to be treated with a little respect rather than chased and shouted at.

That was the style – speak to the people who were likely to be the trouble and treat them right. I'd go to a wild area like Nitshill, speak with the main people and strike a deal. In a sense I was marketing my reputation, not just as an ex-player but as someone they knew they could trust. Ironically, the police started recommending us.

Premier Security would eventually build up a turnover of £5 million per year but these were the early days and I was hungry for legitimate work. I'd developed a range of services providing bodyguards, protecting sensitive meetings, clubs and so on. Throughout it all I'd kept in touch with Ben, Billy's friend from prison who'd asked me to take care of those cargo ships years ago. Ben was long out of prison and a successful businessman. Through the years he gave me constant support and encouragement to go straight, to apply myself to legitimate enterprises. Ben's influence gave me ambitions and I made contacts with influential people. So I was in London to discuss security for a legitimate meeting when the police arrived in my hotel room.

The guy standing in the corridor didn't say he was the police but the hotel manager. He explained that some coppers were downstairs asking questions about me and I should go down to find out what they wanted. With the old feeling of dread in my gut I rode down in the smooth lift, wondering what the hell it was now.

When I walked into the manager's office I was bundled to the ground by armed men and handcuffed. By their dress, communications systems and weapons they were not ordinary police. There had been a bit of IRA action in London around that time – had they confused my Scottish accent for Irish? Can you be arrested in Britain for the way you speak? Up in my room they strip-searched me and methodically took the room apart before bundling me into a car and down to the local nick. Only then did they tell me that I was arrested under suspicion of passing counterfeit notes in the hotel. The notes were the genuine article – Scottish notes but legal tender nevertheless.

I was held in custody and repeatedly asked the purpose of my visit, who I was going to meet and why. They were more interested in my business meeting than the origin of the banknotes. Old habits die hard and I refused to tell them who I was meeting. I'd learn a year later that they already knew.

They held me in cells overnight before releasing me early next day with the expected news that the bank notes were genuine. By now I had decided to protect my business contact so went straight to the airport and caught the next flight home. Back in Glasgow, I contacted the man I was meant to meet in London. He wasn't best pleased but thankfully was still interested in using our services. We would do business and I would learn what the fiasco of an arrest in London had been all about. In the meantime I got on with my business and my life.

Late one night I'd been waiting outside a club for a friend when I spotted a girl I knew looking for a taxi. It was Angie, the daughter of Davie Bryce, the guy who ran Calton Athletic, the football team therapy for ex-heroin addicts. Angie was the girlfriend of my good mate, Stevie Moffat, so I paid the usual courtesy of offering her and her friend a lift home, making sure she was all right. Her friend turned out to be Sandra Arnott who turned my head instantly. A few dates later and I was confronting the usual problem – Sandra's mother didn't want her lassie associating with Paul Ferris. In time that was sorted out – I get on really well with parents, always have.

I was also beginning to appear on TV programmes on crime. I thought it important that the public should understand why someone should choose a life of crime. That's not a job for psychologists, sociologists or journalists but for an ex-criminal. I appeared with John McVicar in a series called Battered Britain, a World in Action programme about Woodman called 'Dennis the Menace', and a chat show with Elaine C. Smith – she of Mary Doll in Rab C. Nesbitt and a stack of other roles. On that programme there was an ex-football hooligan, a Chicago cop, Hugh Collins, who'd been jailed for life for stabbing a guy to death in a Glasgow bar, and me. As we sat there waiting for the cameras to roll, Elaine C. Smith came over to me and said, 'Paul, the sound people think that guy's you.' The Chicago cop was dressed in an extravagant double-breasted suit with huge lapels, spats, a wide-brimmed fedora and had gold dripping from every finger. The rest of us looked normal.

At the end of the show Hugh Collins pulled me aside and said, 'When we met in jail Arthur Thompson junior offered me £30,000 to kill you.'

I replied, 'Why didn't you take it?' He looked quizzically and struggled to answer so I continued. 'Because you wouldn't be here having this conversation tonight.' Walking away, I felt a bit sorry. Hugh Collins as a young guy had pushed a blade too far in the wrong place. It has happened to so many team guys and could've happened to many more, including me. He'd spent his adult life in prison, out of the way. He was no player with a track record, just another young bloke rotting away in prison. There were queues of more proficient hit-merchants ahead of him who would've worked for less. Anyway, Arty asked almost everybody he met to kill me. That Collins saw his conversation with the fat joker as significant just proves what a sheltered life Hugh Collins had led.

My London contact was on providing security to sensitive meetings between some overseas businessmen. Preparing for the work, I was down south frequently, being briefed on the requirements. It became obvious that Kuwait oil was the subject in question. As I understood it there was a huge underground reservoir of oil, mainly in Kuwait but that it could be accessed from Iraq. There was an embargo against Iraq trading in that oil. However, a group of Iranians were willing to buy the oil at a low price, planning to sell it on to Pakistan. You didn't need to be an expert in world affairs to work out that this was a highly sensitive matter in international politics.

The final meeting between the Iranian and Iraqi businessmen was to take place in the restaurant of Waterloo Station, a spacious place built on three tiers. The Iraqis, including a cousin of Saddam Hussein, were jittery and had chosen that very public place to meet. The meeting took place on the middle tier with my people patrolling the ground and top floors. As the time ticked by, I noticed a peculiar flow of people on the top tier overlooking our customers below. One group had been at their table for much longer than you might expect. The adjoining tables were being filled by different types at different times – students, young couples, businessmen – while there were many other empty tables throughout the place. I was being paid to be suspicious.

I passed a note to my main contact, pointing out the location of the people and suggesting they might be national security, MI5. As I watched him read, I felt a touch embarrassed. Here was this wee guy from Blackhill imagining he was caught up in a James Bond movie. My contact looked up, smiled and nodded. When his note came back it read, 'Yes, we knew they'd be here. I suspect you've met some of them before – on a previous trip to London!'

So the armed arrest at the hotel was MI5 sussing me out. If they'd go that far what else were they doing? Here was me trying to make an honest living and staggering accidentally into the spy business. Wrong turning, Paul.

Later I made a point of contacting Ben, wise in the ways of diplomacy and international affairs. What I described didn't faze him at all. In fact he made me feel a little backward since I'd accepted the contract without anticipating the security services looking over my shoulder. Ben had had horrendous problems leaving Iran and afterwards. He advised that, like him, I should avoid all similar dealings in the future – to stick with straightforward business ventures. As usual Ben was right, but I was left with this nagging doubt that the national security services would leave me alone.

As soon as I saw the guns I thought I was a dead man. Somehow, I'd always known this would be the way. Whenever you were least expecting them and turned your back they would appear. The car came screeching down the road and spun to form a blockade. Men in uniforms held the guns, police uniforms of skip hats and flak jackets. So what? It was the police I'd most feared for years. They'd tried before and have long memories.

I was committing a crime but not one that required this show of force. So I worried that this was the time they were going to shoot me. Since that night in Rothesay a bullet in the head from the police was as likely as from a paid hit-man. I'd walked away from violence to earn a legal living – isn't that the time they came to finish you off? Turning your back to hang up a picture? There are certain people who will not allow you to retire. For a few minutes on that London street I expected to die.

Two of the policeman lifted me through the open car window, hoisting me straight out. It was then I reckoned I was safe from death since hit-men would've shot me where I sat. In the driver's seat was my good friend, Arthur Suttie, who hadn't even known that I was up to a trick. What was he thinking sitting there? He wasn't left alone for long – they smashed his side window and yanked him out too.

Arthur was Ben's father-in-law, a right gentleman who'd taken me under his wing. An old-timer from the London scene, Arthur had been an expert safecracker when young. As in the old tradition Arthur Suttie stuck to that type of work, was non-violent and had given up on crime an age before. He was happy to take me under his wing, keep me right and encourage me. Arthur was respected by all the faces from the London firms – the Krays, Joey Pyle, Frankie Fraser

– and had made sure they knew the truth about Arthur Thompson and that fake letter. I'd taken him along on this trip and felt I'd let him down but I was about to find out I didn't know half of it.

We'd just visited a guy called John Ackerman in his Islington council flat. Unbeknown to Arthur, I'd picked up a box of what I understood to be £200,000 of forged notes and some printing blocks. The deal was to link with a European group who'd received EU grants and would exchange the money for Deutschmarks. Ackerman had made the approaches and I'd been tempted. Eventually, it could have brought me in a sizeable fortune – the final buffer between me and the temptations to return to a life of crime. No violence and no guns – it was to be one last throw of the dice.

When the police searched the car and found the box they didn't find counterfeit currency but three MAC-10 sub-machine-guns capable of firing 1,200 rounds a minute, two sawn-off shotguns, a Thompson sub-machine gun, handguns, silencers and ammunition. The police weren't ordinary officers but members of the National Crime Squad, the UK equivalent of the FBI, recently formed under the directorship of Roy Penrose. For two years I'd been watched by MI5 in what they called Operation Shillelagh.

The arresting police took photographs of everything around the scene. Finally they all lined up posing with their two prisoners like a posse recording the capture of two outlaws. I could see what they were doing and smiled. Elsewhere, they would be arresting poor Connie Howarth, Arthur's friend, driving another car as part of the cash scam and now lumbered with this. As the police were booking me, all I could think of was Sandra and my son Dean, born three weeks earlier. How I'd let them down.

Ackerman was arrested too but promptly turned Queen's Evidence and supergrass. Once started they couldn't stop him from yapping and he made 24 lengthy taped interviews against people. Ackerman had been a major arms trader for years, handling thousands of weapons. Through him they later got to a guy called Anthony Mitchell, a special police constable, who manufactured the arms. They also arrested a friend of mine called Joe Macaulay in rather suspicious circumstances.

Joe had been travelling from London to Glasgow by train and had gone to the buffet for a drink. Two guys were smoking a joint and offered Joe a puff. Joe declined the dope, being wary of guys

THE FERRIS CONSPIRACY

234

who went out of their way to make conversation. Both men said they were from Glasgow. 'Dennistoun area,' said one.

'Which street?' asked Joe. The guy blushed red and stammered. 'You're a fucking copper, aren't you?' stormed Joe. 'Why don't you people leave me alone?' Joe told them in no uncertain terms where to get off. Short, sharp, brief and to the point.

At Preston the train was boarded by a squad of police who arrested Joe as being drunk and disorderly. They found a revolver and ammunition in his luggage. Eventually the police admitted Joe had been under observation and photographed at my place of business on two separate occasions. He went down big-time under a blaze of publicity describing him as the 'Drunken Scottish Gunrunner'. What the police weren't to know is that Joe Macaulay doesn't drink alcohol – ever. They used that as a ruse to pick him up without revealing the surveillance. He'd been seen in my company, had visited London and telephoned me – what more reasons did the security forces require?

In my own trial I admitted my intentions to commit a currency offence but denied gun-running. Prosecution witnesses involved a stream of people shielded from public view and identified only by a letter – the secret service. I was prepared to go down if it would help Arthur and Connie. This was not heroism but simple justice. It had been my plan and we'd been set up because of me. Typically they refused and we all took our chances with the jury.

At the Old Bailey Arthur Suttie and Connie Howarth got five years each. I was found guilty of conspiracy to sell weapons. Summing up, Judge Blacksell said, 'I have no doubt you are a dangerous and ruthless professional criminal.' I wanted to butt in and tell him that was all in the past but he continued, 'Those who choose to deal in such arms can only expect prison sentences of great length.' True to his word the judge proposed to jail me for 15 years until the barristers interrupted. There was this farcical debate where both the defence and the prosecution advised the judge he'd exceeded his powers and the maximum sentence for conspiracy was ten years. Clearly the judge thought I was being let off too lightly and slapped me with the ten years.

Up in Glasgow I imagined a cheer rising from certain police stations and The Licensee's gaff. All I could think about was whether Arthur Suttie was going to be okay in prison, if Paul and Dean were

*going to be okay and how much I'd let my young Sandra down.
Would she cope on her own?*

Ackerman, arms dealer and supergrass, was jailed for six years only. He didn't serve much of his sentence before word was circulated by the authorities that he had died of a heart condition. In fact he had been smuggled out of the country with a new name, identity, home and a handsome pension. Last heard of he was seen sneaking around the red-light district of Amsterdam.

Roy Penrose, director general of the National Crime Squad, with a budget of £10 million and 1,500 hand-picked detectives, described the arrest of Paul Ferris as the biggest accomplishment of his career. He did not go as far as to thank John Ackerman.

By Reg McKay

56.

A SENTENCE OF DEATH

I was 35 years old and facing the English prison system for the first time. Here I was in a system with few friends, doing the longest stretch of my life when I'd planned to put it all behind me. I was proven wrong about the friends right away.

Paul Massey and the Salford Gang stood right by me, letting it be known I was okay and helping me out in practical ways. I met up with old associates like Mick Healy and we sorted out some difficulties, becoming good friends. It was then that Mick told me all about the confessions of William Lobban, Judas. Mates of Arthur Suttie searched me out. At one time, just before his death, I spent time with Charlie Kray and made a point of watching out for him in case any ambitious kid tried it on. As a Glaswegian I was sceptical about the brouhaha about the Krays and the old-time gangsters but Charlie converted me. He was an ace bloke who represented everything I mistakenly thought Arthur Thompson had been all those years ago.

Joey Pyle, a man of immense influence on the London scene, had been sent copies of the fake Crown Office letter. Arthur Suttie was a close friend of Joey Pyle and put him right on the letter and on me. In prison I felt the warm glow from this kindness as Joey Pyle and his like put the word out among his allies. Men would come up to me in prison and offer their hands which otherwise might well have held a weapon with my name on it.

I started off in Bellmarsh Prison alongside people like Edgar Pierce, the Mardi Gras Bomber. Charles Bronson, the self-proclaimed most dangerous man in Britain, was there and up to his usual nonsense – hostage-taking. One time he took Adnan Hoshan, one of the so-called Sudanese Airbus hijackers, captive and refused to let him go till he was served with ten hamburgers or whatever. Other prisoners were weary of Bronson because he spoiled things for them for no good reason. Adnan on the other hand I really liked. He was a gentle, artistic guy who'd decided to hijack the plane on the spur of the moment, pretending a bottle of sauce with tape wrapped round it was a weapon. Adnan would've been killed had he returned to his homeland so was pleased to be in a British prison – Charles Bronson and all.

My good pal, Jaimba McLean, set off to visit me but was nobbled by plainclothes detectives. They knew where he was going and who he was going to see. For hours they interviewed him in a hot, stuffy, windowless room. Jaimba was sweating profusely and repeatedly asked for a drink. After several hours they handed him a half-empty can of Coke which he guzzled in one. After they released him to return home, within an hour he was hallucinating. Within a day he was arrested for breach of the peace – one of the lowest charges on the Scottish criminal justice list. Still, they held him in a padded cell, force-feeding him drugs. Eventually they took him to the Sheriff Court that had been cleared and sealed off. On the spot, he was declared insane, sectioned and sent to the State Hospital in Carstairs. Jaimba festered in a drugs-driven stew for a year in the company of the most dangerous, unpredictable people in the country. When they released him he had a dependency on lithium.

When they'd lifted Jaimba they claimed to have information he was going to help me escape. For the same reason I was shoved into the segregation unit at Belmarsh. Unhappy as I was, I reckon I had a better deal than my pal. No evidence was ever presented or charges brought in connection with my alleged escape plan.

By way of Full Sutton Prison I moved to Frankland Prison in Durham still carrying my Category A status as a security risk in spite of behaving as a model prisoner. Frankland was closer to home and the best prison I've ever been in. It's the only time in any prison I've felt treated as a human being by everybody. Back home the bored tabloids started yapping about me being scared to return to Glasgow. Not at all, I just know when I'm well off. A transfer request to a Scottish prison would be like a journey back to the dark ages. The prisons there are still primitive, brutal and run by too many screws intent on punishing anyone they can get close to. I was for staying put.

My sentence had been reduced to seven years on appeal and I could begin to envisage freedom. At Frankland they encouraged you to pursue your rights – something I've always been keen on – so I asked for access to my prison file. Mostly I found what I expected, then I came across a clipping of one newspaper article. I happen to know that the Scottish Prison Service and Strathclyde Police have a standing order with a Glasgow clippings service for every newspaper article written about me. There are thousands and must cost the state a fortune. Of all those only one found its way into my prison file.

It was from **The Herald**, the best-selling broadsheet in Scotland, and published on 24 July 1998, the day after I was sentenced at the Old Bailey. My conviction had run on the front page, was granted editorial comment and a background piece on page eight, all written by the same journalist, James Freeman. Freeman had been writing about me for years and wavered between outrage and objective reporting. In this instance he was sloppy and lethal.

Freeman advised readers that he had seen 'proof positive' that I was a paid police informant. He went on, 'The proof comes from a letter written by a very senior Crown Office official in 1992 to Ferris then at Barlinnie awaiting trial.' Mr A. Vannet's name was being taken in vain yet again six years after he'd established the letter to be a forgery in open court during the most high-profile criminal trial in Scotland in modern times. Six years after **The Herald** had written about Mr Vannet's evidence. Freeman didn't even check his own archives – the first thing any journalist would do with every story. He surely didn't make any effort to contact Mr A. Vannet, whom he would have found employed in the procurator fiscal's department less than one mile away from **The Herald**'s office.

The Herald quoted from the letter selectively. Had they printed the whole text, their own literate readers would've spotted the glaring spelling errors. Did James Freeman, experienced journalist, not notice the mistakes or did he choose not to print them?

Did **The Herald**'s editor think twice before publishing the piece? Did the newspaper check with their lawyers? **The Herald** is owned by the Scottish Media Group who also own STV. Do they use the same group of lawyers as in the days of Don Lindsay and the smothered tapes and film of police corruption? Or did they think it didn't matter – he's just a gangster from Blackhill, a convicted criminal, so *what if someone kills him because we printed lies masquerading as facts?*

Freeman was either an incompetent journalist or deliberately out to do me serious harm. In fact he wrote that the information was 'calculated to raise the equivalent of raised eyebrows in the East End circles'. A polite way of saying DEATH SENTENCE and he knew it.

My solicitor, John Macaulay, agreed with the seriousness of The Herald's report. On my instructions, he wrote to Freeman, his editor, Harry Reid, and the newspaper's managing group, now called the Scottish Media Group. I asked for a retraction and correction of the mailicious falsehoods they had published. Through their solicitors my complaint was 'rejected in its entirety'. To me, that was proof positive, to quote Mr Freeman, that my enemies extended to the editorial reaches of The Herald. Forget about me for a minute. This is also about 'Scotland's Quality Newspaper', as The Herald styles itself, maliciously and deliberately peddling false information to its readership. If this is quality journalism, I wonder what gutter journalism looks like? Freeman had been known to be spending a lot of time socialising with senior police officers. Sleeping with the enemy? Gone native? Call it what you will, I call Freeman a traitor to his profession and a lackey of the police. He is an example of the final thread in the web of conspiracy and unholy alliances – the control of information. Propaganda parading as facts – the journalist, his editor and his management should be ashamed.

After his trial as Paul Ferris's co-accused in 1998, Arthur Suttie said, 'I know all the top players in Britain – hard men but moral men. I've been in the dock with quite a few over the years. Paul Ferris was the best. He offered to take all the blame to save the others.'

By Reg McKay

57.

LOOKING BACK IN ANGER
by Reg McKay

The Apprentice has become more reflective as he has grown older. Still in his thirties, he has done a lot of living and made many mistakes. He ponders on those errors from time to time in an effort to learn fully and move on to be a better person.

The early gang violence when he glorified the disfigurement and death of others, young boys who should have been playing football or courting the girls. They were just like him though not so fast, not so vicious. There was no glory in gore.

The people he had worked for without question. The young boxer he slashed when he should have cut the throat of that foul-mouthed businessman. The jobs he carried out for Arthur Thompson senior in Glasgow and London he would have walked away from if he'd known the man's character. If he'd turned away sooner maybe lardy Arty wouldn't have been so loud-mouthed, so threatening.

Poor Blind Jonah, he should've had a word. The guy was solid but got mixed up with the wrong team. The Thompsons left him to die in the end. They just stood back and let their enemies stab and chase and haunt him to death. But that Lobban, that Judas, he was another mistake, 'I should've trusted my intuition and put him down years ago.'

McGraw, well there's a man who never did his own dirty business, ever. Never trust a butcher with a clean, white overall. There was a while The Apprentice didn't pay much attention to the Ice Cream Wars and the jailing of TC Campbell and Joe Steele – it was all before his time. But the more he saw of The Licensee's trading in flesh the more he knew the wrong men were in prison. Having that poor Doyle family burned to death and then blaming two innocent men had to be the lowest. Besides, everybody knew McGraw could have had TC and Joe released at any time using his battalion of paid police. Why didn't he?

McGraw had claimed Joe Hanlon's blue Ford Orion, the one he and Bobby Glover were found dead in. Joe had registered it through McGraw's taxi firm for convenience. The Licensee gave it a cheap valet and stuck it out on the streets of Glasgow as a taxi, driving around tormenting Sharon, Eileen and everyone who loved Bobby and Joe. The Apprentice had considered killing the greedy bastard and torching his garage. But he was angry, hurt, furious and The Apprentice made a point of working only when calm, careful and lethal. There would come a time though.

The Licensee was having his problems, being chased by the tax people and getting terrified for his life. The Apprentice wondered if McGraw was losing his head. In the same month The Licensee had sold his taxi firm, looked to buy a couple of ice-cream vans and hired some Serb guerrilla bodyguards. The last thought made The Apprentice chuckle, 'Aye, but who'll mind the minders though?'

58

LOOKING FORWARD IN HOPE

Life could be worse, I could be in the slop-out queue at Bar-L or in the Wendy House under a constant blaze of white light. Frankland Prison has allowed me to relax, think about the future, make plans for my sons and the sons of my friends, Bobby and Joe.

In 1999 my brother Billy was finally released after 26 years of a life sentence. Now we've changed roles with him out in the world and visiting me here. It's funny but I feel like the older brother as he spins around burning up all the energy of a man 26 years younger than his age. We look forward to being at liberty together for the first time in our adult lives.

But there is life in prison and some of it unexpected. Interesting people like Kevin Lane, a top man, who'd clearly been set up as a contract killer and was fighting to clear his name, and Grant Turnbull, diagnosed HIV+ in 1980 in Dumfries Prison and treated like the walking plague by the screws for three years – in spite of being told he'd six months to live. Lots of good guys with stories to tell of injustice, inhumanity and conspiracy.

A prisoner sidled up to me and introduced himself as Mick Steele.

'You might want a look at these papers, mate,' he said, stuffing a bundle of official-looking documents into my hands. What he passed to me was an intelligence surveillance summary of an investigation into what has become known as The Essex Boys murders. Leah Betts, aged 18, had died after taking an Ecstasy tablet. The high public furore resulted in a lot of attention being paid to the Essex scene. One gang was suspected of supplying the huge Essex market with E. Then things started to go wrong and three men – Tucker, Tate and Rolfe – were found dead in their Range Rover, shot through the back of the head. A vast police and secret service investigation ensued. Mick Steele had been convicted of the murders though he was mounting an appeal.

I read the papers with mild interest till I came across the entry for 1 February 1996. 'Suggestion that D arranged the shootings and that PAUL FERRIS from Scotland may be responsible for the murders. That FERRIS flew down from Scotland about eight days before the murders. That FERRIS is an associate of the A family.'

The information failed to shock me. It was simply further proof that when your name is on the list they watch you all the time, suspect you of everything and will get you – honestly or otherwise. It's no consolation that around 50 suspects were also mentioned, including Paul Betts, young Leah's father.

Around me in Frankland Prison there were men from all over the country. Contrary to the public stereotype, not all of them claimed to be innocent – but some did. As I got to know them I realised that police corruption and their unholy alliance with certain gangsters licensed to commit crimes with immunity was not an isolated affair. Glasgow could have been Middlesbrough, Liverpool, London, Manchester, Newcastle, anywhere. The cells of Frankland are full of people who need no convincing on police corruption.

Even Sir David McNee, in charge of the bizzies in Glasgow before becoming Commissioner for the Metropolitan Police, said there was a place for 'pious perjury'. I think Sir David meant it's okay to lie as long as you're wearing a police uniform.

I do hope that the honest police, well-intentioned prison wardens and objective journalists win the day. I hope that people will listen to the cries of the incarcerated with an open mind and a willingness to hear their calls of injustice. I hope that young people will be given more choices and be allowed to choose a life free from crime. That politicians stop their moral chest-beating and take responsibility for poverty and exclusion. That violence will be seen for what it is, a last resort for those who believe they have no other way to go. I hope these things but I believe that life will rumble on as before. Too many in power, too many in authority, too many of the wealthy need us – the underclass, the unemployed, the criminals.

In truth, my hopes are more ambitious: that when they eventually allow me to walk away from prison they accept it as an end to the game. We'll call it a no-score draw. We'll call it quits. Just let me go *back to my family and work honestly to make their future a good one.*

But be warned – follow me, harm me or mine, conspire against me, fight me and I'll fight you right back.

WHERE ARE THEY NOW?

BLACKHILL: As this book was being written Blackhill was being demolished and redeveloped.

THE WELSH BROTHERS: All bar two are dead.

ARTHUR THOMPSON JUNIOR: His murder remains unsolved.

BILLY THOMPSON: A known drug addict, he was recently seriously assaulted. At the time of writing he remained in a critical condition in the neurological unit of the Southern General Hospital.

WILLIAM LOBBAN (JUDAS): In hiding in England – still has his wristwatch.

DONNIE McMILLAN: Played a bit part in Lynne Ramsay's film *Ratcatcher*. Still acting the gangster.

PAUL HAMILTON: His murder remains unsolved.

DENNIS WOODMAN (DENNIS THE MENACE): As of February 2001 back in prison in England.

JOHN ACKERMAN (ARMS DEALER AND SUPERGRASS): Last seen in Amsterdam living under a false name supported by a UK government pension.

TAM BAGAN: Shotts Prison for armed robbery. Has taken up painting and claims he is reformed.

JOHN HASSE: In February 2001 in Liverpool jailed for 13 years for guns and drug offences. During the course of his trial Customs and Excise and various police forces revealed that he had collaborated with them for years. Many of his victims claim they were fitted up and are working on appeals.

MARTIN HAMILTON: Jailed for life in November 2000 for torturing an 18-year-old man and his girlfriend, several charges of assault and supplying Class A drugs.

GREG DIDDLE (EX-DETECTIVE): Last known to be employed by a private firm.

JAKEY WADDLE (EX-DETECTIVE): Was witnessed fitting kitchen in The Licensee's home. Last seen running an ice-cream van.

SGT GRADY MIDDEN: Last seen employed by Strathclyde Police in Paisley.

STRATHCLYDE POLICE: When the security services and the police in Ireland were investigating Thomas McGraw, The Licensee, on numerous charges they declined to consult with Strathclyde Police.

JAMES FREEMAN: Still employed by *The Herald* in the spring of 2001.

THOMAS McGRAW (THE LICENSEE): Last heard of he had moved to Tenerife.

THE APPRENTICE: When last seen was planning a short trip to Tenerife.

WILLIAM LOVE: Withdrew his evidence against TC Campbell and Joe Steele. Not enough to win appeal. Later one of the three Law Lords would confess he had misread papers.

TC CAMPBELL & JOE STEELE: Held in Shotts Prison unjustly after 16 years. Last seen, the Commission had to take legal action forcing the Crown to free all legal papers in connection with their appeal. The Commission are due to announce on their appeal in March 2001. Free the Glasgow Two.

PAUL MASSEY: Serving 12 years for wounding. Unjustly convicted. Fighting to prove his innocence.

TONY McGOVERN: Shot dead on the streets of Glasgow in September 2000. His murder remains unsolved.

JAIMBA McLEAN: Since being drugged and admitted to the State Hospital, Carstairs, has suffered further breakdowns and hospital admissions.

RUSSELL STIRTON: Continues to lead a happy, crime-free life.

ARTHUR SUTTIE: Free and still a good friend to Paul Ferris.

BILLY FERRIS: Free at last.

JOE HANLON: His murder remains unsolved.

BOBBY GLOVER: His murder remains unsolved.